Ignatius Loyola and Francis de Sales

TWO MASTERS — ONE SPIRITUALITY

Cross and Crown Series of Spirituality

LITERARY EDITOR

Reverend Jordan Aumann, O.P., S.T.D.

NUMBER 32

F. CHARMOT, S.J.

IGNATIUS LOYOLA
AND
FRANCIS DE SALES

Two Masters - One Spirituality

TRANSLATED BY

SISTER M. RENELLE, S.S.N.D.

B. Herder Book Co.

ST. LOUIS AND LONDON

A translation of *Deux Maîtres: Une Spiritualité: Ignace de Loyola—François de Sales,* published by Editions du Centurion, Paris, 1963.

NIHIL OBSTAT
Very Rev. J. S. Considine, O.P.
Censor Deputatus

IMPRIMATUR
Most Rev. Cletus F. O'Donnell, J.C.D.
Vicar General, Archdiocese of Chicago
December 16, 1965

The Nihil Obstat and Imprimatur are official declarations that a book or pamphlet is free of doctrinal or moral error. No implication is contained therein that those who have granted the Nihil Obstat and the Imprimatur agree with the contents, opinions or statements expressed.

© 1966 by B. Herder Book Co.
314 North Jefferson, St. Louis, Mo. 63103
London: 2/3 Doughty Mews, W. C. 1
Library of Congress Catalog Card No. 66-17096
Manufactured in the U.S.A.
Designed by Klaus Gemming

PREFACE

We regret deeply that we must forego including a brief account of the childhood of St. Francis de Sales in our present study. However, several are available, all containing descriptions of the most charming traits that have ever appeared in the lives of the saints. The purpose of this work is not to compare the youth of St. Francis de Sales with that of St. Ignatius Loyola; they were very different one from the other. We propose merely to show how the Holy Spirit elevated them through their knowledge of Scripture—especially of St. Paul and St. John—and, by means of their personal experiences with souls, implanted in them the same concept of the mystique of Christ and the same practical spirituality. In a similar manner, two torrents, gushing from two mountains distant one from the other, sometimes join their courses and form a single cataract before losing themselves in the sea.

Of what interest—dare we say necessity?—is this study? Chiefly, we intend to compare the spiritual methodology of the two saints, not to describe a historical situation. Perhaps the historians of spirituality will find in this comparative study some light on the development of the action of the Holy Spirit through the course of the ages, just as theologians like to trace the line of development of certain dogmas. Nor is it our intention to complete or modernize the very satisfactory work of the hagiographers. Father Liuima's *Aux sources du traité de l'Amour de Dieu* [1] contains a complete bibliography, should anyone wish further information.

In all knowledge, especially in the domain of the sciences, there are two kinds of genius: the genius of invention or dis-

---

[1] Since this is primarily a devotional rather than a scholarly work, full bibliographical information for works cited is given only in the Bibliography on page 250. In general, quotations will be acknowledged merely by inserting the author's name and page numbers of his work immediately after the passage quoted. Footnotes will be used only for comments.

covery, and that of the practical utilization of forces of nature already known. The same holds true of the spiritual life. There are the apostles, who received the definitive revelation, the great mystics, who were favored with visions and other interior directives, and the incalculable number of saints who put into practice the laws and counsels of those whom the Holy Spirit enlightens for the greater good of the Church. St. Paul said clearly to the Corinthians (1:14) that all do not receive the same charisms in one charity. St. Francis de Sales was richly endowed with graces to understand the spiritual life and to direct souls; perhaps no other spiritual master received these graces so abundantly and so clearly. We do not claim that he had the genius of discovery in mysticism and asceticism to a greater or less degree than St. Ignatius Loyola; it would be vain to try to discuss it. We only wish to prove that if the Holy Spirit gave St. Ignatius Loyola a truly exceptional insight to the difficult roads by which, despite the obstacles and multiple illusions of nature and the devil, we can attain sanctity and the imitation of Jesus Christ, St. Francis de Sales received from the same Spirit an equally exceptional ability to interpret clearly and skillfully the doctrines, rules and counsels of the Fathers and mystical and ascetical writers who had preceded him, together with an incontestable superiority in the fruitful application of the Christian mystique elaborated by the author of the *Exercises* to all souls, wise or ignorant, rich or poor, holy or sinful, mystical, active, or of any sort whatever, and to the temperaments, the natural and supernatural dispositions of each one of them.

Some readers—priests, religious, lay—claim that St. Ignatius is a difficult author, whose talent is too mediocre, whose language is too foreign, whose visions are too extraordinary. It is true that some of his texts are obscure and equivocal; they have been and are still being discussed. Sometimes thoughts which are not properly his are attributed to the Saint, for example, notions on the purposes of the *Exercises,* on love, the greater glory of God, indifference, vocation, prayer, the "election," the discernment of spirits, the three degrees of humility, the utilization of the third and fourth weeks of the *Exercises* and the meditation *ad amorem,* which should crown the *Exercises.* In regard to his institute, the wisdom of which has been greatly admired and followed by many, some persons have criticized his ideas on religious government, blind obedience, the methods of the apostolate, the role of the liturgy. We do not yield to these criticisms, but we do think that God favored St. Ignatius in giving him St. Francis de Sales as interpreter and commentator. He was the learned scholar whose works displayed the greatest clearness, significance, adaptation to souls, charm, unction, savor—all qualities with which St. Ignatius, in spite of prestigious intelligence, was not gifted to the same degree.

The Society of Jesus should be grateful to God that St. Francis de Sales elucidated, explained, expanded the doctrine of its founder with an incomparable mastery, so highly praised by the Popes and by all spiritual writers. Souls of all nations and all ages, reading his works seriously and *in toto,* attach themselves fervently to the spirituality of St. Ignatius. We hope that they will draw a double profit from our study, namely, (1) that of knowing and following more effectively the *Exercises* of St. Ignatius, and (2) that of nourishing their souls with the principal works of St. Francis de Sales: *The Introduction to the Devout Life, Spiritual Interviews, Treatise on the Love of God, Spiritual Correspondence.*

We advise all souls who conduct the Exercises of St. Ignatius and those who wish to probe their depths by meditation and prayer, not to separate St. Francis from St. Ignatius. We beg those who wish to absorb the true Salesian spirituality from Francis' works not to separate St. Ignatius from St. Francis. Study and experience have convinced us that it is in the union of these two great masters—in the convergence of their lights, in the identical spirit which animates them—that souls will find all the truth of the mystique of Christ, the source of all sanctity for those engaged in the active life.

Before they plunge into the exhaustive reading of St. Francis de Sales' works, we advise the "Philotheas" (as he called them) to read a short account of his life. And perhaps we should warn certain critical readers at the outset that when we compare the spiritual systems of these two great saints—a comparison which is rather a "convergence"—we do not intend to take away from St. Francis de Sales his own originality, his own genius, his dependence on Holy Scripture and the Fathers of the Church (in particular on St. Augustine), his personal and direct knowledge of the mystical and ascetical authors of the different schools that preceded St. Ignatius. It would be an error to think that St. Francis de Sales owes *everything* to St. Ignatius and *nothing* to his own supernatural lights, nothing to his lofty contemplation, nothing to the Flemish contemplatives, nothing to Bérulle, nothing to Mme. Acarie, nothing to St. Jane de Chantal, and so forth. We could have studied the "convergences" between his doctrine and that of St. Augustine, or St. Teresa, or St. Bonaventure, whose name he received at baptism and to whom he was greatly devoted. It would probably require several volumes to demonstrate his profound knowledge of Holy Scripture, the Greek and Latin Fathers, monastic life, and his influence on contemplatives of various countries, saints who have themselves composed works on the mystical life.

We have preferred to compare the two spiritualities which we know best, hoping that the one may be further clarified by the other. Even so, our undertaking is limited and unpretentious.

CONTENTS

PART ONE

Spiritual Contacts

1 St. Francis Chooses St. Ignatius

HISTORIANS of spirituality unanimously place St. Francis de Sales, whom Pope Pius IX proclaimed "eminent doctor equal to the ancient Fathers," among the masters of mystical contemplation, sometimes called in our days the "mystique of God" or of Christ. He was steeped in this mystique of God, the same mysticism into which St. John, St. Denis the Areopagite, the Greek Fathers, especially St. Clement of Alexandria, and later St. Augustine, were initiated, and the stages of which were illustrated by Ruysbroeck, St. John of the Cross and St. Teresa of Avila. He had plumbed its depths in his own meditations and in his spiritual direction of St. Jane de Chantal, a few other Visitation Sisters and several authentic mystics, such as Mme Acarie. Two books of the *Treatise on the Love of God* give evidence of his knowledge, his mastery of this subject.

The young Francis de Sales, admired and sought out by all because of his copious readings and his associations with the most influential and famous leaders of the religious society of the seventeenth century, might have been carried away by this strong current of contemplative mysticism if he had not willingly and knowingly, for the same reasons that we shall reveal later, preferred the spirituality of St. Ignatius, the spirituality that today we call the "mystique of Christ." In order to understand how fully deliberate this choice of Ignatian spirituality was, we must realize that he had read widely and deeply the works of all the schools of spirituality. Perhaps no one else of his time was as well informed as he. Let us keep this in mind as we continue our study of the parallelism existing between the two great spiritual systems.

The famous writers of the Flemish school: Ruysbroeck, Thomas à Kempis, Eckart, Tauler, Suso, were all familiar to him. Since he was a native of Savoy, we are not surprised that he, more than those from other regions, had read the works of St. Catherine of Siena, whom he loved very much, St. Catherine of Genoa, St. Philip Neri, and other less famous Italian authors. A deep knowledge of the Spanish school, made famous by Carmel, was almost imperative for a cleric of his times. When, in 1607, he thought of writing his *Treatise,* the great Spanish mystics were attracting devout souls. He read their works in their own language, being fluent in Spanish as well as Italian. In his *Treatise* he cited a few great names of the sixteenth century: García of Cisneros, John of Avila, Peter of Alcántara, Bernardine of Loredo. He also recommended a knowledge of the spirituality of Louis of Granada (d. 1588), Louis de la Puente (d. 1624), St. Teresa of Avila (d. 1582) and St. John of the Cross (d. 1591).

By frequenting the most fervent and enlightened society, mystical groups and congregations, the young Francis de Sales was initiated into the secrets of every important spirituality. Dom Richard Beaucousin (1561–1610), a Carthusian of Paris who was called by his brethren the "eye of the contemplatives," presided over a group of holy persons who had created a mystical renewal in France: Bérulle, Father Pacificus, a Capuchin, Gallemand, Mme Acarie. Francis de Sales was, so to speak, their moving spirit. He was present at the meetings, he was consulted and heeded, he advised, he acted. Antoine Dufournet (p. 243) wrote: "We know that not a single article of the future rule of the Carmelites in France, not a single statute was adopted before it was discussed with our Saint." Indeed, in his *Supplique* to Pope Clement VIII, St. Francis de Sales mentioned his active participation in the deliberations and adds his testimony as bishop, asking for the Apostolic Bull in order to confirm its establishment. We are correct, therefore, when we say that the convent of the reformed Carmelites of Paris was founded "under the auspices of the Bishop of Geneva" (*Œuvres,* XIII, 118).

His influence was not only that of a bishop; it was felt still more in his direction of consciences. The members of the group of mystics, to quote Charles-Auguste de Sales (I, 322), "chose him for their director and spiritual Father, unfolding to him the most hidden recesses of their consciences, drawing a marvelous sweetness and light from his opinions and counsels." In his writings St. Francis tells us that he had "the leisure to direct the good Gallemand two or three times" (*Œuvres*, XII, 118). For six months he was Mme Acarie's regular confessor. Almost every day he discussed "various opportunities for the service of God" with her. In his later years he ingenuously reveals his admiration for this holy soul, the consolations he enjoyed from his contacts with her, and the regrets he felt for not having profited more from these meetings. "O what a fault I committed when I did not profit from her holy conversation, for she freely revealed her whole soul to me; but the great respect that I bore her prevented me from asking her the slightest question" (C.-A. de Sales, I, 324). His friendship and esteem for Pierre de Bérulle are well known. Names of the other mystics of the same period often recur in his writings.

Nevertheless, St. Francis de Sales, informed and sought after as he was, preferred, in general, to follow the spirituality of St. Ignatius, which he knew perfectly and which for several reasons—the same ones which had oriented St. Ignatius himself in his *Exercises* and in founding his institute—had convinced him that the Holy Spirit was leading him into the practice of the admirable ways (Ruysbroeck called them "extraordinary") of St. John of the Cross and St. Teresa. It seemed to him that he had to engage himself in the "mystique of Christ," that of the apostles and the first Christians. St. Ignatius had simply revealed practical and fruitful methods of accomplishing this.

We are a little surprised at the mistrust and severity of these two great saints, Ignatius and Francis, when they judged the writings of some devout persons who declared they had been favored by sublime elevations. While still very young, St. Francis wrote in his *Introduction to the Devout Life:*

There are certain things which many persons consider to be virtues, but which in reality are not. I mean ecstasies, raptures, insensibilities, impassibilities, deific unions, elevations, transformations, and similar experiences, treated of in certain books that promise to elevate the soul to a purely intellectual contemplation, to an essential application of the spirit and a supereminent life. Note well, Philothea, that these perfections are not virtues. They are rather rewards that God gives for virtues, or small specimens of the happiness of the life to come which God sometimes presents to men to make them delighted with the whole, which is only to be found on high in paradise. For all that, we must not aspire to such graces, since they are by no means necessary for the service and love of God, which should be our only intention (*Œuvres*, III, 131–32).

And again, he repeats the same advice in the *Introduction to the Devout Life:*

Let us willingly leave these supereminent favors to elevated souls; we do not merit so high a rank in the service of God. We shall be too happy to serve him in his kitchen or in his scullery, to be his lackeys, his porters, his chamberlains. Afterward, if it seems good to him, he may admit us to his cabinet or private council. Yes, Philothea, the King of glory does not recompense his servants according to the functions they perform but according to the measure of the love and humility with which they exercise them (*Ibid.*).

At the end of his life he had not changed his opinion. He wrote to the Baroness de Chantal:

As for me, ecstasies, trances and those deific affections, elevations, transformations and such graces, those which we consider distractions from serving our Lord in his humanity and in the members of his Mystical Body, those which have no purpose except in the divine essence, let us leave them for rare souls, advanced souls who are worthy of them. We do not deserve such high rank in the service of God. We must serve him first of all in low offices before being drawn into his cabinet (*Œuvres*, XIV, 109).

And Msgr. Jean-Pierre Camus reports this observation of his highly venerated friend:

I hear of nothing but perfections, and yet I see very few people who practice them. Each one follows his own manner in pursuing them, and thus the seeking becomes a true idol of Michas. Some place their virtue in austerity; others in abstemiousness in eating; some in almsgiving, others in frequenting the sacraments of penance and the Eucharist; another group in prayer, either vocal or mental; still others in a certain sort of passive and supereminent contemplation; others in those gratuitously given, extraordinary graces. And all of them are mistaken, taking the effects for the causes, the brook for the spring, the branches for the root, the accessory for the principal, and often the shadow for the substance. For me, I neither know nor have experienced any other Christian perfection than that of loving God with all our heart and our neighbor as ourselves. *Every other perfection* without this one is a *false* perfection; it is a gold of base alloy and counterfeit. They deceive us, forging other perfections for us, giving us a Lia for that Rachel and a statue for this David. Those who attempt to nourish us with any other food deceive us (*Œuvres*, I, 60–61).

All these sincere avowals, so often repeated, leave us no doubt of his convictions and his decision to unite, as he often said, the prudence of the serpent with the simplicity of the dove. In concrete terms, he positively did not wish to wander from the path that St. Joseph and the Blessed Virgin, then the apostles and especially St. Paul, had followed. He knew only Jesus crucified; and he was particularly fond of these words: "I am meek and humble of heart. Come to me, you who suffer, and I will comfort you." "Blessed are the poor, the meek, the peacemakers, the persecuted," and so on.

In the following pages we shall show for what reasons and with what fidelity and constancy he was inspired by St. Ignatius, and how he followed him even in the smallest details as an intelligent and fervent disciple, though in his own personal way. Before expanding this, we shall quote his fundamental counsel: "Let us endeavor sincerely, humbly and devoutly to acquire those little virtues which our Savior has set forth for our cultivation and care. These are patience, meekness, mortification, humility, obedience, poverty, chastity, diligence, holy fervor, tenderness toward our neighbors, bearing with their imperfections, and so forth" (*Œuvres,* III, 132). "Little" does not mean "easy" and lacking reward, but hidden, modest, without glamor in the eyes of the world. "Praising God," he added, "for the supereminence of others, we must keep ourselves in our lower but safer way, not so outstanding but better suited to our insufficiency and smallness. In this, if we conduct ourselves with humility and faithfulness, God will unfailingly raise us to heights that are truly great" (*Ibid.,* 133).

Do we wish to know what he means by "little virtues"? He does not hide it: they are "humility, contempt of the world and oneself, simplicity. Its exercises are love of abjection, service of the poor and the sick; its place, at the foot of the Cross; its rank, last; its glory, that of being despised, its crown must be its wretchedness: *little virtues*" (*Œuvres,* XIV, 109). "I say that we must practice the little virtues without which the great ones are often false and deceiving. Let us learn to endure willingly words of abasement and those which tend to disparage our thoughts and opinions; then we will learn how to suffer martyrdom and to be annihilated in God, disinterested in all created things" (*Ibid.,* 110). He proposes as a model the valiant woman of whom the Wise Man said: "She puts her hands to the distaff, and her fingers ply the spindle" (Prov. 31:10).

"Meditate, raise your spirit, direct yourselves toward God, draw God into your spirit; these are strong things. But do not forget your distaff and your spindle; spin the thread of the little virtues, devote yourself to the exercises of charity. Whoever tells you differently deceives you and is in error" (*Ibid.*). At least ten times in his letters he recommended the asceticism of what he calls the "little virtues" as being fundamentally necessary for deep mysticism. And more often than we would imagine, he repeated these same lessons for those he was directing.

From these avowals, repeated unreservedly and unhesitatingly, and from many others too numerous to be cited, we must certainly conclude that St. Francis de Sales lived and encouraged the souls he directed also to live according to the "mystique of Christ" which St. Ignatius had taught him through his *Exercises*. The pupils in the colleges of the Fathers of the Society, such as the young Francis and many other persons, embraced their doctrine and confidently followed St. Ignatius.

Let us be excused for repeating here what we have already stated in our Preface, namely, that through reading and association with the souls of the mystics of his time and by his own personal experiences he was acquainted with the most elevated ways of contemplation. To imagine that he did not have a profound admiration for and a very lively attraction to the most perfect union with God would indicate complete ignorance of his soul, his life, his prayer, his thought. He mistrusted the nonconformities of the imagination, not those of mysticism.

2 *In the School of St. Ignatius*

IN THE SECOND PART of this book we shall, to the best of our ability, unfold the spiritual doctrine of St. Francis, comparing it to that of St. Ignatius, on which it largely depends. For the moment we wish only to report some *facts* of their relationship. These data reveal not only the love of St. Francis for St. Ignatius, but his total formation by the Society of Jesus and its founder. Between the ages of seven and nine (1574–76), Francis attended the *collège* of La Roche-sur-Foron in Savoy;

then he went to the *collège* at Annecy for his secondary studies (1576–83). Peter Favre, who was born in 1506 at Saint-Jean de Sixt and became the first priest of the Society of Jesus, had also studied at La Roche.

Francis repeatedly and tenaciously asked his father to permit him to attend the Jesuit school in Paris. Finally his father, who feared the dangers of the city of Paris for his young son, gave him permission to pursue the intellectual, moral and spiritual education of the Jesuit Fathers at the famous *Collège de Clermont*. Here he acquired a very extensive and careful training in letters, philosophy, theology and Sacred Scripture. We will speak of this again later. Let us in the meantime indicate only the outline of his studious adolescence. He was fifteen years old (1582) when he entered the famous *collège*. We must here take note of certain details which, although somewhat lengthy, are not superfluous since we are describing the formation of a character at school as well as at home. We know that the young student from Savoy was received by the Father Rector with extreme satisfaction, even though the school was quite crowded at that time.

Here is the daily schedule of the Fathers which Francis had to follow in part: the signal for rising sounded at 4:00 for the stronger students, at 5:00 for the others. A quarter-hour later prayers began, and lasted forty-five minutes. Professors and students devoted themselves to study until time for Mass, at 7:00. After Mass those who wished to breakfast, did so. At 8:00 classes began and continued until 10:00 for philosophy, 10:30 for letters. Then a Mass was said for those professors prevented by preparation for their classes from attending the earlier Mass. Dinner was at 11:30, followed by an hour's recreation, after which all returned to their studies. At 3:00, after the course of theology which Maldonnat began at 1:30, the classes were resumed and lasted until five o'clock for philosophy and 5:30 for letters. After formal classes the students reviewed their lessons for the day, either in groups or alone. Fifteen minutes of physical exercise was then granted them before supper at 6:00, which was followed by recreation until 8:15. In addition to this horarium of classes, Francis pursued his exterior practices of worship and other requirements of his domestic life, vacations, holidays, amusements, and so forth.

The number of Jesuits with whom Francis came in contact was probably approximately the same as in 1587 (the year for which we have a record): sixteen priests, eight scholastics, nineteen theology students, thirteen coadjutor brothers, and thirteen novices who had been driven from Verdun by Protestant troups; a total of nearly eighty religious. Francis de Sales associated with them daily. Anyone who has ever been a pupil of the Jesuits, no matter at what period of their history, knows with what care, devotion and fatherly solicitude they devote themselves to the intellectual and spiritual formation of their students and how they give a special preparation to those they feel can fulfill duties leading to the greater glory of God. (Cf. Charmot, *La Pédagogie des Jésuites,* Paris, 1943.)

There is no doubt that Francis de Sales, outstanding in every aspect among the 1500 students of this extraordinary *collège,* was the object of special vigilance and affection. He had everything necessary to attract the attention of the Fathers, the Scholastics, and even the Brothers: an education in which nobility of family was mingled with simplicity of manners, an exceptional intelligence, virtue without weakness, a true and earnest piety, a charm which even from his infancy attracted persons of all rank and all ages. At Clermont he profited to the highest degree from the formation given by the teaching and conversations with the Fathers and Brothers. We read in his *Memoirs* of this period: "The devoted zeal of the professors, making their instruction an instrument of the apostolate, the cleverness of their methods and the animation of their classes, the enthusiasm of students happy to escape outmoded procedures, happy also with the affection which indicated they had dedicated and devout masters," all contributed to the prosperity of the *collège.* On August 26, 1571, the Protestant Hubert Languet, the Duke of Saxony's Parisian agent, declared to Camerarius: "The professors of the *Collège de Clermont* surpass all others in their reputation."

We note that in this school, where there was an intense intellectual and social life, Francis de Sales had been chosen from among all to be prefect of the Sodality of Our Lady. By reason of this, he exercised a sort of moral authority over the other pupils. The responsibilities and honors of this office attached him more intimately to the Fathers of the Society.

Writing on the early history of the *Collège de Clermont* from 1564 to 1588, Carayan (*Documents inédits,* Poitiers, 1863) related:

As for the more reformed religious houses, like those of Chartreux, the Capuchins and the Minims, we can truthfully say that this *collège* at Paris has been like their common seminary. In addition to what has been said above, the Sodality of Our Lady helped greatly: members of this organization included scholars, several prelates, doctors, counselors, lawyers and merchants. It was customary for the great theologians to preach there; meditations, penances, confessions and Communions were very frequent, devotion was easily sustained by means of the High Masses and Vespers which were chanted with great ceremony every Sunday and on feast days.

By these few details, once we know the mind and soul of St. Francis de Sales, we realize how enthusiastically he impregnated himself with the spirituality of St. Ignatius, the activating principle of the Fathers' life and conversations and the one which directed and stimulated all their pedagogy. The contacts that he established at that time with several of the Fathers were so beneficial that he continued them throughout his life.

After he had finished his studies at the *Collège de Clermont,* his father, not without reason ambitious for his son, sent him to the famous law school at Padua so that Francis might become a prominent magistrate. Since classes at the University began in November, Francis must have arrived at Padua in the fall of 1588, when he was about twenty years old. But Providence, holding other views than those of M. de Boisy, proposed to make the young Francis a saint as well as a scholar. Therefore she placed in his path one of the most famous men of the Society of Jesus, outstanding in all fields, Father Antoine Possevin. Officially, he was professor of theology; but he taught theology as only the most erudite and intelligent men can teach it when they are enlightened by the Holy Spirit. Inspired by God, Francis did not hesitate for a second to take this remarkable Jesuit as his professor and as director of his conscience.

What did Possevin teach him? Certainly the Patristic writers, Tradition, Scripture; we will demonstrate that soon. But as his director he revealed to him St. Ignatius' illuminations very thoroughly. No one could do it better than Possevin, endowed as he was with gifts of nature and grace for this sort of teaching. He showed Francis the value and human usefulness or the methods of prayer, the struggle against faults, the examinations of conscience, the particular examen, all of which Francis applied immediately to his interior reform, perhaps in too theoretical a manner. He kept his esteem for these practices all his life. Possevin initiated him especially into the discernment of spirits, the art of knowing souls and the divers movements of the interior life. The theologian was also a psychologist of a very rare type; no one in the primitive Society except St. Ignatius was equal to him in this respect. The *Annotations to the Exercises* presented to him an art that was difficult and only slightly diffused, that of leading individual souls in accordance with their extreme diversities. That is why the Pope himself had chosen him from among several others for pontifical diplomacy; he had been sent to treat of very delicate affairs with men of quite dissimilar nations. He had a very highly developed sense of finesse. Francis de Sales, by putting himself under his tutelage, developed his own gifts of discernment as St. Ignatius had traced them in the *Exercises*. The two saints are, so to speak, two wellsprings of spirituality bubbling up from one and the same spirit. (Cf. Charmot, *op. cit.*, pp. 552–59.)

Francis' relations with Antoine Possevin were constant. In a letter of December, 1594, he congratulated himself for having been his spiritual son. A few months later he rejoiced that his friendship continued without eclipse, that he could meet his mentor and receive his advice. Addressing his friend, Antoine Favre, he rejoiced at possessing Father Possevin's good will. Even after he was named bishop, he still considered himself fortunate in having been his spiritual son. On his side, Father Possevin, some fifteen years later, assures us that he loved Francis "above all his spiritual children." Father Antanias Liuima (pp. 115–43) has recorded an almost complete list of the numerous friendships Francis enjoyed among the Jesuit Fathers. We shall borrow a few extracts from this large group. Francis was to remain faithful throughout his life to the directors of his youth. When Antoine Possevin was drawing close to his *venerabile vecchiezza,* the bishop of Geneva "confided his conscience to Father Jean Fourier, to whom he was bound by a very special friendship"; he reveals his heart to him in order to "set all the pieces . . . in their place"; he discloses his ideas for beginning the Congregation of the Visitation; he likes to refer to himself as "son and most humble servant" in letters that he wrote to other Fathers.

Robert Bellarmine was the source and model for his *Controversies*. Francis corresponded with him regarding the Congregation of the Visitation. Despite the great distance that separated them, he also wrote to Peter Canisius, whose virtue he admired; he asked him for an explication of a text and begged him to include him in the number of his sons in Jesus Christ. He rejoiced at sharing the friendship of Leonard Lessius, as well as his views on predestination. He asked for Jesuits to help in his mission at Chablais, and rejoiced at their successful efforts at conversion; he established a *collège* at

Thonon, staffed by Jesuits; and on the occasion of their jubilee he interceded on behalf of the Jesuits that their power of absolving heretics should not be withdrawn. Father Aignan Moreau helped him establish a convent of Visitandines at Moulins; Father Etienne Binet advised him concerning the vocations of several religious, as did Father Bénigne Arviset. So great was his confidence in them that he wrote on July 29, 1597, to the Duke of Savoy: "Nothing more useful can happen to this province of Chablais than that we should establish a *collège* of the Society of Jesus in the city of Thonon." Two collaborators "of great merit" in the mission of Chablais were Fathers Jean Saunier and Alexandre Hume. Father Hugon Parra requested a convent of Visitandines at Aurillac. He recommended Jesuits to help in the visitation of monasteries. Father Liuima, who cites these numerous texts and gives the sources for them, declares that his enumeration is far from exhaustive.

On the subject of dispensing from vows, he took his example from the *Rules of the Society*. In the difficulties attendant upon the spiritual government of religious women, he had recourse to "the good Jesuit Fathers." He had contacts with Father Pierre Lallemand, received from him *"advis asseurés"* and significant help in establishing the Congregation of the Visitation. Together they examined vocations. He wrote to Cardinal François Tolet, S.J., that he was happy with the state of Jesuit affairs in France because this excellent Society could contribute infinitely to the renascence of virtue and piety. To Mother Claude-Agnes de la Roche, superior of the Visitation at Orléans, he wrote: "Maintain firm relationships with the Jesuit Fathers and communicate freely with them." Written in June of the year 1620 or 1622, this letter gives evidence of the continuance of his feelings to the end of his life. From the same period a similar counsel was given to the superior at Nevers: "You may speak freely to the Jesuit Fathers, and put great confidence in them, but with much respect. If a Sister feels the need, she may even speak in private to them."

For him, the Jesuits are a sort of supreme authority. Let us recall the frequently quoted text in which he calls them powerful spirits in the service of the Church, exalts their fearless courage, their indefatigable zeal, their charity, their profound learning, the example of their holy and religious life, and the fact that by their studies they fill the world with learned men.

The *Introduction to the Devout Life* was published on the insistence of Father Jean Fourier, then translated into Italian "by several Jesuit Fathers." A little later it was translated again into Italian by Father Antoine Antoniotti. This second translation was much better than the first, in the opinion of St. Francis de Sales. After the death of the saint, Fathers Nicholas Caussin and Jean Suffren completed his project of giving to "Philothea" a more complete directive for the guidance of souls.

Dom Mackey, the great editor of Francis' works, thus summarizes the Jesuit help: "The Society of Jesus, which he had loved so well, contributed powerfully thereafter to spreading everywhere his spirit and his maxims. Among the Fathers who had known him most intimately, Father Binet, the Provincial of France and his long-time friend, Fathers Arnauld and Suffren, . . . Fathers Dragonel and Caussin also spread his teachings, the former in Christian counsels, the latter in spiritual direction. Father Talon collaborated with the Commander of Silléry in the preparation of the great edition of the complete works of our saint." This cooperation continued and was climaxed with the recent edition from Annecy under the direction of Father J.-J. Navatel, S.J.

His friendship for the Fathers of the "holy Society" is ordinarily expressed in very affectionate terms. We find a special mention for Father Jacques-Philibert de Bonivard, with whom he is bound in an "inviolable," paternal, fraternal and filial affection. We have also some documents on his friendship for Father Nicholas Polliens, in whom he had "a most special confidence," and whom he wished "to honor all his life." He owed him a special honor. In his humility he wrote to Father Polliens: "Your holy charity deceives you in my regard, in that it represents me as worthy of your affection and that of all your Fathers and Brothers, although in truth I lack all the required conditions to receive this happiness. My only claim to it is that I wish to yield to no one the honor and respect that I owe to you all, and most especially to you."

Here is his "little message of friendship" to Father Jean Fourier who was seriously ill: "I have learned from M. d'Hostel that our reverend Father Rector is very ill, and if I thought I could be useful to him I would visit him in person; but since that could render him no service, I will visit him every day in spirit, offering the most holy Sacrifice for his health. And yet, Father, I beg you to present to him my most affectionate recommendations and to tell him that if my prayers are heard in heaven he will soon find himself in his church and in the midst of his community, giving thanks for his recovered health, to use it for a few more years for the glory of God and the consolation of his neighbor."

Father Ignace Armand wrote to him concerning the projected Visitation:

Your Excellency, several persons have spoken of your intention. . . . It is true that once more they are saying you are erecting a hospital rather than a devout community, but who would not laugh with you, my most honored bishop, at the foolish brains of the children of the world? . . . It has happened before, relative to a few religious women, leading a very austere life which prevented them from receiving girls who were sickly or of indifferent health, that the world complained that they wished to receive only the healthy and robust, and taxed them with an indiscreet rigor. You have, Your Excellency, begun a seminary of special imitators of the meekness of the Word-Made-Flesh, who rejected no one. You have found the nucleus and secret in your Visitation, which is not at all too soft for the strong, nor too austere for the weak. The children of the world censure that and say that you are establishing a hospital, or too soft a life. These are the rattlings of brains empty of the maxims of the Crucifix, who do not know what the effects of this Word cost nature; nor what it means to die to self

so as to live in God, to renounce self so as to bear the Cross. . . .
Ah, who would not have pity for a virgin, one having her lamp
glowing in her hand, filled with good oil, and yet unable to enter
the convent to celebrate her marriage with the Lamb because her
shoulders were not strong enough to bear a robe woven of camel-
hair, like that of the great Baptist, nor her stomach sufficiently
strong to fast half the year and to digest nothing but roots? As for
me, Your Excellency, I believe that your dear daughters will be
the true spouses of Jesus. This good Lord was living with St.
Martha and did not refuse to go to the feast. Your Congregation
will rise up to imitate the hidden life, the contemplative life, the
good life of Jesus. Let us find in the plan of Your Lordship the
poverty and the mortifications of Bethlehem, and the reasonable
comforts of Nazareth, the solitude of the desert, and the sweet
conversation of Bethany.

It is unnecessary to bring a greater abundance of written
documents to show the intimacy of St. Francis de Sales and
the Fathers of the Society. The relationship was born at the
Collège Louis-le-Grand; it did not cease to grow during the
whole life of the priest, the missionary, and the bishop, even
to his death. The Society owes him very much; it has always
given testimony of great gratitude. He, too, owes much to the
Society, especially to its founder, St. Ignatius.

3 *Fundamental Agreement*

FEW PEOPLE outside the Society read the books of St. Ignatius. A certain number of priests and laymen find him dry,
austere, having no literary attraction. They are repelled not
only by the style, even in translations from the Spanish, but
also by the doctrine itself and the manner in which it is presented. What doctrine? Is it that of the Gospel, of St. Bene-
dict, of St. Augustine? Many persons are not able to read him
because the doctrine is not sufficiently explained or elucidated

by the Saint himself. They have caviled about the *Exercises.* Often poorly understood in his brevity, Ignatius has been accused of being either too Spanish or two imaginative, too active or too courtly, too military or too semi-Pelagian, too methodistic, too voluntaristic. They have asserted that he falsified the straight line of prayer, that he made it a human pedagogy. His Institute, too, less criticized and even exalted by some souls, has sometimes been the object of false and malevolent interpretations. Certain parts, such as the rule of "obedience of judgment" and "blind obedience," those of government and of the apostolate, have been censured as too clever and too political. Briefly, St. Ignatius needed counselors, lawyers, defenders, exegetes in his Society in order to be understood, accepted and followed by his contemporaries, and in our days by the historians of spirituality. That is why his doctrine—at least on certain points—is obscured by legends and errors. Many souls do not read him, do not know him; many judge him unfavorably and, not understanding him, assert that they do not like him.

We could, then, believe—if we lent an ear to the legends —that the doctrine of St. Francis de Sales is entirely different from that of St. Ignatius; some have even called it opposed to his. Nevertheless, St. Francis de Sales has never placed the least restriction either on the *Exercises* or on the Institute, not even on the commentaries of the Jesuit Fathers that the read with his customary penetration. We shall see that voluntarily, humbly, tenaciously, he made himself the disciple of St. Ignatius, followed him in everything, and often literally.

Let us say immediately that his *Treatise on the Love of God* and, if we wish, his letters of direction, his spiritual interviews, expound in the most exact and most precise fashion the doctrine of the *Exercises* and the spirituality of St. Ignatius. In this chapter we will content ourselves with very general views on the fundamental agreement of these two saints.

Not one of the principal points which St. Ignatius propounds briefly and that are thought to be most personal to him has been passed over by St. Francis de Sales. Whether it is a question of the love of God and of neighbor, of indifference, of sin, of the last things, of the role of the will and of grace in the spiritual life, of temptations, of discernment, of good, bad or suspect movements of the soul, of the examination of conscience, of the reform of life, of faith, hope and charity, of vocation, of prayer, of the spirit of Christ, of the moral virtues, such as humility, poverty, justice, obedience; whether it is a question of the imitation of our Lord in Bethlehem, in his hidden life and in his public life, of the contemplation of Jesus crucified and risen again; or again of the conquest of souls, of methods to be used toward the poor, the great, pagan or Christian nations—in all, we find in the works of St. Francis de Sales what we find in St. Ignatius, with no important divergence. St. Francis does it in his usual manner, that is, with lucidity, transparency, charm, the adaptation of asceticism and the mystical ways to circumstances, to temperaments, to states of souls, to variations in the human spirit, to times and customs.

But, as it is the universal custom to criticize, St. Francis has also been reproached for having proposed a Christianity that is too flowery, too easy, too relaxed, too "sweet," just as Ignatius was reproached for being too harsh. The one was not austere enough, the other too much so. Briefly, they were not in perfect unanimity, even though some have wrongly thought so.

Let us, then, attempt a confrontation on four major points of asceticism and two basic points of mysticism: love of God, indifference, obedience, abnegation or death to self, prayer, contemplation. St. Francis treats these matters with an intransigence which St. Ignatius does not surpass and which perhaps he never attained. Francis is contagious; Ignatius is didactic, structural.

Thus, no one can believe that St. Ignatius loved God more or less than St. Francis; still, he wrote nothing similar to the

Treatise on the Love of God. Furthermore, some have imagined that philosophy was the basis of the *Exercises* because Ignatius directed them to the end of creation. But St. Francis makes us penetrate into the secret abysses of the soul of Ignatius by disclosing the attractions of the love of God under all its forms. He communicates to us in burning accents, comparable to those of St. Augustine, St. Bernard, St. Francis of Assisi, St. Teresa or St. John of the Cross, his eagerness to respond to the graces of the Holy Spirit. The basis of the *Exercises* is the love of God the Creator: *prior dilexit.*

St. Ignatius twice asks his retreatant to develop the virtue of *indifference:* in the foundations and in the exercise preparatory to the election. He does it in a word and with frightening rigor. St. Francis makes it loved. He uses the same word, despite whatever displeasing connotations it may have; he calls it "loving indifference." He explains it at great length with a marvelous felicity of expression; he shows the necessity for it and the advantages of it; he describes particular cases for its use; he extends it to the other virtues, to the will that is already dead in that of God. He exalts liberty, peace, joy and the strength which results from them as well as the love which is their source—in brief, all that engages the soul to make itself indifferent, without pain, without trouble, without hesitation. St. Ignatius, through St. Francis, reaches his ends.

Obedience, the virtue which Ignatius makes characteristic of religious life in the Society, is neither neglected nor softened by St. Francis. He recommends it in all his works, showing the same preference for this virtue. He writes in his *Constitutions:* "The obedient man, according to Scripture, will tell of victories. In order, then, for this Congregation to be able to surmount the spiritual enemies and tell our Lord some day of holy victories, it must be established in *perfect obedience.* Therefore all the Sisters will obey the superior, like their mother, carefully, faithfully, promptly, simply, frankly, and cordially, that is, with complete filial affection" (XXV, 57).[1] And the elaborations, the praises, the examples that he gives to exalt this virtue yield in no way to the texts of St. Ignatius. But they are presented with a more smiling countenance, under a more attractive form.

Self-abnegation is also a capital virtue for St. Ignatius. Francis prefers to call it "abjection," but it is the same abnegation, or death to self, which he recommends throughout his ascetical works and in his letters. He seems even more demanding than St. Ignatius when he repeats: "Love your abjection." The letter to the Baroness de Chantal (August 6, 1606) repeats this word, insists on the perfection of humility which is the love of abjection. And he goes so far as to propose this question: "Do you wish to know which are the greatest abjections? They are those which we have not chosen and are least agreeable to us." He enters into minute detail and does not cease to push the soul to extremes. I have chosen an example almost at random, since there are hundreds of them, all equally forceful. In a homily on the immolation of Abraham's own will, he cried out:

O Lord Jesus, when will it be that, having sacrificed all that we have, we will immolate to you all that we are? When will we offer to you as a holocaust our free will, the child of our spirit? When shall we bind this will and extend it on the wood of your cross, share your thorns, your lance? When, like a small lamb, may we be the victims, agreeable to your good pleasure, dying, burned by the fire and cut down by the sword of your holy love? O free will of my heart, what a good thing it would be to be bound and extended on the cross of the divine Savior! What a desirable thing it is to die to self so as to burn forever as a holocaust to the Lord! O Theotimus! Our free will is never so free as when it is the slave of the will of God, as it is never so much a slave as when it serves our own will. Never does it have so much life as when it dies to

[1] See also *Entretiens spirituels,* X, "On Obedience" (p. 165: "We must advance like a blind person in this Providence . . ."); *Treatise,* IV, vii and viii, and especially VIII, xiii, IX, X; also *passim* in the correspondence.

self, and never does it have so much death as when it lives only for self.

Who has ever spoken with greater force? "Let us renounce this unfortunate liberty, and let us forever subject our free will to the heavenly love; let us make ourselves slaves for the love which makes slaves happier than kings." St. Ignatius did not dare speak of "unfortunate liberty" and the "slavery of the will." Finally, let us sacrifice "this free will and let us make it die to self, so that it may live for God." That is the pure Salesian doctrine. And, in terminating his *Treatise*, St. Francis wrote these famous words: "Theotimus, Calvary is the mount of lovers. All love which does not take its origin in the Passion of the Savior is frivolous and dangerous. . . . Love is unhappy without the death of the Savior. Love and death are so mingled in the Passion of the Lord that we cannot have one in our heart without the other" (XII, xiii).

No, St. Ignatius never wrote anything stronger than this on death to self. And we easily agree, he could never, by the grace of literary style, add such an attraction of beauty to the austerities of virtue.

One word only on the mystical life. The mystical life was evidently familiar to St. Ignatius. His spiritual journal shows him constantly elevated to the highest summits of union with the Holy Trinity. It is certain that religious souls who are called to supernatural favors will find in his *Exercises* the surest road to fidelity to grace. But he seems to refuse to trace out the mystical paths for them; he abandons them to the great theologians of the contemplative life. St. Teresa and St. John of the Cross came after him, and the Holy Spirit elevated them by his all-powerful and personal breath. In his *Treatise on the Love of God,* St. Francis employs the experiences of his own prayer life and those of the great souls who revealed the passive ways to him, to disclose to religious what St. Ignatius would probably also have counseled them, without writing it out. Books VI and VII of the *Treatise* complete the *Exercises* by giving the clearest and surest lights and direction to souls favored with exceptional gifts. In that he seems to complete St. Ignatius. But he is fully in agreement with him in counseling the spirituality of abnegation and the discernment of spirits such as they are found in the *Exercises* for souls who are called to the mystical life. We will discuss these points in greater detail later.

4   *Francis de Sales, Disciple and Teacher*

ST. FRANCIS DE SALES is much indebted to the great founder of the Society of Jesus for his thought in all domains of the spiritual life. He is superior to him in culture, in the expression of the thought, and in its adaptation to lay and religious souls. The numerous sons of St. Ignatius, in turn, owe him much. Indeed, he presents the spirituality of St. Ignatius in a fuller, more explicit manner, sometimes more profound, certainly more attractive, than has any other commentator or any Jesuit author. No one can equal him. We shall try to characterize what we can call the Salesian harmony with the Ignatian spirituality.

Culture

The learned equipment—if we can use such a term—of St. Ignatius is relatively small (See Bibliography). What he retained from his studies in Alcalá, at Salamanca, and at Paris is almost insignificant. He was inundated with so many mystical lights by the Holy Spirit that historians did not bother to list the titles of the books which he had read and the courses he had taken or given. However, he did achieve the superior grade of the *Maître dès arts*. For a more serious study of theology he selected the teaching of the Dominicans, at the convent of Saint-Jacques in Paris. From these professors he gained not only a solid theological background but a great admiration for St. Thomas Aquinas. Father Jacques Laynez, who was very close to him, wrote: "No one praises him for his literary worth, his philosophical worth, his theological worth." His historical readings were limited to a few authors. The Fathers of the Church were not unknown to him, but those he had read thoroughly were relatively few. Holy Scripture was very familiar to him. He meditated on it, long and extensively. There is no doubt that he arrived at the University on a level superior to that of St. Francis of Assisi, but his greatness, like that of *Il Poverello*, is of an order different from that of the learned teachers who instructed him. Nevertheless, St. Ignatius wished that the members of his Society should be as well-instructed as possible. On this point he differed from St. Francis of Assisi, who, it is said, discouraged learning as a temptation for his friars.

The culture of St. Francis de Sales is peerless, far surpassing that of St. Ignatius. Francis received from his family and from the beautiful land of Savoy his first impressions and his first customs. He owes to God and to his parents a nature exceptionally rich in gifts—gifts of the intellect, of the will, of the heart, as well as the equilibrium and general harmony of his physical endowments. He acquired from his family and the environment of their society a distinction of the higher standards which permitted him to please, without any effort, King Henry IV and all the nobles of Paris; he likewise attracted the children of the most wretched villages, the peasants, the poor, every human soul, introvert or extrovert, happy or suffering. The splendid variety of his country, Savoy, was not only a continual pleasure for his childhood, but an abundant source of the beauties which he enjoyed with a pure love for all things. These represented the goodness of God; these he knew how to use as symbols and metaphors in all his writings.

Paris, with its bustle and animation, stimulated his imagination. It was truly the "city of light" for him, for his memory was capable both of retaining what was truly beautiful and useful and also of forgetting what was not. His intellect was challenged by his studies at the *Collège de Clermont:* Latin, Greek, French, Hebrew, philosophy, theology, the sciences, and at the same time by experiences and associations with human nature of all ages and characters.

At that time Latin and Greek were studies for their own sakes; the humanists of the sixteenth century saw in these languages the triumph of the Renaissance. St. Francis de Sales wrote Latin, just as he wrote French, with incomparable ease. We can see this clearly in the letters he exchanged with his friend Antoine Favre from 1596 to 1597. Both of them dashed off polished Ciceronian phrases, not without a certain preciousness. The Jesuit Fathers gave instruction of great professional value, famous throughout the world, to use the words of Father Maggio, who was Visitor at the time. The latter wrote to the Father General:

This establishment is like every other nursery of youth, but more than others it has attracted the attention of princes from every part of the kingdom, even from foreign countries. Many foreign leaders write to our Fathers, proposing a multitude of questions, and they come in crowds to consult them. That is why it is always necessary to furnish this *collège* with distinguished superiors and learned professors, capable of preserving its reputation by their prudence, their eminent learning and their outstanding virtues" (Fouqueray, II, 186).

This familiarity with the Greek and Latin languages permitted Francis de Sales to read easily not only the masterpieces of ancient literature but especially the Fathers of the Church, such as St. John Chrysostom and St. Augustine, whom he quoted frequently. In addition, he wrote French with such perfection that Victor Bérard was to say of the *Introduction to the Devout Life* that it is "the introduction to the French language." Did not the Bossuets, Racines, Pascals who were the great luminaries of the language in the seventeenth century receive, like Francis de sales, the same Greco-Latin formation? St. Ignatius lacked this type of education.

On October 1, 1584, Francis had finished his studies of rhetoric and was admitted to the class in philosophy. During the first two years, this meant the study of logic and the sciences, that is, reading and commentary on the works of Aristotle and St. Thomas. The third year of the course (1586–87), under the direction of Arnaud Saphore, was devoted to mathematics, physics and metaphysics. Of Francis' other professors, we shall include only Father Jean Suárez (not to be confused with the great philosopher Francis Suárez) and Majoris (1580–88). As evidence of the type of education Francis received, we can examine two manuscript notebooks that are still extant. One of these is kept in the presbytery of Saint-Sulpice; it treats of logic, and is dated 1585–86. The other contains notes on courses in ethics taken in 1587; it is preserved as a relic at the Grand Séminaire at Grenoble. The calligraphy indicates the "character of a holy young man, his nobility of race, his tranquil soul and his glowing piety." The latter qualities are substantiated by the fact that the names of Jesus and Mary always appear at the beginning and end of his work.

The last year spent at Paris was devoted to the study of theology. Francis wrote: "In Paris I learned many things to please my father, and theology to please myself." That is why he pursued this study at Padua, continuing it throughout his life. The Fathers Jean-François Suárez and Jean Chastelier were his teachers, superior intellects whom Francis de Sales held in grateful memory. Gilbert Génébrard, one of the most brilliant theologians of his day, who employed Greek and Hebrew like his mother tongue, also had a profound influence on this incomparable student. Under his guidance Francis read the Greek and Latin Fathers, and also Holy Scripture.

Eventually the student surpassed many of his professors whose names are now forgotten. He was praised as one of the most learned and finely educated humanists of his day. Nineteenth-century authors, such as Sainte-Beuve, Strowski, Petit de Julleville, have confirmed these judgments of the seventeenth century. We wonder how a man could acquire in a short time such universal learning. Instead of dazzling our readers with these documents, we prefer to cite the apt, thorough judgments of Bossuet (1627–1704) and Bourdaloue (1632–1704), who are better known to us than many other authors. Bossuet wrote:

Three things especially have given him much renown in the world: learning, as doctor and preacher; authority, as bishop; leadership, as director of souls. Knowledge makes him a torch to illumine the faithful; the episcopal dignity put this torch on a sconce to enlighten the whole Church; and the direction of souls has applied this kindly light to the leading of individuals. See how brightly this sacred torch gleams; admire how gently it warms. The unction of his knowledge softens hearts; his modesty in authority inflames men to virtue; his sweetness in direction gains them to the love of our Lord. This, then, is an ardent and gleaming torchlight; if this knowledge gleams because it is clear, it warms at the same time because it is tender and affectionate; if he shines in the eyes of men by the brilliance of his dignity, he edifies them all by the example of his moderation; finally, if those whom he directs find themselves happily enlightened by his salutary counsels, they also find themselves touched by his charming sweetness" (*Panégyrique de saint François de Sales,* III, 578).

Bossuet developed these thoughts, describing his principal characteristics in an over-all view. On the other hand, Bourdaloue and the Abbé Dufournet analyze him very succinctly. "He was one of the most learned prelates of his century;" wrote Bourdaloue, "his profound capacity was admired by the first men of the world, for example, the Cardinals Baronius and Bellarmine" (*Œuvres complètes,* X, 287). "He was a great author," stated Dufournet, "one of the most eloquent of his time; he was one of those Christian humanists who with the clear definition of moral concepts and relations among men restored to divine creation its true character" (p. 83). We cannot express the height and originality of his humanism better than that.

Pope Pius IX, on July 18, 1877, in the Bull naming Francis a Doctor of the Church, proclaimed that the illustrious bishop of Geneva "revived the example of the Fathers of the Church . . . and that in him was fulfilled that statement of Sirach:

> Many will praise his understanding;
>> his fame can never be effaced;
> Unfading will be his memory,
>> through all generations his name will live;
> Peoples will speak of his wisdom,
>> and in assembly sing his praises (39:9–10).

The Pope "placed this indefectible light, St. Francis de Sales, the nineteenth Doctor of the Church and the first of the French language, on a candlestick." St. Ignatius, enlightened as he was by the Holy Spirit, never, either in his childhood or in his maturity, acquired a culture comparable to that of St. Francis de Sales. Providence leads each saint in a different manner.

Dazzled by the extraordinary talents of his son and by the praises he heard everywhere, M. de Boisy aspired to a glory, loftier in his opinion, than that which humanism, science, *belles-lettres*, philosophy and theology could give him. Wishing to make a great magistrate of him, he sent him from Paris to continue his studies at the University of Padua. But the ways of God were not the ways of the ambitious father.

At Padua, Francis—austere, ascetical, suffering and very studious—spent three busy years which were productive in all ways, and not merely for his intellectual development. He included the Italian language, natural history and medicine as accessory acquisitions to his principal studies: jurisprudence, to conform to the wishes of his father, and Holy Scripture and theology because of his own interest. At the same time he nourished his intellect with the works of St. Augustine and the *Summa* of St. Thomas.

Let us turn now from these work-filled years to the culmination of his studies. In the year 1591, the famous scholar Guy Pancirole gave him the *Doctorat des droits, in utroque jure,* that is, in civil law and in canon law together, which was the special diploma of the University of Padua. After a moving eulogy of the varied accomplishments of Francis de Sales, Guy Pancirole asked the prior to announce the results of his examination.

We, Jules Urbani, vicar general of the Most Reverend and Most Illustrious Lord Bishop of Padua . . . have examined the outstanding Francis de Sales, son of the illustrious Lord Francis of Savoy, originally from Thoren in Geneva, who, after studying the sciences, has appeared before us. In his examination, he conducted himself so well, so admirably, so eruditely, so honorably, so praiseworthily and so excellently, and has given such great proofs of his intelligence, his memory, his learning and all the rest of the qualities required in the most accomplished jurisconsultants, that he has not only responded to the great expectation of all his hearers, but has even surpassed it.

Francis, in a beautiful discourse, expressed his admiration and gratitude to Guy Pancirole, "prince of jurisprudence," Jacques Ménochius, Ange Matteazi, the most learned Otellio, the most excellent Castellano, and so forth. It was a day of glory for Francis' father, M. de Boisy. The goal he had desired for so many years had finally been achieved. His son was going to be the light of the Parliament of France. But he did not know that Francis, with the help of Father Possevin, had decided that he was going to become a priest. And so he did. Soon afterward he was made bishop. He became, as Bossuet expressed it, "the torch of the whole Church, not only of the jurisprudence of Savoy."

Expression

Francis de Sales is also outstanding for the expression of theological truths and of the form, both human and supernatural,

that can be given to each virtue. All authors competent on
this point exalt his exceptional gifts which, it seems, no other
spiritual writer ever equaled. Let us quote, for example,
Sainte-Beuve. Others have not said it better.

When I named Montaigne, it was perhaps only in one sense:
the author of the *Essais* endeavored to make philosophy accessible
and pleasing to all rather than the severe and roughcast study that
it was. Francis de Sales did the same thing for devotion. He wished
to make it familiar and popular. . . . The inspiration of Francis
de Sales is tender, affectionate, and burning with love of neighbor.
He is among those who on awakening in the morning and finding
themselves filled with sweetness and a singular sprightliness, could
say in all truth: "I feel a little more loving toward souls than
usual." He began his book, the *Introduction,* rather lightly; he
compares the variety with which the Holy Spirit disposes and
shades the teachings of devotion, and assigns them to each one
with the same art that the flower-girl Glycera employed in making
her garlands. He attaches himself to worldly people, he lures them,
ensnares them with the talent for pictures and images with which
nature has gifted him. . . . He cannot keep from smiling and
seeming almost to amuse himself with words, even when he is
fundamentally most serious. He resembles those bees of which he
speaks so often; we could say that he is playing while he is working. "There are," he said one time, "bitter hearts, acid and sour
hearts, bitter by their very nature, who make all that they receive
equally sour and embittered." His nature is quite the opposite;
his is the meekest, the most even-tempered and at the same time
the most active and peaceable of hearts, the cleverest at converting all things to improvement; he mingles with others in order to
pour out on them consolation and love. He is in love with souls
so as to cure them; he insinuates himself into them in order to make
an entrance there for that "interior and cordial affection which
renders all actions agreeable, sweet and easy." Devotion for him
is only a "spiritual agility and vivacity" which animates all the
elements of life. "Let us do good works promptly, diligently and
frequently." He does not approach souls with the threatening tone
of controversy, nor with the hauteur of pride; he never attacks the site, as Bossuet said, "from the side of the eminence

where presumption is entrenched"; he approaches by the most accessible point, he wins the heart, he hurries all along the low valleys, always at his constant, unwavering pace, until he has succeeded in entering and is lodged in the citadel (*Causeries du lundi*, VII, 28).

There were then, as always, some souls who loved to put thorny questions to him, in order to wound and irritate him. Sainte-Beuve cites the example of one letter which "showed how St. Francis de Sales eluded and warded off difficulties, or rather, how by his elevated manner, sweet and calm, he prevented them from ever arising."

This gracious amiability is far from being a sign of weakness; it is rather an effect of strength and poise of character. Sainte-Beuve pointed this out very effectively:

Let us observe St. Francis de Sales such as he was . . . in his strength and his interior force. Let us untangle the well-spring from the brook of his lively imagination, fertile and so pleasant that it seemed at first to be childish; for he not only had Amyot in his speech, he also had some Joinville, of the time of St. Louis. Let us separate, then, these gentlenesses and flowers in order to arrive at that soul so sweetly ardent and strong, and that character so firm, yet clothed in suavity. It is he himself who, in order to avoid that union he felt within himself, said to us: "There are no souls in the world, I think, who love more cordially, tenderly, and —I say it in all good faith—more devotedly than I; and indeed, I abound in love . . . , nevertheless, I love independent, vigorous souls, those which are not feeble. . . . How can it be that I feel these things, I who am the most affectionate man in the world?" (121st letter to Mme de Chantal). No one has painted a better portrait of a spirit nor rendered so vividly things which seemed inexpressible: light, sweetness, clarity, vigor, discernment and heavenly dexterity, the ordering and economy of virtues in a soul, all represented there and painted there with a firm and definitive stroke. Such pages do not enter literature and cannot be submitted even to admiration (*Ibid.*).

Henri Bremond, who in this regard is one of the best judges of our times, likewise praised St. Francis de Sales.

Would you think that I exaggerate in affirming that the publication of this book (*Introduction*) is a memorable date in the history of Christian thought and life? Charm of style, excellence and depth of moral analyses—no educated person is insensible to the secondary merits of Francis de Sales; less unanimously do we appreciate the basic originality which makes his book unique and of capital importance. . . . Its novelty is not in its doctrine but in the special choice he wished to make among the teachings of his predecessors, in the principles which directed, sustained and animated his diligent synthesis. . . . The great merit of Francis de Sales is having given them a limpid, charming voice, of having imposed them on the world by the double authority of his own genius and personality.

Whatever attempts may have been made in the past, the Church, at the beginning of the seventeenth century, still waited for the man of genius who could adapt Christian thought to the needs of the multitude. Francis de Sales appeared and placed, if we may so express it, the whole Christian renascence at the disposition of the most humble (II, 68).

We could never say such a thing about St. Ignatius, who is sublime for doctrine, but difficult to read, nor about several other Jesuits of the same period who tried—with too many faults and only mediocre success—the same literary venture as St. Francis de Sales. Henri-Coüannier, in a very fine analysis of the *Introduction*, wrote:

Francis has neglected nothing that might please the reader. Therefore his "poor little book," as he called it, was printed more than forty times during his lifetime. Its success did not diminish throughout the seventeenth, eighteenth and nineteenth centuries, and today it numbers more than a thousand editions and is as popular as it was at its birth.

This thunder of acclamations did not move the author. He learned that Henry IV, who professed to admire him so much, declared that this book surpassed his expectations. The Queen sent it, decorated with diamonds, to the King of England; General de Feuillant said that this was the most perfect book that he knew; the Archbishop of Vienna begged Francis to devote himself thereafter to letters; the Superior General of the Carthusians advised him to renounce any further writing since he had just attained perfection and any further work would necessarily be inferior. This latter compliment offended Francis a little; he thought only of serving God, of making him loved, and cared not one bit for his own fame.

This "thunder of acclamations," as Henry-Coüannier said, was not restricted to the single work of the *Introduction to the Devout Life.* Francis de Sales did not suffer any loss of his talents in the continuation of his life and writings. On the contrary, we find them again, with a more accomplished and more extended perfection, in his *Treatise on the Love of God,* in his *Spiritual Conferences,* in his conversations, reported in *The Spirit of Saint Francis de Sales* by Msgr. Camus, and in his extensive correspondence. They continued until his death. Indeed, we can say that he died as he wrote and as he accomplished all things: with a simplicity, a purity, a disinterestedness and a grace which are the marks of his genius.

5 *Apostolate*

ST. IGNATIUS can be considered—and indeed he is considered—as father, brother, director and model of souls by religious men and women, members of secular institutes, and laymen who understand the apostolate according to the ideal of the *Exercises* (the kingdom of Christ, the two standards) and wish to follow the rules of fidelity to "the hierarchical Church, our Mother and Mistress" (*Regulae ad sentiendum cum Ecclesia*). The same can be said of St. Francis de Sales, bishop, pastor and universal doctor. In a more personal and precise fashion he has both traced and traversed the roads common to the active Orders: the conversion of unbelievers and heretics, the eucharistic and community transfiguration of parishes, the Christian formation of children, succor given to the poor, prodigal care of the sick and the dying, and so forth.

This apostolate cannot be discussed thoroughly in a few chapters. It would be necessary to write several books to recount the history of his victorious struggles with Protestants, his catechesis, his zeal as pastor, the formation of his priests, his charity as good shepherd, his love for the poor and the sick. We sincerely regret being obliged to limit ourselves to only two testimonies. At the Mass and the *Te Deum* celebrated at Notre-Dame of Paris for his centenary celebration, Msgr. de Bazelaire spoke thus:

> The grandeur of Savoy is above all in its Christian faith. It separated from the Piedmontese monarchy and cast itself into the arms of France to keep intact the sacred deposit of the faith of its ancestors. It brought to Mother Church a treasure more precious than that of its lakes and mountains. It brought its soul, an upright soul, with the uprightness of the children of God, a soul modeled for a long time by centuries of Christian living, a soul imprinted with the love of Christ and marked by its attachment to the Church.

We should add here that it brought to all the nations of the world a holy Doctor whose spirituality has saved, brought and will bring to the highest sanctity more souls, it seems, than many other holy Doctors, after the Fathers of the Church. Msgr. de Bazelaire continued:

Ah, these beautiful famlies of Savoy in which young and old gather each evening for prayer in common and each Sunday for the parish Mass. They are given birth by a people hard at work, a people strong in the trials of life, a people united in respect for Christian traditions, a people blessed by God. Land of fidelity, Savoy had before her eyes the example of her saints. . . . Reconquered for the faith from Protestantism by St. Francis de Sales, she has lived in a climate of Christianity which has given her a spiritual countenance. Here and there convents, abbeys, monasteries dotted its countryside. The prayers of monks, the

words of preachers, the influence of religious of all Orders, the
authority of her bishops and of the clergy, circulated a current of
Christian life, and in spite of wars, conflicts, the good and evil influences of politics, assured the permanence of the divine protection. This blessing was exercised through the Middle Ages, the
Renaissance, and even to our modern times. How can we be surprised at the flourishing of missionaries who, during the last century, spread throughout distant countries, in the midst of pagan
peoples? (*Centenaire de la Savoie*, p. 39).

Summing up in a few pages what was discussed at length
by so many historians, Henri Daniel-Rops emphasizes the
catechetical work of St. Francis.

From this immense effort accomplished by the Church since she
became aware of its problems and perils, and in order to renew
itself from the interior, to return to its true fidelities and to oppose
the arms of light against her enemies, it seems that a man has
been chosen most especially by Providence to contain in his being
and in his fruitful life the very essential and most determinant
spirit for the future: St. Francis de Sales (*Eglise de la Renaissance
et de la Réforme*, pp. 465–76).

The historian expressed it first in a general manner:

It is sufficient to evoke divers points of the great plan of renova-
tion accomplished by Catholicism during the sixty years which
followed the closing of the Council of Trent in order to measure
the historical importance of this man. In the defense of the faith,
he is in the first rank; the re-conquest of lands occupied by heretics
—that is the task to which he vowed his youth; the reform of the
clergy—obstinately he consecrated himself to it for twenty years.
A new Order came from his hands and, in order to re-introduce
into the weighty mass the leaven of the Gospel, who is more efficacious than that tireless preacher, the author of the innumerable
editions of the *Introducton to the Devout Life*?

Then he recalls his rapid elevation to the episcopacy:

But what a bishop! In the small city that Annecy was at that time
—Geneva, of whose see he bore the title, was in the hands of

Théodore de Bèze—he lived modestly, more like a monk than a dignitary. Everywhere he organized catechism classes and he even taught the little children himself. To all the people whom God confided to him he wished to bring truth and life.

He preached constantly, but his preaching was instruction:

Are these sermons, these familiar interviews on such an exquisite tone, in which he mingled anecdotes, comparisons, questions thrown out to the audience, and with an infinite amount of good feeling and finesse? What a marvelous preacher was he who took as a principle: "I would not like anyone to say, 'Oh, what a great preacher! Oh, how well he speaks!' but only, 'My God, how good you are, how just you are,' and such things."

Let us be excused for not entering into the details of the prodigious apostolate of St. Francis. Our subject is more restrained. All the historians of Savoy, all the biographers, make us admire this harvest of which the multitude of seeds were sowed by the holy apostle of Chablais—later the marvelous bishop of Geneva—in Paris and his own diocese.

PART TWO

Ignatian Spirituality

6 *Discernment of Spirits*

THE *Exercises* of St. Ignatius are based on two essential principles of theology, the very foundations of the mystique of Christ: (1) *Sine me nihil potestis facere*. Nothing, absolutely nothing, can be done except through the Holy Spirit. (2) The Spirit of Christ demands the *cooperation of souls* through a docile and generous activity. This second principle results in the *Exercises*. The first principle demands not only prayer but the discernment of the Holy Spirit, since we can easily confuse it with our own natural spirit or with the spirit of the demon. (According to the Gospel, the demon tempted even Jesus in the desert.) The discernment of spirits is, therefore, essential to understanding the purpose of St. Ignatius, that is, the election of God's way for each soul. From the point of view of discernment, St. Ignatius was a creative genius. Nor does St. Francis de Sales have an equal in this regard.

We distinguish three types of discernment: (1) that of the ways of God, (2) that for individual souls, and (3) that of the three sorts of spirits.

Discernment of the Ways of God

Jesus said: "I am the Way, the Truth, and the Life." By following him we have the truth and the life. If we do not follow him, we do not receive his Holy Spirit, nor do we attain the eternal beatitude of God. St. Ignatius in his *Exercises* does not teach us this way; Holy Scripture alone reveals it. But Ignatius has taken us through Scripture completely, from the Incarnation to the descent of the Holy Spirit on the apostles. His *Spiritual Journal* gives us a first proof of this essential importance of discerning God's will. This journal is not a logically composed book, written painstakingly in solitude; it is a brief jotting of notes by the Saint to preserve his experiences, inspired either directly or indirectly by the Holy Spirit. The source of the observations in this little book and the method by which he obtains the precise knowledge of the ways of God are: assiduous prayer, fervent assistance at Mass, mortification, purifications, confirmations by a lively faith. In the preface to this *Journal*, Father M. Giuliani, S.J., shows in detail "that Ignatius constantly practiced the same method, allowing the grace of God to enlighten him slowly and to conduct each problem to its solution." He awaits, first of all, light from his prolonged and repeated prayers. "These Masses and these meditations cause him to advance day by day in the knowledge of god's mystery and in docility to the Spirit: the journal is manifest proof of this" (p. 11).

Let us add this fact, strange though it may seem. In general, Ignatius implores the "confirmation" of lights which direct him, that is, "that God grant him a seal to the decision already taken in his soul, and no longer awaits anything but the final sign in order to become an act, his act, which will in reality be God's act in him." It is of great value to quote the following statement, since it enlightens us how to seek the ways of God.

Before the Mass of the 18th, Ignatius asked for "confirmation" and thought he was denied it; on the 23rd he wrote on the margin of his manuscript, "Confirmation of Jesus." Between these two moments lies one of the greatest mystical experiences related in his journal. God at first seemed not to answer, but delayed only that he might better console him who sought him. Indeed, on February 19, the divine "understanding" was such that Ignatius had the feeling of being illuminated beyond all knowledge; he contemplated "in feeling or in seeing" the relations of the Persons in the bosom of the Trinity" (p. 23).

The total confidence we have in the Ignatian method is based not only on the certitude of the holy founder but also on the initial and continued approbation of his book by the popes. Let us recall only that statement found at the end of

Pope Pius XI's statement on July 25, 1922, because his words seem to conform to the spiritual direction of St. Francis de Sales:

Truly, the excellence of a spiritual doctrine completely guaranteed against the perils and errors of false mysticism, the admirable facility with which these *Exercises* can be adapted to persons of every class and every state, whether they are members of religious orders or leading a life in the world, the perfect connection of its parts, the marvelous clarity of order in the truths proposed for our meditation, and finally, the spiritual teachings which help men shake off the yoke of sin and heal their moral miseries—all these lead souls to the heights of prayer and divine love by the sure way of abnegation and victory over their passions. Without any doubt all these advantages explain superabundantly the efficacious nature and power of the Ignatian method.

We can be sure that in the eyes of those who have read the works of St. Francis de Sales attentively and exhaustively this high recommendation of Pope Pius XI merely repeats what other Roman Pontiffs have already expressed. Before substantiating this statement, let us recall Pope Pius IX's eulogy when he proclaimed Francis "Doctor of the universal Church." We cannot be surprised by this identity of views and methods when we realize with what intelligence and filial love Francis made the *Exercises*. Confiding in the lights of St. Ignatius and inspired by the same spirit, he followed the same methods to discover the ways of God and his designs for him and others. He thus arrived at an astounding wisdom. Even some lay persons, like Sainte-Beuve, and theologians, like Bossuet, also admire him.

In his *Histoire du bienheureux François de Sales,* Charles-Auguste de Sales (I, 327) attests that Francis made a retreat of twenty days before his episcopal consecration. He became accustomed to following the *Exercises,* influenced as he was by his Jesuit education at Paris and his more intense formation at Padua.

According to the Brief of Doctorship, Francis owes his title of "Doctor of the universal Church" not only to his published works, such as the incomparable *Treatise on the Love of God,* but also to his correspondence.[1] Furthermore, if we consider the letters that he wrote to a great number of correspondents, it will be clearly evident that Francis de Sales can be favorably compared to the most important of the ancient Fathers of the Church when he explains and defends the Catholic Faith, when he elucidates questions of the faith and applies these truths to conforming his life to the moral truth of Christianity. He wrote with great spiritual authority and abundant knowledge to the Sovereign Pontiffs, to princes, magistrates, priests, his collaborators in the sacred ministry. His zeal, his exhortations, his admonitions, his counsels purified regions of their heretical pestilence, established Catholic worship there, and widely extended the Catholic religion. His letters, sent to a great number of persons, provide a rich harvest of ascetical teachings. We admire unreservedly the inspirations of the Spirit of God pervading his correspondence; the suavity of the author implants in souls the seeds of the cult of the Most Sacred Heart of Jesus, which we, in our difficult times, regard as so important for the increase of piety and the uplifting of our souls.[2]

---

[1] *Maximam etiam rei asceticae segetem epistolae ipsius ad plurimos datae suppeditant, in quibus illud plane mirabile est quod spiritu Dei plenus et ad ipsum suavitatis auctorem accedens, devoti cultus erga Sacratissimum Cor Iesu semina miserit, quem in hoc nostra temporum acerbitate maximo pietatis incremento mirifice propagatum, summa cum animi nostri exultatione conspicimus.*

[2] *Quinimo, si ipsae epistolae ab eo ad plurimos scriptae considerentur, cuique compertum erit Franciscum ad instar gravissimorum inter veteres Ecclesiae Patres, a compluribus, de iis quae ad catholicam fidem explicandam tuendamque, quaestione ea dire enucleandas ac vitam ad Christianos mores componendam pertinerent, rogatum saepe fuisse; ipsumque multa persecutum copiosissime ac docte, apud Romanos Pontifices, apud Principes, apud Magistratus, apud sacerdotes cooperatores suos in sacro ministerio, adeo valuisse, ut ejus studio, hortationibus, monitis, consilia saepe inita fuerint quibus regionis ab hœretica lue purgarentur, Catholicus cultus restituetur, religio amplificaretur.*

During the retreat preparatory to his consecration as bishop, under the direction of Father Jean Fourier, whose sanctity he proclaimed to Pierre de Bérulle, he wrote "with his own hand" "an episcopal rule" which was inserted into the first process of canonization. His retreat extended from November 18 to December 8 and ended with a resolution to make a retreat of "eight days or more when he can" every year; he then described the principal exercises recommended by St. Ignatius. An editor's note informs us: "Our Saint was always faithful to this resolution. Ordinarily he chose the days of Lent and the *Château de Sales* for his place of retreat." It was there and on such an occasion that in 1604 he had an ecstasy in which he learned that he would found a religious order and he saw "the phantasms or ideas of the principal persons by whom this order would take its beginning" (C.-A. de Sales, *Histoire*, VI, 311). In 1615 he was again spending the last days of Carnival at Sales, no doubt preparing for his retreat (*Ibid.*, XVI, 313–320). The next year he consecrated the novena of Pentecost to this recollection (*Ibid.*, XVII, 214 ff. See also XXI, cxxi, cxxii and cxxxii). Mother de Chantal was also in retreat at this time.

On January 8, 1620, he wrote to Mother de Chantal: "What shall I say at the beginning of this year? I am *Roi de bon jeu* in your house (he had drawn the piece of cake with the charm in it on the feast of the Kings), and the Sisters seem very happy about it. At the beginning of next week I shall make my retreat, for an extraordinary renewal of spirit which our Lord is inviting me to make, so that as these transitory years pass I may prepare for eternal ones" (*Œuvres*, XIX, 100).

In his history of the Church, Father F. Mouret speaks very favorably of the *Exercises*. He places them in opposition to the heretical tendencies of the times:

No one has ever spoken of the marvels of the divine life with such great depth and sureness of doctrine. Protestantism had recently denied outright its existence in souls. Perhaps we have not sufficiently noted how the negations of Luther found their best refutation in the positive work of St. Ignatius and St. Teresa. According to the thesis of the heresiarch, man sanctifies himself neither by his works nor by his personal efforts, but only by the application of the merits of Christ which cover his soiled soul like a mantle, without changing its interior. The *Spiritual Exercises*, by their marvelous efficacy in converting souls, showed how much the efforts of a man wisely disciplined by divine grace could accomplish (V, 571).

Francis attached such great importance to retreats, even for seculars, that in his *Treatise* he described them as a "holy method, familiar to the ancient Christians, but lapsed into disuse until the great servant of God, Ignatius Loyola, again put them into practice a generation ago." According to him they are a necessary means to "review our lives and restore all the pieces of our hearts into their places." He wrote to the Baroness de Chantal on January 10, 1606, that he was going to follow the *Exercises* with Father Fourier at Chambéry, whom he expected "to calm my poor soul all upset by so many affairs."

As Bishop of Geneva, he said that the *Exercises* converted more sinners than they contained letters. He founded a retreat house for men and granted women living in the world the privilege of retiring to the Visitation for recollection. He considers this withdrawal from everyday cares essential to spiritual progress. On February 2, 1616, he wrote to Mother Favre, superior of the Visitation at Lyon: "In answer to my Lord the Archbishop . . . on the alternative he proposed to me . . . I unreservedly leave the choice to him, except that of the principal end of our Congregation which provides that widows . . . can retire there until any impediment to their profession or taking the habit is removed and that women of the world can enter there to make the *Exercises* and to practice their devotions according to their circumstances." He wrote to Cardinal Bellarmine (July 10, 1616) noting as a

happy specialty of the new congregation that it was au-
thorized to "admit married women who wish to undertake a
new life in Christ and to make, with the preparation of some
spiritual exercises, what they call a 'general confession' and
who need to withdraw for several days to some place removed from the bustle of the world. We cannot sufficiently
estimate what abundant fruits this holy and brief hospitality
produces."

The spiritual direction of the Baroness de Chantal is particularly interesting from the point of view of method. We find
there all the means which St. Ignatius used: prayers, Masses,
examens, questions pro and con, election according to the
Holy Spirit and reason; the "confirmation" expected from God
is not absent. How many times St. Francis made the over-
eager soul of St. Jane de Chantal wait until in her prayer she
should have the "confirmation" that her project was certainly
the will of God. The foundation of the Visitation in particular was decided in the Ignatian manner, according to the
"*Spiritual Journal* of the Saint," that is, after years of prayer,
several "confirmations" of the Holy Spirit and even one or
more visions. For St. Francis, the *Exercises* were then the best
itinerary to follow when seeking the will of God.

Discernment of Souls

First of all we must distinguish: souls of good will and souls
recognized as striving for perfection. The first, the souls of
good will, endeavor to purify themselves of their sins and to
conform their life to the known will of God. The rule, given
by our Lord and proclaimed vigorously by the Evangelists
and by St. Paul, is charity, universal and without exception.
To these souls St. Ignatius proposes the *Exercises* in the
measure in which they are able, with God's grace, to follow
the law of Jesus Christ. He requires of them integrity, sincerity, generosity, and he proposes to them the meditations of
the first week, that is, the general and particular examina-

tions of conscience, confession, Communion, the first rules for discernment of spirit. By these means the retreatant will acquire knowledge of God, of himself and of the world; he will be initiated into the discovery of the demon's snares; he will learn how to struggle against evil tendencies and temptations; he will break with perverse habits; he will make effective resolutions; he will order his life according to God; he will devote himself to the persevering observance of the commandments of God and the Church; in brief, he will live as a good Christian. The first part of the *Exercises* must be proposed to all sinners, to all souls. One sermon, or even a series of sermons, is not sufficient. It is necessary to be isolated in a secret place, to meditate, to pray, to be instructed and directed.

The Curé of Ars spent his life pursuing the strayed and wounded sheep; he went out each day to meet the prodigal child. In the same way, we ought to encourage the maximum number of souls to make the Ignatian retreat. The retreat master will see in the first week whether the soul is implementing the program traced out by Ignatius and whether the Exercises should be continued. He sees the soul called by God to a higher degree of virtue, to the evangelical counsels, to a more perfect spiritual life, and even to the apostolate; he will encourage it to pursue for one week, two weeks, or even for a month the work elaborated by St. Ignatius and divided into three "weeks," more or less prolonged. One cannot flatter himself at having made the *Exercises* if he interrupts their course; he must arrive at the end without avoiding the difficult phases.

St. Francis de Sales directed a great number of souls. Henry Bordeaux has written—and no other author disputes it—that

never did St. Francis de Sales flatter or scorn anyone; he was no more concerned with the title and rank of Madame de Chantal, Madame de la Fléchère or Madame de Charmoisy than with the insignificant villager, Pernette Boutey, of whose death he could not learn without "wiping his eyes," because he knew how great she was before God; or with the poor widow of Annecy whom he perceived "following the Blessed Sacrament, and while others carried long white wax candles she carried only a small tallow dip, made by herself, until the wind extinguished it" (p. 179).

"Everyone had access to him." That is true to the letter. "To the great annoyance of his servants, the first one to come entered his office, even ragmen and charlatans. An old blind woman recited her woes interminably, and he felt himself indebted to her. He was on equal footing with the poor and with the children whom he loved to teach catechism. The calm and serene death of a peasant whom he had heard speak so well of God that he wanted to go see him, filled him with emotion." He fled the court when they intrigued to make him frequent it: "Well-born spirits do not amuse themselves with these trivialities of rank, honors, salutations—they have other things to do; that is the concern of ne'er-do-well spirits." When Henry IV himself invited him to Paris to make him one of the great bishops of France, he answered wittily: "Sire, I beg your Majesty to excuse me; I cannot accept this kind offer. I am already married; I have espoused a poor wife and I cannot leave her for a richer one."

Evidently a diocese is less burdensome when the bishop concerns himself only with generalities. But Francis de Sales was essentially a pastor of souls and director of consciences. In the Preface to the *Introduction to the Devout Life,* he declares in his own manner the joy he experiences when directing souls individually. This page is worth quoting:

It is painful, I grant, to give individual direction to souls; but it is a pain that brings comfort, like that felt by the laborers in the harvest and the vineyard, who are never better pleased than when they have the most to do and when their burdens are the heaviest. . . . It is that when the tigress finds one of her whelps which the huntsman leaves in the way to beguile her while he carries off the rest of the litter, she puts it upon her back and yet does not feel herself encumbered. On the contrary, she is more active in the course that she takes to bring it back safely to her den, for natural love lessens the weight of her burden. How much more willingly, then, will a fatherly heart take charge of a soul in which he has found a desire for holy perfection, carrying it in his bosom as a mother does her little child, without being wearied by so precious a burden! But his must indeed be a fatherly heart. Therefore apostles and apostolic men call their disciples not only their children, but even more tenderly, their *little children*.

Each soul found Francis as unhurried as if he had no other in the world under his care. For each one he found a special counsel, the one needed, the healing word, the comforting admonition. "We must not be surprised," he wrote, "if each herb and each flower in a garden requires a particular care." "Far from complaining at the number, the insistence, the fancies or repetitions of these penitents, he worried about them all as if each was the only one." Without doubt, he was harassed by souls ill with scruples, worries, melancholia, as are so many nowadays, for they are found in every age. "He recalls in his correspondence a passage from the ancient Fathers of the Church which says that hens always have much work when they are leading their chicks, and that is why they cluck continually. . . . He, likewise, is ceaselessly solicitous for his flock."

Does not our Lord show us the picture of the Good Shepherd abandoning his flock to seek the straying sheep? And in the confidences given to certain privileged mystics, such as St. Margaret Mary, does he not say that for *her alone* he would have died on the cross and would have instituted the sacrament of the Eucharist? St. Francis de Sales imitated Jesus in his apostolic zeal. "Our Lord," said Madame de Chantal in her deposition, "regulated the charity in this holy soul; for, as many souls as he loved *particularly*—vast numbers of them —that many different degrees of love had he for them; he loved them all perfectly and purely, according to their rank, but none of them equally. In each one he noted his most estimable qualities in order to give him proper rank in his love, according to his duty and according to the measure of grace in each of them."

Bossuet, in his panegyric (II, 580), cites as a precious document this statement of Cardinal du Perron: "The great Cardinal du Perron has given us a beautiful testimony. This rare and admirable soul, whose works are the strongest rampart of the Church against modern heretics, has said several times that anyone could convince the erring, but that if he wished to convert them he should conduct them to our prelate (Francis de Sales)."

Before directing the Visitandines in the religious life, and some of the holier ones in the mystical paths, St. Francis directed lay persons, whose names have remained famous. Let us cite, for example, Mme de Charmoisy, Mme de la Fléchère, Marie and Hélène Lhuillier of Fransville, the countess of Dalet. Historians have recounted the spiritual adventures of many others and have tried to portray some traits of their characters. Their director, Francis de Sales, is found confronting all the difficulties that can be met with in the lives of young girls, married women, mothers of families, widows, religous women, priests, religious superiors, and more. There are, as we all know, some inextricable situations in families, in social relationships and in business. Perhaps today they are even more serious, but even in the seventeenth century souls were assailed, sometimes tempestuously, by all the suffering and the anguish of living. It has been said that the works of St. Francis de Sales which are known to us do not include letters of direction of souls engaged in some pathetic or degrading passion. But we know by the deposition of Mme de Chantal that the Bishop of Geneva restored calm of families prodigiously troubled, at a time when the violence of both love and hate was extreme and often led to exile, disinheriting, and even to bloodshed.

St. Francis had received from God the gift which St. Ignatius should have had and which he esteemed so highly, namely, that of penetrating the state of joy or suffering of each soul which came to him, and the ability to prescribe the best remedy. His book, *Introduction to the Devout Life,* contains many directives for persons living in the world. It corresponds with all the subjects which St. Ignatius felt should be considered for the first week. Francis treats them with greater detail and, perhaps, with greater delicacy.

Discernment of Souls Striving for Perfection

The discernment of individual souls had been recommended by St. Ignatius as a prime necessity both for receiving candidates into the Society and for permitting retreatants to prolong the *Exercises* for a full month. A "general examen" which studied all aspects of the postulant's life should precede entrance into the novitiate. The candidate should be questioned on his past, his present, his dispositions and capacities for the future; information should be sought from competent, trustworthy persons. Not only a true and exact assurance of his good health, his good qualities and his weaknesses, from all points of view—intellectual, moral, and spiritual—were required, but also knowledge of his family, his origin, his rights, his duties, even—with prudence—his serious failures against the commandments of God and the Church. Briefly, St. Ignatius did not wish to receive any man into his Society unless he knew him well. The novitiate was also a sort of universal experience which should reveal the whole man. The novice had to pass through trials in which he would be judged capable or incapable of living according to the rule of the Society.

This is also true of the *Exercises.* The number of precautions written by St. Ignatius in his little *Manuel des retraites* is more extensive than one would imagine. First of all, St. Ignatius agreed to prolong the *Exercises* for a month only for certain well-chosen persons, and not for all those who asked. He always prepared them, sometimes for months or for years, and the preparation showed whether or not it was necessary to continue the *Exercises* during thirty days of retreat. Twenty "annotations" elucidate the manner in which the meditations and other spiritual exercises should be proposed, ways to hasten or slow down the movement of the four "weeks," to compress, to repeat each daily task, considering the physical, moral and spiritual state of nature and grace in each individual. These "annotations" prove beyond question the truly extraordinary importance St. Ignatius attached to the psychological make-up of each individual retreatant.

But even though we know the principles of St. Ignatius with certitude, we know almost nothing about the manner in which he applied them in dealing with souls. A few cases, such as that of Nadal, have been preserved in the *Monumenta*, but an infinity of others have remained secret. This is not true of St. Francis de Sales. He is totally in agreement with St. Ignatius on the necessity for individual psychological considerations for discerning spirits. But the application that he makes of the Ignatian rules is clearly shown in his correspondence and through the personal testimony of thousands. The story of these Salesian "directions" is by far the best commentary on the principles and rules of St. Ignatius contained in the book of the *Exercises* and in certain explanations, more or less authentic, included by some editors.

Many spiritual directors are not enlightened by theoretical abstractions and do not modify their practice, their routine, in any way. But St. Francis de Sales is a master, a doctor, a saint, for whom the discernment of souls was not only a prime necessity—as it was for St. Ignatius—but also a consummate art. In his time, he was perhaps the most prodigious director who *applied* the rules. The study of the Salesian and Ignatian methods is very difficult, since their application of the rules varies with each soul and according to the successive dispositions and unforeseen movements of the Holy Spirit.

Let us choose the privileged case of the direction of St. Jane de Chantal. There we shall see how St. Francis used the seventeenth, eighteenth, nineteenth and twentieth annotations to the *Exercises*. This will necessarily be only a cursory study.

First phase: *Francis agreed to direct a soul, even one which by many titles seemed to be raised on high, only after having recognized beyond a doubt that this direction was the will of God.* He followed the rules of the election, sometimes even waiting to receive a light from the Holy Spirit. He wrote to Mother de Chantal, suffering from doubts:

The choice which you have made [of him as her spiritual father] has all the marks of a *good and legitimate election;* do not doubt that any longer, I beg you. You have indubitable and infallible signs that it is the will of God that this great movement of soul has brought you to me almost by force and with great consolation. The lengthy consideration I have devoted to this matter before consenting to direct your soul, the fact that neither you nor I have trusted only ourselves but have applied the judgment of your confessor, a good, learned, and prudent man [Father de Villars, rector of the Jesuits at Dijon], the fact that we have waited in order to cool off the agitations of your conscience if they were poorly grounded, even the inspiration of our prayers, not of one day nor of two weeks, but of several months, are further evidence of the holy will of God.

What Jesuit, accustomed to the prudent methods of St. Ignatius, would not recognize his system of directing in this text? And what follows seems to reflect still more the lights of the *Exercises*. First of all, the action of the demon is to be perceived and feared. "The movements of the evil spirit or of the human spirit vary considerably. They are frightening and violent, but not constant. The first advice they hurl at the disturbed soul is *not to heed any counsel,* suggesting that these are the counsels of people with little ability or experience. They pressure the soul, they wish us to cut off an activity before having treated it sufficiently, to be content with a short prayer which serves only as a pretext to establish the more important things." But Francis, like Ignatius, insisted on the capital point: "There is no equality in our deeds." That is to say, the demon has no part in them. "That was neither you nor I who made the treaty; that was a third person who in that matter could look to *God alone.* The difficulty that I presented at the beginning, proceeding only on the considerations that I should have given it, must be wholly resolved. I wished to follow neither your desire nor my inclination, but only God and his providence."

"Stop there, I beg you, and dispute no longer with the enemy on this subject; tell him boldly that it is God who wished it and who did it." However, prayer, reason, and purity of intention are not the only factors. The Holy Spirit, as St. Ignatius says on the first two occasions of the election, intervened directly in the souls of St. Francis and St. Chantal. Charles-Auguste de Sales (I, 377–78) reports a vision in which the holy director saw a woman dressed in black, like a widow, accompanied by two religious. "He heard interiorly that these three persons were to be the first religious of his Institute" (Hamon, I, 489). This vision was confirmed by an analogous vision of St. Chantal's. Riding one day in the fields,

she suddenly saw, at the bottom of a hill, not very far from her, a man resembling our blessed Father Francis de Sales, bishop of Geneva, dressed in a black cassock, with his rochet and biretta, just as he had been the first time she saw him at Dijon. . . . While looking unhurriedly at this admirable prelate, she heard a voice saying to her: "There is the man beloved by God and men, into whose hands you should entrust your conscience." The vision disappeared from her bodily eyes, but remained so impressed on her holy soul that about twenty-five years later she said in confidence to a certain person (Mère Françoise-Madeleine de Chaugy) that it was as fresh in her mind as the day on which she received this heavenly favor, which was then followed by several others (*Ibid.,* p. 502).

Second phase: *Having decided to undertake the direction of "this soul" St. Francis tried her as an instrument for an important work, without making his projects known to her. It* was his plan that she found a religious institute to which Jesus proposed to confide the revelations of his divine heart. Even the director did not know all the riches of his great design. But, like St. Ignatius, he was convinced that in responding wholly to God's love, it is of primary importance to be detached from created things. Therefore, the holy director, having decided to fulfill the will of God, required of Jane de Chantal the complete renunciation of all that a Christian mother considers good and precious: her country (Burgundy), her children, her friendships, her relatives, her habits. For example, he wrote to her: "Keep in mind the maxim of St. James that worldly friendship is the enemy of God. Take care not to receive or foster any worldly friendship under any pretext whatever. This is a very important point." We see very well whither the director was heading: "The fruits are: distraction of heart, nebulousness of spirit, disgust of soul, dissipation of the interior faculties." Would the Baroness who put herself under his direction be capable of beginning her formation with such sacrifices? "Cut off those friendships and do not dally about doing it gradually; you must use the scissors and the knife. The knots are thin, but are interwoven, twisted together. You think you are strong enough to untie them and unlace them, but your fingernails are too short to tear through all those knots. You must cut them with a sharp knife. The cords are of no value; do not spare them." Would her soul hesitate to pursue this road with such a director? "It is not I who say this," he finished, "it is God."

At another time a situation arose which permitted the Saint to try her again. Mme de Chantal saw dying in her arms one of the nieces of Francis de Sales, Jeanne-Françoise, whom she had agreed to entertain at her house during the vacations. In order to save the girl, before consulting her director, she offered God her own life, and even the life of one of her children. She also made a vow to give one of her daughters to the house of Sales. Subsequently informed of this death, these prayers, and these generous offerings, the director, inspired by God, far from congratulating her for her devotion and her great courage, immediately sent her a letter in which he censured her, an admirable letter which no worldly person would have written. These few lines are very revealing of Francis' direction:

> I do not think it is good that you offered your life or that of one of your children in exchange for that of the deceased. No, my dear daughter, we must not only accept what God strikes us with, but we must also acquiesce that it be in the manner which pleases him. We must leave the choice to God, for it belongs to him. From these temporal losses, my daughter, with which God touches the lute-strings of our heart as he chooses, will result a beautiful harmony. "Lord Jesus, without reserve, without an *if*, without a *but*, without any limitations, may your will be done, to father, mother, daughter, in all and everywhere." I do not say that we should not wish and pray for their preservation, but, my dear daughter, we should not say to God: "Leave this one and take that" (*Œuvres*, XIII, 328–33).

Other circumstances, frequent in the life of the holy baroness, were seized upon by St. Francis de Sales to obtain from his *dirigée* the virtues that St. Ignatius recommends so strongly in his fifth and twentieth annotations. Detachment and generosity are proof that we shall not stop on the road but continue the efforts of the *Exercises*. We are only at the beginning of the soul's ascension, called by God to perfect union with him. But from the beginning, Francis de Sales, according to his principles, granted or withheld admission to the Visitation to certain souls. He said he did not wish a congregation of mollycoddles and weaklings.

Third phase: *Convinced by many trials that Jane de Chantal could reach sanctity and become the founder of a religious congregation, he asked of her total confidence in her director and complete freedom of spirit.*

In this, the third phase of his direction, these two attitudes may seem contradictory; they derive, however, from a single

principle: dependence on the Holy Spirit. Francis de Sales
does not agree with those directors who wish the soul to
make a vow or a promise of submission to him. In this he is of
the same mind as St. Ignatius, expressed in the fourteenth
annotation. Direction can be that of the Holy Spirit only if
the soul, disengaged from all human attachment and animated by lively faith and filial abandonment, sees in her director the presence, the word and the will of God. "When the
director sees the retreatant advance in consolation and great
fervor, he must warn him not to make any insufficiently considered or precipitous promise or vow."

St. Francis de Sales holds absolutely to liberty of spirit in
confidence:

I have never understood that there was any liaison between us
which bore *any obligation except that of charity and true Christian
friendship*, St. Paul's "bond of perfection." And truly it is that, for
it is indissoluble and never suffers any rupture. All other bonds are
temporal, even that of obedience, which can be broken by death
or many other causes; but that of charity increases with time and
takes new strength by its duration. . . . There, my good Sister,
. . . there is our bond, there our claims which the more they bind
and press us, the more they release and liberate us. Their only
force is suavity, their only violence, sweetness; nothing is so pliable
at that, nothing so firm. Consider me, then, closely bound to you
and take care not to seek more unless this bond is contrary to some
other bond, either of a vow or of a marriage (*Œuvres*, XII, 285).

This letter was written at the time—the exact date is
unimportant—when Mme de Chantal had another director.
Frequently Francis de Sales would say, often repeat: "It is
my opinion that I have nothing at all but God and all souls
for God." He was pleased by the purity of her love. Nothing
is more beautiful than this letter of July 7, 1607, a masterpiece and a model: "How I desire your consolation, my dear
daughter. But only if it is the good pleasure of his divine
Majesty, for if he wishes you on the cross, I acquiesce to his
will. Come, come, my daughter. We are well on our way.

Look neither to the right nor to the left." He said that this uprightness strengthened his heart. Let us read the following evidence of his candid simplicity:

I love this incomparable love (the love that I bear for you). . . . It is unwavering and without measure or reserve, but sweet, easy, most pure, most tranquil. . . . These are the signs of the Holy Spirit. . . . Briefly, if I am not mistaken, all is in God. Why, then, should I not love it? But what am I saying? Yes, I would not erase the words; they are too true, and have no danger in them. God, who sees the hidden corners of my heart, knows that there is nothing there except what is his and accords with his wishes. I desire, through his grace, to be nothing to anyone and let no one be anything to me.

Now, what he demands of his own soul he also demands of the soul he is directing. When he expresses himself thus, "our unique soul," "our most unique heart," "our unity," it means that director and directed love God alone, only for God and in God, with the same liberty. He uses these terms to the end of his life. He asserts that his affection is "whiter than snow, purer than the sun." "What a consolation in heaven," he wrote in the same letter, "to be led into this ocean of charity" (*Œuvres*, XIII, 84). Henri Bremond was correct when he wrote:

It was the goodness, the beauty of God that they loved and that they sought, with which both of them were impregnated when they reposed one in the heart of the other. Both of them were a radiation of these divine perfections which their human eyes could not yet see face to face, but the light for them was soft and did not conceal from them the fire in which, forgetful of the ray and of themselves, each day more closely, sooner or later they must finally be engulfed (p. 142).

When the soul had arrived at that summit, which is also a point of departure, its director could promise to draw great fruits for the last weeks of the *Exercises*. The soul will learn how God communicates his Spirit in order to make himself loved without measure. Perhaps he will grant his grace of mystical union, of spiritual marriage for which it has been prepared, although it has neither requested it nor earned it by its own efforts. There is no reason for God to refuse it graces superior to those which the *Exercises* do not explicitly define but for which they open the door.

St. Francis de Sales knows all the ordinary and extraordinary ways of grace. Souls as abandoned as that of St. Jane de Chantal must receive two new graces which correspond to the second and the third weeks of the *Exercises:* the radical despoilment of self, even to the third degree of humility, and then the mounting of Calvary, even to the death on the cross. The letters of the holy bishop return with an incredible strength and frequency to these two points, without which the supreme end of love cannot be attained.

St. Ignatius had required of the retreatant, from the beginning of the second week, a total oblation of self, an active oblation which enkindles the holocaust of all self-love. St. Francis de Sales is no less demanding and formal. One cannot trifle with God.

I wish you to continue the exercise of despoilment of self, abandoning yourself to our Lord and to me. But, dear Mother, I beg of you, intersperse a few actions of your own in approbation of the spoliation, for example, ejaculatory prayers: "I most earnestly wish it, Lord"; "Withdraw completely all that covers my heart"; "Lord, I except nothing; snatch my self-love from me"; "O self, I leave you for always, until my Lord commands me to take you back."

Still, dear Mother, if you please, it is not necessary for you to take any other sustenance; but, as you see, leave off what you still have and live as a poor little worthless creature before the throne of God's mercy; live completely divested of all, without ever asking for any action or affection from creatures. Make yourself indifferent to those it will please him to give you to command, considering that it is I who will serve you as your support. If you take a director of your own choice you will not deny your self-will and thus will always have your own choice, which is, however, what you should flee above all things.

These renunciations are admirable: from our own esteem, from what we were according to the world (which was truly nothing except in comparison with poor wretches), from our own will, from complacency in all creatures and in natural love, and, in short, from our self, which we must bury in an eternal abandonment in order not to see nor to know it any longer except when God orders us and according to what he orders us. Write me if you find this lesson good.

God wishes to possess me forever. Amen. I am his here and there —in myself or in you—as you very well know, for you are inseparable from me except in the exercise and practice of the renunciation of our whole selves for God.

After this divestment, does any obstacle to perfect union still remain? Yes, several. First of all, strangely enough, there is the obstacle of the virtues, or attachment to the virtues.

That is all very well, dear Mother. Truly it is necessary to remain in this holy divestment until God reclothes us. Remain there, said our Lord to the apostles, until you shall be clothed from on high with virtue. . . .

Certainly your imagination errs in representing to you that you have not left off the care of yourself and the affection for spiritual things, for have you not abandoned all and forgotten all? Say this evening that you *renounce all the virtues,* desiring none of them except in the measure that God wishes to give them to you, rejecting any concern for acquiring them except in proportion as his goodness will employ them for his good pleasure.

Our Lord loves you, Mother; he wishes you to be entirely his. Let no other arms but his support you; rest on no other bosom but his and that of his providence. Do not direct your glances elsewhere, but fasten your mind on him alone. Hold your will so simply united to his in all things that he will be pleased to act with you, in you, through you and for you; let nothing come between you. Think no longer of friendship nor of the unity which God has established between us; think not of your children, nor of your body, your soul—nothing at all, for you have given all to God. Clothe yourself with Christ crucified. Love him in all his sufferings. Make ejaculatory prayers to him. Whatever you must do, do no longer because it is your inclination but only because it is the will of God.

My health is very good, thank God. This morning I began my review of conscience which I shall finish tomorrow. I feel deep in my heart a new confidence in serving God better in sanctity and justice all the days of my life; and I find myself stripped of worldly desires, thanks to him who died stripped of his every garment in order to lead us to live a denuded life. Oh, Mother, how happy were Adam and Eve when they had no garments.

Live happily at peace, my very dear Mother, and be re-clad with Jesus our Lord. Amen (Letter to St. Jane de Chantal, August 10, 1619).

St. Jane replied that she had received this grace of spiritual nudity with ineffable joy. This was the fruit of direction. On another occasion she wrote to her spiritual father:

My God, how deeply the knife has penetrated! Can I live long in this feeling? At least, I desire that our good Lord will hold me in his resolutions, if it pleases him. How much strength your words have given to my soul! How it touched and consoled me when you said to me: "How many blessings and consolations I have received from knowing that your soul is stripped before God!" Jesus wishes you to continue this consolation and he wishes this happiness for me.

I am filled with hope and courage, most peaceful and tranquil. Thank God, I am not impatient to see what I have stripped off; I remain rather simple. I see it as something afar off but I dare not approach and touch it. Suddenly I turn aside. May he who has thus despoiled me be blessed! May his goodness strengthen and fortify me for the execution, when he wills it. When our Lord gave me that sweet thought that I sent you on Tuesday of letting myself go to him, I did not think that so soon would he begin to despoil me of myself, making me thus put my hand to the task. May he be blessed in all, and may he be willing to strengthen me!

I do not tell you that I have little light and interior consolation; still I am at peace everywhere and it even seems that our Lord, these past few days, has withdrawn a little that sweetness and suavity which gives the feeling of his dear presence. Today again, more or less, there remains very little for me to rest upon and so repose my spirit; perhaps this good Lord wishes to put his holy hand in all the places of my heart so as to take everything from it and to despoil it of all. May his holy will be done!

Oh my dear Father, I happened to remember today that one time you commanded me to despoil myself, and I said, "I don't know of what." And you said to me, "Have I not told you very often, my child, that I would despoil you of everything?" O God, how easy it is to leave off what is outside us, but to leave our skin, our flesh, our bones and to penetrate into the innermost marrow—which is, it seems to me, what we have to do—that is a tremendous thing, difficult and impossible, unless we are helped by the grace of God. The only glory, then, is due to him; may it be given him forever.

My dear Father, never will I reclothe myself with that consolation without your permission. It seems to me that I must do nothing further, have no thought, no affection, no will except what is commanded me. I finish, then, by sending you thousands of greetings, and telling you what I seem to see. It seems that I see the two portions of our spirit as one, singularly abandoned and dwelling in God. Amen, my dear Father. May Jesus live and reign forever! Amen (August 9, 1619).

Why have we insisted at such great length on this point of renouncement? Because nothing is more conformed to the second and the third week of the Ignatian *Exercises,* and because without this grace the soul cannot arrive at the highest union. Francis de Sales is not satisfied until the soul has mounted Calvary, which in his *Treatise* he calls the "Mount of Lovers." His favorite expression is associated with that of love: "death to self." In his correspondence as well as in his *Treatise on the Love of God* the name of Jesus Crucified, in whom we must die and who must die with us and in us, recurs constantly. "Are not God's crosses sweet and full of consolation? Yes, provided that we die in them, as did our Savior. Courage, now, my dear daughter, let us die, if it is expedient." To clothe Christ Crucified by the Holy Spirit and then by love, that is the Pauline formula, essential to Ignatian spirituality. St. Francis de Sales, as we see again and again, traces all perfection to it. It is a formula familiar to the Visitandines.

The Cross redeems us, and the Resurrection of Christ makes us live the life of the Trinity. Thus Bremond, who omits some capital points in his *Histoire littéraire,* is very careful to point out how St. Francis de Sales conducts souls to mystical union. It is the explicit end, not merely of the *Exercises* but of the spiritual life itself. Souls following these points throughout their life can attain this end only after much effort. In general, theologians teach that the graces of higher prayer are given to these souls only if God invites them gratuitously to this "extraordinary" repast. Francis de Sales has always been esteemed as a mystical doctor; one of the greatest, the surest, the clearest. Therefore we see, as Bremond said, that the most vigilant Orders have adopted this book of mysticism without the slightest hesitation. The Jesuits themselves, he added, ordinarily severe toward any spirituality which ventures away from the "beaten paths," have warmly accepted this mystical work because their Society is in some manner recognized in the work of their former student. Bishops, priests, seculars, Oratorians, Capuchins, Jesuits and others, having been influenced by a sole and single force, are carried on by the same current.

Directors are always more or less enlightened by the lights of the holy souls whom they are directing. For example, Father de la Colombière received many graces from his associations with St. Margaret Mary. The same is true, to a lesser degree, of St. Francis de Sales and St. Jane de Chantal. The latter, because of her Carmelite influences, her personal experiences with mystical prayer, could contribute to the composition of certain chapters of the *Treatise on the Love of God.* "The book of the love of God," its author wrote to her, "is written especially for you." Bremond comments on this statement: " 'For you' is not enough. 'According to you, listening to you, looking at you, raising myself little by little to the life I saw you were living,' that is what he should have said, and indeed, it is what he did say many times over." And in order to write his masterpiece, Francis de Sales probably did not need these additional lights which came principally from the foundress of the Visitation but also from other souls whom we have already mentioned, e.g., Mothers Favre, de Bréchard, de Châtel, de Blonay and de la Roche. All gave a faithful account to their holy director of the favors heaped upon them, and they served also as witnesses to the mystical phenomena described in his admirable treatise. The life of Mother Anne-Marie Rosset in particular was an uninterrupted succession of supernatural operations of the highest order. Bossuet did not fear to describe her soul as being in an anticipated state of the blessed, while Mère de Chaugy wrote of her: "We know that our holy Founder had her in mind when composing several chapters of his sixth, seventh and eighth books on the love of God."

What personal part, then, should we attribute to St. Francis? That of *Master,* that part which St. Ignatius gives in his *Exercises* to the director of the retreat. Let us add that of bishop, saint and founder of a contemplative religious congregation. For many years he had enjoyed exceptional experiences of the mystical life. And the sanctity that he demanded of his new institute was not inferior to that which St. Teresa proposed for her daughters at Carmel. Bremond did not force the meaning of the texts of the *Correspondence* nor of the *Treatise* in favor of his thesis of the "mystical invitations." All historians agree with him in affirming that St. Francis de Sales is one of the greatest masters of contemplation.

In regard to those of its children who were making the *Exercises* of St. Ignatius, the Society did not hold them back on the road leading to the highest mysticism. Those who have been favored with exceptional graces in their prayer are numerous. This is also true of the religious of the Visitation. The spirituality of St. Francis takes into account our weaknesses and spirit and body. But, trusting in grace, it puts no limit to the power of love. Like God himself, Francis

as an eagle incites its nestings forth
  by hovering over its brood,
so he spread his wings to receive them
  and bore them up on his pinions (Dt. 32:11).

7   *The Alternance of Spirits*

ST. IGNATIUS' TEACHING in the *Exercises* on the discernment of spirits has been studied a hundred times. According
to his formula, spirits are the good and bad angels, or, if you
prefer, the Holy Spirit and the demon. They act on our intellect—indeed, on all our faculties—and even on our bodies,
but we must not confuse them with personalities themselves,
under the pretext that they are "spirits." We will not study in
this résumé the thoughts and counsels of St. Ignatius; our purpose is simply to show the close parellelism between the spiritual systems of St. Ignatius and St. Francis de Sales.

In the works of the latter, his superiority over St. Ignatius,
which we have already pointed out in regard to the other dis-
cernments, is evident. The rules of St. Ignatius are utilized
there, not in an abstract form but with the explanations, comparisons, examples and practical counsels which the author of
the *Exercises* did not give, but which add a concrete value for
personal guidance to the Ignatian teaching.

The rules of the first week are not quoted, copied or repeated, but reproduced in the *Introduction to the Devout
Life* (Part IV) and in a multitude of letters. The rules of the
second week are expounded explicitly in all his works, in his
correspondence with the holy souls of Carmel, of the Visitation, and of the world. We shall omit the teaching of the *Exercises* for the first week on sin, mortal and venial, on the
general examen (thoughts, words, acts), on temptation, on
scruples, on confession, on the reform of life. It is, indeed,

common to all theologians, and the manuals of moral theology make the necessary distinctions. But St. Ignatius and St. Francis de Sales are in agreement in their insistence on the necessity of distinguishing the spirits which move the soul in its various moods and humors in retreat and in its whole spiritual life.

The *alternance* of spirits is a constant fact to which St. Francis de Sales often returns in his correspondence. He wrote: "God continues the existence of this great world in perpetual change: day always changes into night, spring into summer, summer into autumn, autumn into winter, winter into spring. One day never exactly duplicates another; some are cloudy, some rainy, some dry, some windy—a variety which gives great beauty to this universe. It is the same with man, who is, according to the saying of the ancients, a *microcosmos,* for he is never in the same state, and his life on this earth rolls by like the waters, flooding and receding in a perpetual diversity of movement. And never a single one of these days, not even an hour, is entirely like the other." Therefore he invites us to keep a "continual and inviolable equanimity of heart in such inconstant happenings and although every thing about us turns and varies, we must remain constantly immobile, so as to look at and tend toward God." He encourages us by the comparison of the boat which follows its compass needle despite contrary winds.

And here again, the thought of St. Ignatius is developed: "Let everything be overturned, upside down, not only around us but in us, that is, let our soul be sad, joyous in sweetness, in bitterness or in peace, in trouble, in clearness or in shadows, in temptations, in repose, in pleasure, in disgust, in dryness, in tenderness, let the sun burn it, or the dew refresh it. Yet, always and forever the point of our heart, of our spirit, of our superior will—which is our rudder—must incessantly look and tend perpetually to the love of God, its Creator, its unique and sovereign good." This characteristically Ignatian idea, found already in the "foundation of the *Exercises,*" and recurring particularly in the discernment of spirits, is illustrated a hundred times by his disciple.

Francis himself, despite his long experience, his equanimity of humor and mastery of passion, does not escape these divers movements. He wrote in confidence to the Baroness de Chantal, to her "alone":

I feel a little more loving toward souls than usual; it is the only advancement I have made since I last wrote you, and in the meantime I have suffered great dryness and derelictions, not prolonged, however, for my God is so good to me that no day passes that he does not flatter me in order to win me to him. Wretch that I am! I do not correspond at all to the fidelity of love which he showers on me. . . . There is always something to be confessed, for I commit faults through ignorance and stupidity, because I do not always know how to find the right way. Savior of the world, what good desires I have! But I cannot fulfill them (*Œuvres*, XIII, 139).

. . . You speak truly, my poor dear Péronne-Marie, when you say that there are two women in you. The one is a certain Péronne who, like St. Peter her patron always was, is a little touchy, sensitive and a little vexed everytime anyone crosses her. This Péronne is the daughter of Eve and, consequently, is in a bad mood. The other is a certain Péronne-Marie who is eager to be all to God and, in order to be all to God, wishes to be completely humble and humbly sweet toward all her neighbors. It is this latter who would like to imitate St. Peter who was so good after our Lord had converted him. This Péronne-Marie is the daughter of the glorious Virgin Mary and consequently has good intentions. These two daughters of such diverse mothers are in constant disagreement. The good-for-nothing one is so bad that sometimes her good mother is hard pressed to defend herself. Then this poor, good daughter thinks she has been conquered and that the wicked one is stronger. But this is not true. Surely, my poor, dear Péronne-Marie, this wicked one is not stronger than you, but she is bolder, more perverse, crafty, and opinionated. When you weep, she is very happy because it is always so much time lost, and she rejoices at causing you to waste your time even though she cannot make you lose eternity.

My dear daughter, pluck up your courage, arm yourself with the patience which we must have with ourselves. Often awaken your heart so that you will be sufficiently on your guard to prevent being taken by surprise; be more attentive to this enemy; wherever you step, think of her, for this wicked girl goes everywhere with you and if you are not careful, she will think of some way to harm you. And when all of a sudden she attacks you, making you tremble and twist a little, do not become angry but call upon our Lord and our Lady; they will extend to you their holy help, and if they do allow you to suffer for a time, it will only be to make you call upon them again and more loudly for help.

Do not be ashamed of all this, my dear daughter, no more than St. Paul who confessed that he had two men within him, one of whom rebelled against God while the other obeyed him. Be very simple, do not become angry; humble yourself without discouragement; take heart without presumption. Know that our Lord and our Lady, having placed you in the bustle of the household, know and see that you are harassed, but they will not allow you to become attached to yourself, provided you are humble and confident. But, my daughter, do not be ashamed of being inefficient and bungling; it is better to be inefficient than wicked. Provided you humiliate yourself, all will turn out well. (Letter to Mme. de Chastel, October 28, 1614).

I see clearly this ant's nest of inclinations which self-love arouses and fosters in your heart, my dear daughter, and I know very well that the condition of your spirit, delicate and fertile, contributes something to that. But still, my dear daughter, in the long run these are only inclinations, since you feel an importunity and your heart complains of them. There is no indication that you consent to them, at least, deliberately. No, my dear daughter, your soul has conceived the God-inspired desire of belonging to no one but him; do not believe that he consents to these contrary movements. Your heart can be disturbed by the feelings of its passion, but I think that only rarely does it sin by consent.

"Unhappy man that I am!" exclaimed the great Apostle (Rom. 7:24), "Who will deliver me from the body of this death?" He felt that his body was an army composed of humors, aversions, attitudes and natural inclinations which had conspired for his spiritual death; and because he feared them; and because he hated them he could not bear them without grief, and his grief caused this outburst. He answered himself that the grace of God, through Jesus Christ, will not guarantee him freedom from fear, from fright, from alarm, from combat, but will prevent him from being overcome.

My daughter, to be in this world and not feel these movements of passion are incompatibilities. Our glorious St. Bernard affirmed that it is heresy to say we can persevere in one same state here below. The Holy Spirit, speaking of man, said the same thing through Job, that never is he in the same state. This is in response to what you say of the lightness and inconstancy of your soul, for I believe firmly that it is continually agitated by the winds of its passions and that, as a result, it is always in turmoil. But I also firmly believe that the grace of God and the resolution that it gives you to remain continually at the peak of your spirit where the standard of the cross is always raised and where faith, hope and charity always proclaim: *Vive Jésus!*

See, my daughter, these inclinations of pride, vanity and self-love are mingled everywhere and thrust themselves perceptibly and imperceptibly into almost all our actions; but, even at that, they are not the motives of our actions. St. Bernard, noticing one day that these inclinations were annoying him while he was preaching, exclaimed, "Go away, Satan. I did not begin for you and I shall not stop for you."

I have only one thing further to say to you, my dear daughter, concerning what you wrote me about feeding your pride by affectations in speech, in your letters. It is true that sometimes in conversation affectation passes unnoticed, but if we ourselves perceive it, we must change our style. In regard to letters, however, it is much more intolerable, because we more easily notice what we are doing. If we detect a notable affectation, we must punish the hand that wrote it, making it write another letter in a different style (Letter to the Abbess of Port-Royal, 1619).

These few extracts of letters show very well what St. Francis de Sales thought about the diversity of spirits. St. Ignatius had called attention to this alternance of spirits, that it was not only a succession but a frequent intercrossing of lines. We are not assured of always "being in orbit," as we say today, for the demon can intervene to turn aside our thought from the sole end toward which we must tend. The wind changes and we think, wrongly, that we are following the straight path. We shall have occasion to speak of what is called in mystical parlance the "angel of light," that is, Satan disguised.

8 *Consolation*

ST. IGNATIUS WROTE "To those who work ardently to purify themselves from their sins and who advance from good to better in the service of our Lord God . . . the good Spirit abiding within them gives courage and strength, consolations, tears, inspirations and peace, rendering their progress very easy and *removing all obstacles so that the soul may advance in doing good*" (N° 315). The good angel touches the souls of those who progress from good to better gently, lightly, sweetly, like a drop of water which penetrates a sponge" (N° 325).

During twenty or thirty years of St. Francis de Sales' life, these rules of the *Exercises* inspired, so to speak, his whole direction of souls of good will. They express a spiritual counsel which he repeated hundreds of times in his correspondence. For example, he wrote to a religious of the Visitation: "Having noticed that when [the motions of the Spirit] come from the Lord, they bear us toward the good with sweetness and suavity. We are indifferent to success because we will remain in peace, provided we have done what was demanded of us. On the other hand, the evil spirit presents our desires for virtue with bitterness, pain, worry and pressure; if we find some obstacle now and then, we are troubled, we strain ourselves" (Letter XLVI). Everywhere in the search for perfection for ourselves and for others, in the exercise of authority, in the reform of communities, in government, in our own zeal, the fault that reproaches souls that are impatient, harassed, agitated, self-willed, nervous, is most often the realization that they are not acting according to the good Spirit, that is, completely sweetly, suavely, with delicacy.

For Francis de Sales, the word "consolation" means three different things. First of all, it is an enjoyment of feeling, satisfied by beauty, truth, friendship, by the admirable life of animals, such as bees, doves, pigeons, by the splendor of nature, mountains, lakes, flowers—in short, all creation. We could here write several chapters on his notion of God's presence in all things, according to the recommendation of St. Ignatius. Let us note in this regard a point that is too rarely observed, namely, that in order to imitate our Lord in the Gospel, Ignatius contemplates all that charms his eyes and ears, as a light on the spiritual life, to such an extent that he urges us to take the bees, the doves, the pigeons, the eagles as models of perfection because of the purity of their instinct. This first consolation is of natural origin, even if its object is spiritual; the liturgy, the naiveté of children, poverty, wretchedness, illness—everything puts his heart in union with the goodness of God. St. Francis wrote to Mère Chantal at Lyon:

I wrote to you while on my way to Sales, . . . and now I am writing to you on my return. I had *three consolations* there and you will be happy to know what they are, for what consoles me consoles you, as another self.

First of all, there was my dear little sister, whom I found more lovable than ever, and more eager to become brave and devout.

Secondly, yesterday was Ash Wednesday and I spent the morning all alone on the porch and in the chapel, where I enjoyed sweet memories of our delightful interviews when you were preparing for your general confession. It is impossible to tell you what good thoughts and affections God gave me on this subject.

Thirdly, it had snowed considerably, and the yard was covered with more than a foot of snow. Jean came out to the yard and swept a certain part of it clear of snow, then threw some grain so that the pigeons who come in a flock to this refectory would have something to eat and could enjoy it with admirable peace and decorum. I enjoyed watching them. You would hardly believe the great edification these little creatures gave me, for they never said a single word, and those who were first to eat some of the grain flew to one side to wait for the others. And when they had left about half the place free, a number of smaller birds which had been watching them drew near. All the pigeons who were still eating withdrew to a corner, leaving the greatest part of the place for the little birds who also came to the table to eat. The pigeons did not trouble them at all.

I admired this charity, for the poor pigeons had so great fear of disturbing the little birds to whom they were giving alms that they huddled together at one end of the table, to carry on the metaphor. I admired the discretion of these beggars who came to the alms-giving only when they saw that the pigeons were at the end of their repast and that there was a sufficent amount left over. In short, I could not hold back my tears at seeing the charitable simplicity of the doves and the confidence of the small birds in their charity. I do not know if any preacher has ever touched me so deeply. This image of virtue did me much good all day long" (*Œuvres*, VI, 313).

The second meaning that St. Francis gives to the word "consolation" is that which St. Ignatius describes in the *Exercises:*

I call it consolation when there is aroused in the soul some interior movement which makes it begin to burn with love for its Creator and Lord, and as a consequence, the soul can no longer love any creature on the face of the earth for its own sake, but only in the Creator of all things. Likewise, when we shed tears from grief at our sins or for the Passion of Christ our Lord, or for other causes directly ordered to his service and praise, this is also consolation. Finally, I call consolation every increase of faith, hope and charity, every interior joy which attracts us to heavenly things and to the proper salvation of our souls, giving it repose and pacifying it in its Creator and Lord" (N° 316).

St. Francis de Sales followed that annotation which recalls joys of the mystical order and gives several examples of what he himself frequently experienced. It seems that he lived in an atmosphere of spiritual consolation, which came to him directly from the Holy Spirit.

This plan gave me a thousand happy thoughts, but I do not wish to tell you about it, except that I was making the octave-day procession for Corpus Christi, bearing the Blessed Sacrament. You see, I was adoring him whom I was carrying, and it came to my heart that this was the true Lamb of God who takes away the sins of the world. "O holy and divine Lamb," I was saying, "how miserable I would be without you! Alas, I am clothed only with your wool, which covers my misery before the face of our Father." On this thought Isaia says that our Lord, during the Passion, was as a sheep that is sheared without saying a word. And what is this divine fleece if not the merit, the examples, the mysteries of the Cross? It seems to me, then, that the Cross is the beautiful spindle of the holy Spouse of the Canticle, of that of the devout Sulamite; the wool of the innocent Lamb is preciously bound to this merit, this example, this mystery.

Now, reverently place this spindle on your left side and spin continually by means of considerations, aspirations, and holy exercises—that is, by a holy imitation. Spin, I say, and draw into the loom of your heart all this white and delicate wool; the cloth which will be made from it will cover you and guard against confusion on the day of your death; it will keep you warm in winter, and, as the Wise Man said, you will not fear the cold of the snows. And it is, perhaps, what the same Wise Man thought when praising this holy housekeeper. He said that she bore in her hand strong things, and that her fingers held the spindle. What are those strong things which are related to the spindle if not the mysteries of the Passion, spun by our imitation? I wished you a thousand and a thousand blessings and that on the great day of judgment we would find ourselves completely clothed, as bishop, as widow, as married person, as Capuchin, as Jesuit, as vinedresser, but all in the same red and white wool, the colors of the Spouse. That, my dear daughter, is what I had in my heart when I held the Lamb in my hands.

Yesterday, (for I must tell you this one more thing), since I was in the city to preach a sermon, I gave a homily to the Poor Clares who had repeatedly begged me to do this. When we came to the point where I was contemplating how they laid the cross on the shoulders of our Lord and how he embraced it, saying that with it he took on himself all our little crosses, and that he kissed them all in order to sanctify them, particularizing that he kissed our dry-nesses, our contradictions, our bitternesses, I assure you, my dear daughter, that I was much consoled and had difficulty in control-ling my tears. Why do I say this? I do not know, except that I could not prevent myself from telling it to you. I had much con-solation in this little sermon, at which were present about twenty-five or thirty devout souls of the city in addition to those of the monastery, so that I felt free to relax the bridle on my poor and slight affections on a worthy subject. May the good and meek Jesus always be King of our hearts.

In the third place, the word "consolation" can mean an ex-traordinary influx of light into the intellect and of super-elevation of the human will without any natural cause nor any bond with the objects which occupy the activity of the spirit or the senses. There is no doubt that it is sometimes sus-pect; we must make the examen necessary to recognize the good Spirit.

Perfect consolation is given especially by the Eucharist and not by contemplation. One of the daughters of St. Francis de Sales, St. Margaret Mary, has illustrated in an extraordinary fashion the ineffable joys which the *real presence,* the *Holy Sacrifice of the Mass,* and *Holy Communion* can produce in certain mystical souls. Is not spiritual inebriation one of the effects of the eucharistic sacrament? How many other souls, in addition to the messenger of the Heart of Jesus have been favored with similar consolations! The consolations of-ten given to contemplatives do not result from their methods nor from their ascetical efforts, but from the gratuitous love of God. St. Francis de Sales, from his frequent personal experiences and those of St. Jane de Chantal, spoke of this in his *Treatise on the Love of God.* This "living flame of love" which also describes St. John of the Cross, whose burning wounds announce the beatitude of the elect, consumed these two souls, that of the Founder and that of the Foundress, the one by the other.

The mystical life flourished in the houses of the Visitation and consequently "all interior joy," as St. Ignatius expressed it, which calls and attracts to heavenly things filled these burning souls without any other cause than the effusion of the Holy Spirit. Mère de Chaugy witnessed this, and noted it in her *Mémoires:* "Immense goodness gratified these dear souls with all sorts of supernatural favors; several, within a very short time, by divine grace, with prayers of quiet, with loving sleep, with the highest union; others, with extraordinary lights of the divine mystery in which they were absorbed in a holy manner; still others with frequent ravishments and holy departures from themselves in order to be completely happy, taken up in God where they received great gifts and graces from his divine liberality" (p. 166).

The Foundress, who was better acquainted with these than anyone else and who knew what God expected from the Visitation, recalls several times in her correspondence that "all those who apply themselves to prayer from the beginning, as they should, and who do their duty in mortifying themselves and practicing the virtues (we recognize here the road traced by St. Francis de Sales) end up . . . in the simple presence of God, through an entire abandonment of themselves to Holy Providence" (*Sa vie et ses œuvres,* III, 337). She adds that "the perfect union of souls with God" is the purpose of the Visitation. "I hold that this manner of prayer is essential to our small Congregation; this is a great gift of God." (*Ibid.,* V, 471).

But we must remember one important point. The distinguishing character of "consolation," according to St. Ignatius, is the *setting aside of obstacles* which prevent the soul from advancing rapidly toward good—and if God wished, toward all sorts of martyrdoms. Nothing is more contrary to true consolation than this relaxation, the "soft pillow of doubt" or of pleasure, facility, "sugar and honey," as it is sometimes called. St. Francis' correspondence, as we shall see later, resembles the "lily among thorns" (Cant. 2:2). He hardly ever writes without making an appeal to great courage and energy. This letter to Mère de Chantal reveals his complete thought on consolation:

> I have written to our Sister N. N. lovingly. I assure you, dear Mother, that it is with my whole heart, for I love this poor girl with a perfect heart. There is no one in the world, I think, who cherishes souls more cordially, more tenderly, and—I am convinced—more lovingly than I, for it has pleased God to make my heart that way. But, nevertheless, I love *independent, vigorous* souls, those that are not *wishy-washy,* for too great tenderness confuses the heart, disturbs and distracts it from the loving contemplation of God, prevents complete resignation and perfect death to self-love. Anything that is not God is nothing for us. How is it possible that I feel this way, I who am the most affectionate person in the world? . . . It is a marvel how I adjust to all this, for I love nothing at all but God and all souls for God (*Correspondence*, X, 216).

Who could imagine that the holy director would write these things to his daughter, Jane de Chantal, making a personal admission that he did not act like others. He sets up a general rule. He has always loved strength of soul joined to "cordiality." For him, "consolation" is strong, enterprising. It advances with large, rapid steps toward God. Therefore, one of the constitutions of the Visitation demands this, and particularly, "from the first reception of those who desire to be members of the Congregation."

He frequently reminds Mère Angélique Arnaud (we shall speak of her later) that the mark of the Spirit of God is consolation. The strict discipline, demanding and harassing, which prevailed at Port-Royal did not conform to the inviolable rule of St. Ignatius. Likewise, let us recall that his calm manner of making Mme de Chantal wait for years because she had always sought rapid and definitive execution of her own plans is very remarkable from the point of view of the discernment of the will of God through consolation. Very many other souls were directed in Ignatian ways by the holy bishop.

We must, then, at all cost, avoid confusing the "consolation" of God with false sweetness, relaxation, well-being, the caresses of nature. St. Francis de Sales knew the beatitude of the soul that rests in God, at least as much as most saints. He had "tasted God," if we can so express it, and in God all Gods creation. This experience brought him more joy than that of those souls, well-born and rich with gifts, who please themselves by living in a climate of beauty, love, confidence, and human exaltation. We defy any and every reader to find in two or three thousand pages written by St. Francis de Sales even twenty lines showing a lack of love and appreciation for the works of God. And yet, an entire volume could not contain the ejaculatory elevations of his heart smitten like a person in love (he liked to use this expression) with the Blessed Trinity. We shall bring out a few proofs of this. The page we quote as evidence of this Ignatian "consolation" is one of those which occur several times in the twelve books of the *Treatise on the Love of God*.

The great St. Bernard, while yet a little boy at Chastillon-sur-Seine, was waiting in church on Christmas night for the divine office to begin. The poor child fell into a light slumber during which (O God, what sweetness!) he saw in spirit, yet very distinctly and clearly, how the Son of God, having taken on human nature, and become a little child in his mother's most pure womb, was virginally born of her with a humble sweetness mingled with a celestial majesty. . . . This vision, Theotimus, so filled the loving heart of the little Bernard with gladness, jubilation and spiritual delights, that all his life he had an intense perception of it. Therefore, though afterwards, like a holy bee, he always drew the honey of a thousand sweet and heavenly consolations from all the divine mysteries, still he had a more particular sweetness in the solemnity of the Nativity, and spoke with a singular relish of the virgin birth of his Master. . . . If a mystical and imaginary vision of the temporal and human birth of the Son of God . . . can ravish and delight so greatly a child's heart, what shall it be when our spirits, gloriously illuminated with the light of glory, shall see this eternal birth by which the Son proceeds, "God of God, Light of Light, true God of true God," divinely and eternally! Then shall our spirit be joined by an incomprehensible complacency to this object of delight, and by an unchangeable attention shall remain united to it forever (Bk. III, ch. xii).

St. Bernard and St. Francis resembled each other as two brothers; they received the same "consolations," as the *Canticle of Canticles* of the great monk of Clairvaux demonstrates. Indeed, a large portion of the sermons of the *Canticle of Canticles* could have been composed by St. Francis de Sales and the effusions of charity of the holy bishop would not have lacked the nuptial love expressed therein. But the purpose of all these divine favors is to impel us to work, to give ourselves, to suffer the passion.

St. Francis de Sales knew very well that St. Bernard had shown by his fasts, his austerities, his missions, his crusades, and also by several sermons of the *Canticle of Canticles* that consolation is given by the Holy Trinity to aid us in following Jesus in his Incarnation and in his Passion. The Son of God lived in an infinite beatitude. But the love that he had received from his Father pressed him with "urgency" to "descend" into created humanity and to die on the cross for the remission of sins. Francis and Bernard are brothers of the same blood. Neither one nor the other could enjoy God for himself, but only for God. They have an equal severity for those who turn away the gifts of God from the glory of God. Francis de Sales did not wish the Visitation to receive souls greedy for well-being or for false sweetness.

We must be careful, so far as possible, not to take those who are too much given to *tenderness and compassion* for themselves, for, to say a word about that misfortune which is often kept secret, such women ordinarily fill a house with tears, complaints, grievings; wear long, melancholy, spiteful faces, and are frequently discouraged at doing good. They think that difficulties are impossibilities, and that whatever is not to their taste is insupportable; and to sustain their cause, they heap up a quantity of sad and scandalous arguments against the rule or against the conduct of those who govern them. If anyone reproves them for their soft and bothersome moods, they redouble them, complaining that those who do not weep and groan with them, complain, lament and protest that they are being afflicted, are lacking in charity. If they are ill and no one goes to the trouble to broadcast how much they are suffering or does not run hither and yon to amass all the remedies which they fancy, then they think themselves unfortunate and neglected, and that no one is concerned about them. In the end, this sort of person must always be looked after and considered; if one does more for others than for them, self-love suggests to their fancy that no one ever does for them what is required. It is a feminine imperfection, capable of troubling, weakening, and disrupting a whole group (*Opuscules*, XXV, 114).

This impatient seeking of sensible consolations comes from the evil spirit rather than from the good. If, by some misfortune, as the saint said, "novices inclined to this too sensitive temperament have been received, they must be corrected in the novitiate."

During the Sisters' novitiate they shall try to fortify their hearts and to become devout, not with a dainty, tender, tearful devotion, but with an equable, sweet and courageous devotion, humble and confident. And in particular, the novice should equalize and stabilize her moods and inclinations according to the dictates of charity and discretion, that is, she should not live according to her moods, passions, inclinations and aversions, but according to order and true piety, weeping, laughing, speaking and keeping silence only through reason and not when caprice or fantasy moves her to do so. She will thus reserve the demonstrations of her ordinary joy for the recreation periods; the inclination to keep silence for the periods of silence; the desire to weep will be indulged when grace will excite her to tears of devotion, but she will not shed them on frivolous occasions. And finally, she will be made to understand that she must make use of her heart, her eyes, her speech only for the love of her Spouse, and not for human moods and inclinations (*Opuscules,* XXV, 120).

The manner of directing the Visitandines after the novitiate supposed that their mistress had given them an energetic formation. Let us read, for example, the *Avis à la Sœur Marie-Adrienne Fichet,* a religious of the Visitation convent at Annecy (1611-18).

In all things, try to mortify yourself and to crucify your passions, inclinations and aversions, with our Lord on Mount Calvary, in order that you may live with him in his glory. Keep this advice of your father in your heart . . . you must live the life of our Lord, always walk according to the better part. Keep this rule, not to live according to your feelings but according to reason. . . . You must at all times be mistress of yourself, that you may always be the daughter of our Lord.

Mortification, abnegation of self-will are required: "There is need to make a great abnegation of our will and affections." He goes step by step to "flay the offering" even to the supreme sacrifice. He wrote:

The Sisters who desire to offer and to vow their persons to God in this Congregation must flay their hearts. . . . And to accomplish this fleecing of the victim, they renounce their inclinations, natural movements, and even the false will of their liberties, in order to live henceforth contrary to their inclinations and according to the perfection of the virtues, contrary to their natural movements and according to the directives of another, contrary to the liberty of their own will and according to the rules and constitutions of the Congregation.

In order that the sacrifice be an acceptable holocaust, "we must warm our hearts and enkindle in them the fire of holy love by various meditations . . . seeking simply, with a completely united heart, the unity of a single and sole love of God" (*Opuscules*, XXVI, 291).

9 *Desolation*

"I CALL DESOLATION the exact contrary of the third rule (spiritual consolation)," wrote St. Ignatius. "Its marks are darkness of soul, trouble, inclinations to lowly and terrestrial things, restlessness in the face of various agitations and temptations which lead to defiance without hope nor love; the soul finds itself completely lax, tepid, sad, as if separated from its Creator and Lord."

St. Francis de Sales, when directing souls, constantly employed this Ignatian rule. It would seem that most of the souls entrusted to him frequently suffered from "desolation." He fought it as the primary enemy of the spiritual life. Let us cite first of all a particular example of desolation in which the holy director shows himself energetic. He was trying to help Elizabeth Arnaud de Gouffiers. Mme de Chantal said of her: "She has a terrible spirit." St. Francis de Sales helped her struggle against personal agitation and the need to become involved in the dissensions, disputes and harassments of the world. She was a study in contradictions: weak in body, wavering of mind, subtle yet enterprising, supple and tenacious, obstinate and ardent. She attracted and discouraged sympathy, wearied her companions of long enduring patience, even that of St. Francis de Sales, through her unreasonable demands and her meddling. Although she was truly generous, to the point of contracting a mortal fever in the service of galley-slaves, the Saint did not see in her the spirit which touches souls by "true divine consolation." Several times he recommended to her the spirit of conciliation and of the renunciation of concerns of "justice." But not meeting with success, he finally wrote her the following letter, in which he had the courage to use these terms:

My dear daughter, how long will you pretend to other victories over the world than those which our Lord has brought to you? When will you begin to follow the example to which he has exhorted you in so many ways? . . . Did he ever plead to have even a place on which to lay his head? A thousand wrongs were done to him; what suit did he ever bring? Before what tribunal did he ever make anyone appear? Never, indeed, did he even wish to name the traitors who crucified him; he invoked on them the authority of mercy. And this is what he has so thoroughly inculcated into us: "to him who would take your coat, give your cloak also." . . . But human prudence will say to me: to what will you reduce us? Are we to let them trample us underfoot, make fools of us? clothe or unclothe us as they see fit, without our saying a word? Yes, it is true. This is what I wish and if I do not wish it for myself, Jesus Christ wishes it for me. The Apostle of the Cross and of Christ crucified cried out: "To this very hour we hunger and thirst and we are naked and buffeted, and have no fixed abode . . . we have become as the refuse of this world, the offscouring of all . . ." (1 Cor. 4:11–13). Oh, you will say to me, "Father, you are very severe with me all at once." It is not all at once, for ever since I had the grace to know a little of the fruit of the Cross, this feeling has penetrated my soul and has never left it. . . . Well, what would you have me say? This letter has been written with impetuosity and interruptions. Love is not prudent and discreet, it makes one go ahead of oneself (*Correspondence*, X, 68).

We are here contemplating a soul the desolation of which St. Ignatius characterizes as "trouble of soul, inclination to things lowly and terrestrial." But St. Francis combats other forms of desolation, for example, "restlessness, defiance, sadness."

St. Ignatius proceeds in a dry, rapid fashion, which unfortunately does not always enlighten souls "desolated" because of the entanglements of the knots which fasten them tightly, like those of a net in which a multitude of struggling fish are trying to escape. St. Francis de Sales, a seventeenth-century master of his pen, like a La Bruyère or a La Rochefoucauld, early in his ministry wrote in the *Introduction to the Devout Life:* "Anxiety is the greatest evil that can befall the soul, sin only excepted" (IV, xi). What experience could have revealed this diabolic ruse to so sure, so peaceable a soul? "Anxiety (*inquietudinem variarum agitationum*) is not a single temptation but a spring from which and through which several temptations arise." After describing the sorrow of an evil which remains in us against our will, he analyzes this malady, the cause of a bad spirit.

If the soul seeks the means of being delivered from its evil for the love of God, it seeks them with patience, sweetness, humility and tranquility, awaiting its deliverance more from the goodness of God's providence than from painful industry or diligence. If it seeks deliverance because of self-love, it will press forward and be ardent in the quest for means, as if this good depended more on itself than on God; I do not say that it thinks this, but that it is as eager as if it thought so. If it does not quickly receive what it hopes for, it enters into great anxieties and impatience, which, not diminishing the preceding evil, but on the contrary making it worse, the soul enters into an immeasurable anguish and distress, with a failure of courage and of strength so great that it seems its evil no longer has a remedy (*Ibid.,* IV, xi).

Every tormented soul recognizes this suffering.

St. Francis makes another remark which shows his great perspicacity: "Sadness, which may be justified in the beginning, produces anxiety. Anxiety in turn produces an increase of sadness, and this is extremely dangerous." This is a strong statement. St. Francis would not employ it if he had not experienced it. St. Ignatius, indeed, said that "desolation put the soul in such defiance that it felt itself without hope, without love, tepid, and as if separated from its Creator." This state is certainly extremely dangerous. As a young student, Francis had experienced temptation to despair. Is there an exit from this frightful interior prison? He asserted first of all that no one could liberate himself. "Birds remain caught in nets and traps because when they find themselves ensnared they helplessly flutter about and struggle to extricate themselves and in that way entangle themselves all the more."

Very frequent is that illusion which pushes the "desolated" to struggle against the demon by themselves. St. Francis returns to this difficulty ceaselessly and in dealing with a multitude of people. As a very perspicacious novelist of the twentieth century has noted: "Our modern maladies such as neurasthenia, nervousness, curiosity, agitation, dissipation, and that very trepidation which prevents the woman of today from remaining quietly at home, precipitating her out of doors, anywhere she can find people, or where she can shine, either in her manner or dress or her conversation, or where there is chatter of the theatre world, or the world in general, they are all secularistic, and they can be understood only by leafing through the correspondence of St. Francis de Sales. These believers complicated the faith, troubled it like 'pure water that has been disturbed.'"

Today the epidemic is becoming more and more serious. That is why the pages which we quote in great abundance reached the greatest number of souls who did not truly know how to leave off their anguish. St. Francis wrote:

I do not wish you to torment yourselves by desires nor by other trifles such as the displeasure at your faults, an uneasiness which no doubt is not pure, since you are "disturbed." Be frank with yourself, then. This is what happens: when this trifle presents itself to your spirit, your spirit becomes angry and does not wish to see it. It fears that it will not stop. This fear weakens your spirit and leaves your poor soul pale, anemic and trembling. This fear displeases your soul and engenders another fear that this first fear and the fright that it gives will cause harm and thus you will be embarrassed. You fear fear, then you fear the fear of that fear; you become angry at your anger. . . . That is how I have seen it in several persons, who, becoming angry, are afterwards angry at having been angry, and all that seems to go around in circles like those made in water when we throw a stone into it, for that makes a small circle, and that makes a larger, and this one makes another (*Œuvres,* III, 373).

Now that procedure is repeated very often with all sorts of sins. St. Francis states that the same situation exists in regard to the exercise of the virtues. "I have told you so often that we must not cavil in the exercise of the virtues; we must approach it wholeheartedly, frankly, in a childlike manner, with liberty and good faith, *grosso modo*. I fear and distrust the spirit of constraint and of melancholy" (*Ibid.,* 312).

The Struggle Against Desolation

Let us return now to the illusion in which the demon is transformed into an angel of light when we are trying to practice virtue. The fundamental idea is that desolation, a great evil, must have its remedies. St. Ignatius knew them from experience, and exposed the most common ones. But since he was addressing directors, he advised the search for personal causes of desolation, which would vary according to natures and circumstances. He also advocated an examination of the procedures of the demon, similar to those of every animal seeking to surprise its prey. On the other hand, St. Francis addressed himself not to the director, but to the soul, yet he follows the line traced out by St. Ignatius: *Proceed, do not recoil, pray, have confidence in the omnipotence of grace.* His manner of attacking the problem, however, is more encouraging. "Whenever you are pressed with a desire to be freed from some evil or to obtain some good, before all else be careful both to calm your mind with repose and tranquility, and to compose your judgment and will. Then gently and meekly accomplish your desire, taking in regular order the most convenient means. When I say gently, I do not mean carelessly, but without hurry, worry, or bustle. Otherwise, instead of obtaining the effect you desire, you will spoil it all and embarrass yourself the more." Thus, Saint Francis recommends his religious to consider illness as great a grace as health, and to love, to desire, to seek poverty, suffering and scorn with the same passion which worldly people devote to the pursuit of riches and honors. This indifference and this preference provide the key for us to escape our desolation. We recognize St. Ignatius (N° 319–325) once more in St. Francis' counsel to have recourse to prayer:

"Is any one of you sad?" says St. James. "Let him pray." Prayer is a sovereign remedy, for it lifts up the soul to God who is our only joy and consolation. In prayer, use words and affections, whether interior or exterior, that tend toward confidence in God and love of God, such as "O God of mercy! My most good God! My sweet Savior! O God of my heart, my joy and my hope! My dear Spouse, well-beloved of my soul!" and the like (*Introduction,* IV, xii).

We know that St. Francis de Sales himself was delivered from the temptation to despair by prayer to the Holy Virgin. But there are too many good things to be said of his confidence in Mary for us not to return to discuss this aspect of his spirituality at greater length. Among the means to combat desolation St. Francis, like St. Ignatius, counseled enduring patience.

I praise God for the constancy with which you bear your tribulations. Nevertheless, I see there still some little anxiety and pressure which hampers the last effect of your patience. "In your patience," said the Son of God, "you will possess your souls." The effect of patience, then, is to possess your soul well, and in proportion to the perfection of your patience the possession of the soul becomes more complete and excellent. Now patience is proportionately more perfect as it is less mingled with anxiety or harassment. God then wills us to put aside these two impediments, and soon afterward you will be delivered from the third.

Courage, I beg of you, my dear Sister. You have suffered the inconvenience of the road for only three years and already you wish to rest. But remember two things: one, that the children of Israel were in the desert for forty years before reaching the promised land, although six weeks easily suffice for this trip under ordinary circumstances. Nor was it lawful for them to ask why God made them take so many detours and led them by such bitter roads. And those who murmured died before they arrived there. The other point is that Moses, the one most beloved by God in the whole group, died on the edge of the promised land, seeing it with his eyes, but not allowed to enjoy it.

May it please God that we pay little attention to the condition of the road we are tracing out; may we fix our eyes on him who leads us and on the blessed country to which he is leading us. What difference does it make whether we go through desert or through fields, provided that God is with us and we arrive at paradise? Believe me, I beg you, avoid evil as much as you can and if you do feel it, at least don't look at it, for the sight of it will give you greater fright than the feeling will give you pain. Therefore, blindfold your eyes against those you wish to attack. It seems to me that you focus a little too much attention on your suffering.

And as for what you tell me, that it is a great trial to wish to practice virtue and not be able to do so, I cannot tell you that you must wish what you cannot accomplish, but I tell you truly that it is a great power before God to be able to wish. Go out of yourself, I beg you, and think of the great dereliction which our Lord suffered in the Garden of Olives. See how this dear Son, after having asked for consolation from his good Father and realizing that he did not wish to give it to him, thought no more of it. He did not press him for it; he no longer sought it; but acting as if he had never reached out for it, he executed valiantly and courageously the work of our redemption. After you have prayed to the Father to console you, if he does not please to do so, think no more of it. Stiffen your courage to do the work of your salvation on the cross as if you never would descend and that never more would you see the air of your life clear and serene. What do you wish? We must see and speak to God amidst the thunder and the whirlwinds; we must see him in the bush, in the midst of fire and thorns. And in order to do this, we must take off our shoes and make a great act of abnegation of our will and affections. But divine Goodness would not have called you to undergo your present difficulties unless he intended to fortify you; it is for him to complete the task. It is true that your trial is somewhat long because the matter requires this, but have patience.

In short, for the honor of God, acquiesce entirely to his will. Have no least thought that you would serve him better otherwise, for we never serve him well unless we serve him as he wishes. God wishes you to serve him without preference, without feeling, with repugnances and revulsions of spirit. This service does not give you satisfaction, but it satisfies him; it is not according to your will, but to his. Do you think that you will never be delivered from your anguish? What would you do? Would you say to God: "I am yours; if my miseries are agreeable to you, increase their number and duration." I have confidence in our Lord that if you would say that, you would think no more of it; at least, you would not torment yourself any longer. Do the same now, and subdue yourself with your work, accepting it as your permanent lot. You will see that when you no longer think of your deliverance, God will think of it, and when you no longer put pressure on yourself, God will run to you. This is enough at this point until God gives you the impulse to declare to him the wish to establish the assurance of your life. That will be when God will make us see his presence.

He also believes that moderate penance is useful for the manifestation of conscience. But he insists especially on perseverance in action with as much good humor as at the time of consolation. "If the enemy, who seeks by sadness to make us weary of good works, sees that we do not cease on that account to perform them and that, being performed despite his opposition, they become more meritorious, he will cease to trouble us any longer." This is an art that we can call "the deceiver deceived." The demon, losing at each throw of the dice, no longer seeks to play. "Sing spiritual canticles, for the evil one by this means has often desisted from his operation; witness the evil spirit that besieged or possessed Saul, the violence of which was repressed by psalmody."

It is good to employ oneself in exterior works, and to diversify them as much as possible in order to divert the soul from the object of sadness. But we must be careful that the pleasure we take in these actions does not cast our heart into a still greater obsession. Thus St. Francis adds: "Perform fervent external actions, even though you perform them without relish, such as embracing the crucifix, clasping it to your breast, kissing the feet and the hands, lifting up your eyes and your hands to heaven, raising your voice to God in words of love and confidence."

What the evil spirit suggests then is the lack of sincerity in these prayers and actions proposed as remedies. What is artificial, he says, cannot heal us. It is a fashion, if we listen to him, of becoming ensnared in his net. "Now, far from being an artifice, this recourse to actions, inspired ordinarily by interior consolation, restores us to God's truth, just as a fish which has been cast upon the bank revives when thrown back into the water."

10   *The Tactics of the Demon*

ST. IGNATIUS in his *Exercises* devoted a great deal of space to the evil spirit, the demon. He believes in the personal existence of this evil spirit and in his actions against Christ. In the four weeks, the retreatant finds himself confronting him as well as Christ, and he must conquer him or be conquered. This is a necessary struggle.

There are, for St. Ignatius, as in Holy Scripture, all sorts of demons: that of pride and luxury, that of despair and presumption, that of fear and pusillanimity, and so forth. In a word, we would say that he thinks there are as many demons as there are vices in man.

The demon acts either alone or in groups. He becomes incarnate, so to speak, in persons, in societies and in material objects. He is everywhere in the world and in everything.

In addition, he is, in his fashion, the master, the leader, the head of a body that is often called "the world" by St. John, reducing it to slavery. He has not only total power in hell, but a universal activity on earth. In the measure and manner willed by God, he is granted the divine attributes of knowledge, cleverness, power, tenacity, superhuman courage. His activity is fearsome, and even the most intelligent people are deceived by his lies, for example, the heretics of each age. His power is enduring; heresies have continued for centuries. Finally, to note his importance, St. Ignatius erects to him a sort of monument in the full center of his *Exercises*. This notice attracts attention because it is built not with stones or with iron, but with fire and flames, as if his whole being was a devouring fire. The demon released his most violent and decisive battle during the Passion of Jesus Christ. After the Resurrection of the Crucified, when he should have despaired of carrying off the victory, nothing could calm his hatred. By every means, and more and more cleverly from century to century, he persevered, making use of all that humanity offered him by its progress; he persists in his attacks against the wisdom and the goodness of God.

St. Ignatius pointed out three characteristics of the demon: (1) the sign of his presence: trouble, desolation; (2) his method: trickery; (3) his arms: wealth, honor, pride.

St. Francis de Sales, unlike Ignatius, did not propose a sort of diabolic epic in the Redemption. His views are nevertheless as profound as those of St. Ignatius. What is certain and remarkable is the fidelity of St. Francis in following the *Exercises* in his direction. We may wonder whether the celebrated nineteenth-century guide of souls, the Curé of Ars, was more perspicacious than St. Francis de Sales or St. Ignatius in his spiritual direction, so different from that of his predecessors. That is an insoluble problem, but from the evidence we have, we could describe the situation thus: the Curé of Ars directed souls without knowing the rules of discernment; he had extraordinary supernatural light. Francis de Sales often directed them by the same light, without applying the methods of discernment; however, it is also true that he often followed the rules which St. Ignatius had taught him. Spiritual authors represent the demon with the traits which the Gospels attributed to him. However, certain special skills of the prince of darkness are pointed out by St. Ignatius and by St. Francis.

Signs of the Presence of the Demon

As there is no smoke without fire, as they say, so there is no trouble in the soul, no agitation, no anxiety which is not suspect. The soul, like the body, has its normal temperature. Above a certain level, there is fever. The normal temperature of the soul, St. Francis—as do all the saints—calls peace. But peace can come from temperament or from favorable circumstances. The demon disturbs our natural peace, but especially our supernatural peace which comes from our Lord: "My peace I give you, my peace I leave you."

St. Francis de Sales has various names for this peace, but they all signify a state which we prefer nowadays to call the "childlike spirit." What this "childlike spirit" contains is profound. St. Thérèse of Lisieux, with a new grace, repeated what St. Francis had said. The devil fears it like a capital enemy and sets about destroying it in a thousand ways, for when bringing trouble he acts in secret. When Francis contemplated the icy peaks of Savoy's mountains, mirrors shining in the sun, it was a sign that there were no clouds; when in a boat he crossed the lake of Annecy, tranquil and transparent, it was a sign that the wind had fallen. "The first time he came," a Visitandine tells us, "he entertained us for about an hour and a half, speaking on tranquility of spirit, with feelings of devotion, and told us several times that we must never put ourselves in pain of anything, nor lose peace of heart because of anything that could happen to us, that his own preference was to be quietly lodged in a corner of a chamber rather than to be in the court amidst the bustle of riches and honors."

In all his works, the spiritual symphony of the holy Doctor

returns to be enriched by new counterpoints on this same subject: "Never yield to the demon of agitation and trouble." His correspondence is a perpetual appeal to tranquility of soul. The twenty "spiritual conferences" which have been preserved for us are familiar conversations in which the Visitandines pose their questions and receive practical answers of which the principle is constantly the same: "Above all, remain at peace." Let us content ourselves with quoting a few passages from the first two.

"The devotion of the Visitation must in no way be soft, but strong. With what strength does it act? Not with that impetuosity, that vivacity, that violence which attacks the neighbor, but with the mastery of self in all changes of nature and of providence." "This devotion must also be strong: (1) in bearing temptations . . . ; (2) in bearing with the variety of dispositions . . . ; (3) in bearing, each one of you, with her imperfections . . . ; (4) in fighting against our imperfections . . . ; (5) in despising the opinion and judgment of the world . . . ; (6) in keeping ourselves independent of all private affections, friendships, or inclinations . . . ; (7) in keeping ourselves independent of the sweetness and consolations which may come to us from God or from creatures, so as never to allow ourselves to be attached to them; (8) in waging a continual war against our evil inclinations, humors, habits and propensities" (*Entretiens spirituels*, 407).

St. Francis chooses his words carefully. He desires us to suffer, to hold fast, to resist, to march straight ahead, without wavering toward any attraction on the right or the left. "This generous devotion . . . enables us without trouble or anxiety to see others walking, running or flying according to the diversity of inspirations and variety of grace which each one receives." It seeks only "the glory of God and the advancement of our neighbor in divine love; and provided it sees its neighbor so advancing, it cares little what road is taken to reach the goal."

Who would expect his conference on the flight of our Lord into Egypt to begin with a long exhortation on his favorite idea of strength in trouble? In the beginning of the conference he says: "Evil, despair, trouble and anxiety are found without any admixture of good, of hope, tranquility, or peace. But in this transitory life, good is never found without evil following in its train; there is no wealth without anxiety, no repose without labor, no consolation without affliction, no health without sickness. In short, in all things here below, good and evil are mingled and commingled; this life presents a continuous variety of divers accidents." It is a piece of luck for the demon, who finds a thousand occasions to disturb us; so much the more because "this change and instability of transitory things" reaches the spiritual life. St. Francis then paints the picture in which "many people let themselves be governed and led by their passions." Then he wrote this page of psychology, so pleasant to read even after two centuries. It is a commentary on the fourth admonition of St. Ignatius.

In what, then, can we display caprice and fickleness? It is in the changes of our tempers, wills and desires. At present I am happy because all things are succeeding as I wished; very soon I shall be sad because a little unexpected contradiction will have arisen. But did you not know that this is not the place where pleasure pure and unalloyed is to be found, and that this life is full of such troubles? Today, because you have consolations in your prayer you feel encouraged and thoroughly resolved to serve God; but tomorrow, when dryness comes upon you, you will have no heart for the service of God. "Goodness," you say, "I am so languid and dejected!" But, come now, tell me: if you governed yourself by reason, would you not see that if it was good to serve God yesterday, it is still very good to serve him today and will equally be very good to do so tomorrow? He is always the same God, as worthy to be loved in dryness as in consolation. Today we desire one thing and tomorrow another; what I see done by so-and-so at this moment pleases me, but presently it will displease me so greatly that I might even conceive an aversion for this person. Just now I love some one very much, and take great delight in his conversation; tomorrow I shall scarcely be able to endure him. And why? Is he not as worthy of being loved today as he was yesterday? If we attended to the dictates of reason, we should see that this person ought to be loved because he is a creature who bears the image of the divine Majesty; and thus we should take as much pleasure in his conversation now as we did formerly.

But all this proceeds simply from the fact that we allow ourselves to be guided by our inclinations, our passions or our affections, thus perverting the order placed in us by God, that all should be subject to reason. For if reason does not dominate all our powers, our faculties, our passions, inclinations, affections, and indeed, all that makes up our being, what will be the result, if not a continual state of vicissitude, inconstancy, variety, changeableness and inconsistency, which will make us sometimes fervent and full of courage, but just as often slothful, careless and idle; at one moment joyous, at the next melancholy? We shall be calm for an hour, and then uneasy for two days; in short, our life will pass away in idleness and waste of time.

On this point, then, we are urged and invited to consider the inconstancy and uncertainty of success both in temporal and spiritual things, so that in the event of sudden occurrences, which because they are quite new and unforeseen might shock our minds, we may not lose courage, nor allow ourselves to be carried away by unevenness of temper amid the unevenness of life; but so that, submitting to the guidance of the reason which God has implanted in us and to his Providence, we may remain firm, constant, and unchangeable in our resolution to serve God with constancy, bravely, boldly, fervently, without any interruption whatever (*Vrais entretiens spirituels*, III, 36–37).

Francis has occasion to repeat this lesson on the "caprice and fickleness" of our moods to all sorts of people whom he directs, because it is the most frequent sign that the demon is going to play his game in obscurity. For example, to the abbess of Puits-l'Orbe (April 15–18, 1605), the director distinguishes the sufferings which give or nourish peaceful abandonment; they come from God, and those which trouble the soul come from the demon. We must necessarily suffer from the interior enemy when God snatches the last skin from the

old man to renew it for the new man who is created according to God; and yet, we must in no way be troubled by that
nor think we are in disgrace with our Lord. But "all the
thoughts which bring us agitation and unrest of spirit are not
from God, who is the Prince of peace. These are the temptations of the enemy, and we must reject them and not give
them any consideration."

It has often been said that St. Francis' ideal virtue was
"moderation," the "golden mean," the *juste milieu*. These expressions are equivocal, for our Saint wishes us to love,
praise, and serve God without measure. There is no "golden
mean" in the action of the Holy Spirit, but a "center" which is
God. Moderation, for him, is not in exercises of piety, mortifications, exterior actions, and so forth, but in peace, whatever
the agitation, the needs, the upsets of the world.

"We must in all things and everywhere live peaceably. Do
we have a difficulty, exterior or interior? We must accept it in
peace. Do we receive a joy? We must accept it in peace,
without agitation. If we must flee evil, we must do so peacefully, without agitation." This counsel can appear hazardous.
The director explains: "In fleeing, we may fall and give the
enemy an opportunity to kill us." And should we not accomplish good with ardor, and even with dispatch? No. "If we do
good, we must do it calmly, otherwise we shall commit many
faults by our precipitation. Even the exercise of prudence
must be calm."

Nevertheless, there is a virtue for the acquisition of which
we must drive ourselves unrestrainedly it seems: humility.
This is the opinion of the Saint, confirmed, he said, by St.
Teresa (*Way of Perfection,* X, 39).

Humility brings it about that we are disturbed by our imperfections, comparing ourselves to others; for why should we be more
perfect than others? And still, we should not disturb ourselves at
their imperfections. Why do we find it strange that others have
imperfections, since we also have them? Humility makes our heart
gentle toward the perfect and the imperfect. . . . Humility makes

us receive pains meekly, knowing that we deserve them. It makes us receive benefits reverently, knowing that we do not deserve them. . . . Let this not annoy us, for we must above all progress meekly and build the edifice step by step, so that it will be more firm. And we must not in any way be alarmed at anything that happens, so that the blessings of heaven come upon our earth like dew on the grass, and that we notice they have descended without our being aware of them (*Œuvres,* XIII, 25 ff.).

No one else has so often and so strongly denounced Satan as the enemy of peace and joy. His signals are agitation, disorder, upheaval. St. Ignatius and St. Francis do not cease to repeat this. What a shame that so few souls recognize his approach or his presence by their interior disturbance.

11 *The Deceits of the Demon*

Fear

THE DEMON KNOWS that fear weakens all souls; it either paralyzes their faculties or arouses their passions. St. Ignatius exposes, by means of comparisons, three tricks of the devil. St. Francis, who also had experience with these deceits and with many others, borrows the same comparisons from his Master. Today, these causes and effects of fear would be expressed in psychoanalytical language. In the sixteenth and seventeenth centuries writers employed figures known to the whole humanistic world.

"The demon," said St. Ignatius, "is like a woman who becomes stronger and stronger against a man who is fearful. There is no beast on earth as ferocious as the enemy of human nature in his desire to pursue his damnable intentions with the greatest malice" (N° 325, R.12).

All these violent expressions are found again in St. Francis de Sales, and the same doctrine on the struggle between a man and a woman, between "vengeance and ferocity" when the man loses courage. We must recognize it, scorn the adversary, and refuse to struggle with him.

I shall suggest the remedy which the Holy Spirit suggests to me. In this temptation it is necessary to maintain your condition of the flesh, that is, not to dispute at all, but to do as the children of Israel did with the bones of the paschal lamb: they did not try to break them but threw them into the fire. We must not respond nor pretend to understand what the enemy said. Let him clamor at your door as much as he will. You must not even say, "Who is there?" What you tell me is true, but he importunes you and his noise makes the members of your household misunderstand each other. We need patience; we must speak only by signs. We must prostrate ourselves before God and remain there before his feet. By this humble confidence he will understand that we are his and that we implore his help, without which we cannot speak. But especially must we keep ourselves firm interiorly, and not open the door under any circumstances, neither to see who is there nor to chase away the importunate one. He will finally stop shouting and leave us in peace. . . . It is a very good sign when the enemy strikes and makes a commotion at your door, for it indicates that he does not have what he wants. If he had it, he would not be shouting; he would enter and stay there. Take note of this, so as not to become scrupulous.

After this remedy, I shall give you another. Temptations against faith are directed toward understanding, in order to arouse it to dispute, to dream and to think about it. Do you know what you will do while the enemy is amusing himself by captivating the intellect? Go out by the door of your will, and make a strong charge against him. . . . Bring it about that instead of disputing with the enemy by your discourse, your affections will charge against him forcefully and even join the exterior to the interior force, shouting: "Traitor! Wretch! You have left the Church of the angels and you wish me to leave that of the saints! Disloyal, unfaithful, perifidious, you presented the apple of perdition to the first woman and now you want me to take a bite of it? Get thee behind me, Satan, for it has been written: "You shall not tempt the Lord your God.""

I do not know if I make myself understood. I mean that we must defend ourselves with affections and reasons, with our emotions and not with our cogitations. It is true that in time of temptation our poor will is completely dry. But so much the better. Its blows will be more terrible to the enemy who, seeing that instead of retarding your progress he is giving you the means to exercise a thousand virtuous affections and in particular, the protestation of faith, will in the end leave you (*Œuvres*, XXVI, 213 ff.).

In his correspondence, St. Francis de Sales invariably advocates this method of warding off the demon without fear, with a courage stronger than his own. And he makes use of terms even more vigorous than those of St. Ignatius.

If the evil spirit gives us temptations against this purity of understanding, we must oppose him, humiliating ourselves before the great power of God, saying, with either our hearts or our lips: "O holy and immense omnipotence of my God, my understanding adores you, too honored to know you and to pay you the homage of its obedience and submission. O how incomprehensible you are, and how happy I am that you are so! No, I would not wish to be able to understand you, for if my small, puny capacity could understand you, then you would be too small." Then, returning to our own understanding—"And what little flea, nourished on my flesh, . . . it is your duty only to adore this abyss and not to plumb it." And sometimes we can reply to the tempter: "O wretch, your presumption in wishing to fly too high has precipitated you into hell; I manage to refrain from such a leap, thanks to the grace of my God" (*Ibid.*).

This warlike accent is not rare in so gentle a man, one who has not the reputation of a soldier, like that of the Saint of Loyola. "Have great courage and long breath; do not lose them for fear of the noise and especially because of temptations against the faith. Our enemy makes a great deal of noise; do not be distressed on that account for he cannot harm you. That I know well. Make fun of him and let him do what he wants. Do not argue with him, but deride him for all his talk is nothing. He did a great deal of shouting around the saints and created a great disturbance. But what of it? There they are, firmly lodged in the place that he himself lost, the wretch" (*Œuvres,* III, 392).

In the same letter, he recommends the reading of Chapter 41 of St. Teresa's *Way of Perfection.* And, indeed, St. Teresa treats admirably the temptations from the demons, especially the discouragement which causes us to review our past faults. St. Francis expresses himself with a sort of gaiety opposed to fear. Let us repeat those picturesque words already quoted: "We must not cavil in the exercise of the virtues, but we must go at them roundly, frankly, in a childlike manner, freely, heartily, *grosso modo.* It is because I fear the spirit of constraint and melancholy. No, my daughter, I desire you to have a great, strong heart on the road to our Lord, but at the same time humble, meek and unwavering" (*Ibid.*). The most beautiful letter the Saint ever wrote on this subject is perhaps that of February 18, 1605. In this letter we can recognize the lively nature of St. Jane de Chantal and the marvelous tact of St. Francis, touching all the chords of her soul, as numerous as those of a harp. He says, in brief, let us not fear the demon.

Secrecy

St. Francis de Sales thought, as did St. Ignatius (*Exercises,* N° 325, R. 13), that secrecy, obscurity, winding back on oneself are the principal tricks of the demon and a great danger for the soul that the demon wishes to seduce. "Take note," wrote St. Francis de Sales, "that the first condition which the evil one puts into the soul he wishes to seduce is silence, as do the seditious leaders of conspiracies and disruptive events; for they demand especially that their enterprises and resolutions be secret. But God, on the contrary, desires discretion as the first condition, not wishing the soul indiscreetly to reveal his graces and favors, but rather that they be revealed to persons of the required qualities, pru-

dently and according to the rules of humble discretion"
(*Œuvres*, XXXVI, 233).

The holy director, knowing what abuses can result from in-
temperate gossiping, demands here a manifestation of conscience in which the soul displays pure loyalty to God. He
wrote in the *Introduction to the Devout Life:* "The sovereign
remedy against all temptations, great or small, is to lay open
your heart and communicate its suggestions, feelings, and
affections to your director." And referring to the *Exercises,* he
adds: "You must observe that the first condition that the
enemy of salvation requires of a soul which he desires to
seduce is to keep silence. Thus those who intend to seduce
girls or women, from the very first forbid them to communicate their proposals to father or husband. On the other hand,
by his inspirations God requires us to make our temptations
known to our superiors and directors" (IV, vii).

If you can disclose the cause of your anxiety to your spiritual director, or at least to some faithful and devout friend, be assured
that you will quickly find ease. To communicate the heart's grief
produces the same effect on the soul as bleeding does on the body
of one who is in a continual fever. It is the remedy of remedies.
Accordingly, St. Louis the King gave this advice to his son: "If
you have any uneasiness in your heart, tell it immediately to your
confessor or to some good person. Thus you will be able to bear
your trouble very easily by reason of the comfort he will give
you" (*Ibid.,* IV, xi).

Humbly and sincerely disclose to your director and confessor all
the feelings, affections and suggestions that proceed from your
dejection. Converse with spiritual persons, and seek their company
as much as you can during this period. Last of all, place yourself
in the hands of God and prepare yourself to endure this trouble-
some sadness patiently as a just punishment of your vain joys. Do
not doubt that God, after he has put you to trial, will free you
from this evil (*Ibid.,* IV, xii).

Go to your confessor; open your heart to him; reveal to him all
the recesses of your soul; take the advice that he will give you with

the utmost simplicity and humility. For God, who has an infinite love for obedience, frequently renders profitable the advice we take from others, but especially from those who are the guides of our soul, when otherwise there might be no great appearance of success; just as he made the waters of the Jordan beneficial for Naaman, whereas Eliseus without any appearance of human reason had forbidden the use of these waters (IV, xiv).

We discover in the letters of St. Francis de Sales very many texts similar to these recommendations on laying bare all the folds and crannies of the heart. The bees are not more assiduous in drawing nectar from flowers in order to produce honey than is St. Francis in extracting from the riches of his own inner life a nourishing food for his spiritual children.

Fully agreeing with St. Ignatius on the deceits of the devil, St. Francis de Sales is more prodigal than he with good advice on the manner of opening the heart and shedding light on what the demon wished to keep in darkness. It would be of little use to convince the directors that the majority of consciences would be afraid to expose to the full light of the sun their true miseries, the poisoned root of all their misfortune, if God did not give them the grace of what we could call the certain diagnosis of the action and snares of the evil one. St. Ignatius certainly had this gift, especially in the choice of candidates for government. St. Francis de Sales is perhaps the great genius or at least one of the great geniuses of "diagnosis" of the secret tendencies which today we would call the "subconscious." It is evidently impossible to describe the movements of a spirit which seeks the truth among the shadows. Here, however, is a passage from Bremond, which indicates approximately the methods of the Saint: "When he writes, St. Francis de Sales is verbose. . . . In public, and even among his close friends, he was, on the contrary, very silent, observing, listening much, with an air of smiling and majestic benevolence, interrupting with only a few words. The young widow, the *'claire-brune'* [St. Chantal], so lively and yet so profound, seemed to him, I think, a mystery" (II,

544). Let us note, for its relevance to the subject of secrecy, what St. Jane tells us: "I shall never communicate to anyone anything even the least bit private, except in great fear, even though the holy meekness of the blessed father invited me to do it and in addition I was dying with the wish to do it."

This comparison was made by Tauler and several others: like a dog who follows the scent of the game that he is to flush, the hunter of souls comes and goes in every direction; he waits, he returns, he goes away again; his patience will be rewarded only at long last and, frequently, on the day that he least expected it. "Reduced to discreet and rapid private remarks, the holy bishop quietly made a few searching probes." Several times he pricked the self-love of the Baroness and her taste for elegance, for finery. One day, a more vigorous temptation required the Baroness to break a too-long silence. It was a Good Friday; she timidly revealed her soul "to the holy prelate from whom she departed so reassured and serene that it seemed to her that an angel had spoken to her." And yet she was only partially relieved of her scruple. Four months of anguish then followed, anguish due to the tyranny of her former director. Finally this scruple disappeared. The bishop of Geneva still did not modify his prudent course. We have letters from that time, marvelous in their suppleness, in which he advises her to advance, to retreat, and finally, to manage her escape. "I admire those who see their soul simply."

Truly, whom or what could he doubt? A theological scruple on the value of a vow which bound St. Jane de Chantal to another? Certainly not. But he wished nothing human to be mingled with a decision the importance of which he was pressing. I believe that he hesitated for the good of both of them, since he had not yet determined his course. This soul which offered itself to his direction, attracted and frightened him at the same time. She bore on her forehead and in her eyes a heroic sign. She was doubly strange, both because of the rarity of her natural gifts and because of the mysterious effects which grace had begun to produce in her. Let her find a spiritual master worthy of her, worthy especially of second-ing the divine operations in her, and she will go far. Is he the predestined master?

The Weak Point

We must be careful not to confuse our weak point with faults. The weak point is the fault, or more frequently, the weakness toward which we tend. We could also call it the "strong point," since it is often pride, tenacity, human respect, reputation, fear of disappointment. It lies in the conscious-ness of its strength, of its value and of its success in attach-ment to its gifts, and so forth. Thus Lucifer (the intelligent one), Judas doubting Thomas, and all the others had their weak point.

Faults committed are often mistakenly considered as in-curable. The predominant fault can be combated because it exists in the will; it is an excessive personal desire which does not deny itself. Rarely do we cling to a fault which humiliates or frustrates us. We correct it if we can, but frequently we suffer from it all our life. The weak point, on the contrary, is more often a force or a pleasure to which we cling. The weak point of St. Jane de Chantal was spiritual excess.

Yet just exactly what is the "weak point"? It is the point in the immense variety of our states of soul to which our self-love forcefully, tenaciously and confidently attaches itself, tempted to renounce the will of God rather than satisfied self-love. There is no soul which does not have one or several weak spots. Spiritual progress often depends on knowledge of these tendencies and on our struggle to attach ourselves vol-untarily to the will of God.

St. Ignatius, extraordinarily perspicacious in the discovery of snares, thinks that the "strong points" of a soul are holy in-difference, the unreserved gift of self to Jesus-Christ, poverty, humility, love of the Cross, docility to the Holy Spirit. These are also the special graces which the retreatant must ask for in the course of the *Exercises*. If one of these virtues is lacking or is gradually weakened by neglect of prayer or exercise, a "weak spot," like an abscess, is born in the soul, and it is a dangerous affliction.

St. Francis de Sales has developed with consummate art the importance of the virtues which contribute to the equilibrium, strength, and constancy of a soul. Ordinarily he called equilibrium "peace," "tranquility," or "meekness." Each person has his weak point; therefore in order to understand St. Francis' marvelous intuition of the true strengths and weaknesses of souls, we should reread his correspondence. Here are only a few examples, cited by Henri Bordeaux, an expert on the psychological point of view, which is also ours.[1]

Madame de Charmoisy had her weak point or points. She was divided between the solitude of the country, where she had lived while married, and the court, for which she had a passionate and consuming love. She did not accept, then, the "tranquility of order." Francis used portions of the directives that he gave her in the *Introduction to the Devout Life*.

Madame de la Fléchère was threatened with "neurasthenia." She worried over "nothing." She attached too much importance to trifles. Now, in our day to day living we cannot avoid these "nothings"; but "we can easily put them in their place, not allowing them to take too large a place in our minds and hearts." We must also advance, the Saint explained to her, "by a variety of small spiritual and temporal accidents, remaining always attached to our Lord who, in this fashion, will lead us by his grace to the immobile state of holy eternity." Her weak spot was quite evident to her confessor. She gave too much importance to her examens. She should become more simple, she should think and talk less of herself, and since her nature was good, and because she had confidence in God, she should let herself advance farther and not

[1] Henri Bordeaux was well acquainted with the families of Savoy. Even though he made several errors in chronology, they do not have great importance for our study. Psychological truth is the same in all centuries.

always be so tense. Using almost the same words as St. John Chrysostom, he adds, "Do not always pick on your dear conscience." The word "dear" is aptly chosen, for that is precisely her weak spot. This soul loves her torment, finds pleasure in it and satisfaction in her need; she would like very much not to be tormented, but recognizes in her torment the delicacy of a soul of quality. This enjoyment is precisely her weakness. "We must not amuse ourselves much in seeking the cause of our dryness and sterility, for we do not know how to discover them; it is sufficient if we humble ourselves very profoundly." Therein lies the truth.

When Madame de la Fléchère became a widow, her weak spot was to seek extraordinary explanations for the death of her husband; she imagined that he had been poisoned. St. Francis de Sales held out obstinately against this fantasy; he persuaded her of the contrary, calmed her, reassured her. She herself was enough to harass herself; she needed him so as not to lose her balance, because the demon, by means of her weak point, led her to discouragement. St. Francis said to her with a smile that God loved harassed souls. "Do not be at all ashamed of being a little bumbling and clumsy; it is better to be clumsy than malicious; provided you humiliate yourself, all will turn out well."

Does this discouragement attack only women? Here is, to convince us of the contrary, a letter to Msgr. Camus, the bishop of Belley, who, among his weak points, thought of resigning as unworthy of his appointment. His friend, Francis de Sales, showed him he was wasting his time and trouble by busying himself with things other than his duty. After having reassured him by two "propositions," he insisted on a third:

Such an idea is very often not free from grave temptation, and most frequently arises through the action of the devil; the reason is that during the time spent in procuring relief from the burden, rarely or never are sufficient pains taken to bear it properly; as he who is deliberating about putting away his wife is scarcely anxious about duly loving her in the meantime. Better would it be then for you to urge yourself to take more pains henceforth than to want to give up all work because hitherto you have not taken pains enough.

Camus was a diligent reader of the Bible, therefore Francis recalled to him the children of Ephrem:

Besides, it is better to raise our eyes to the mountains whence help comes to us and to hope in the Lord, gladly rejoicing in our infirmities that the strength of Christ may dwell in us, than like the sons of Ephrem to turn back in the day of battle. For they who trust in the Lord shall take wings as eagles, they shall fly and fail not, but those who give way shall vanish like smoke. The soldier who timidly returns to the baggage has rest, indeed, but no greater security than he who fights.

It is pleasant to see the two friends, typical theologians, using propositions in their correspondence. Francis adds a "fourth proposition: I seem to hear Christ saying, 'Simon, son of John, or Peter-John [Camus was named Pierre-Jean], lovest thou me?' And Peter-John answering: 'Thou knowest that I love thee.' Then, at length, the Lord strictly commanding: 'Feed my sheep.' There is no greater proof of love than the doing of this work." With such reasons, so well presented by a saint, Bishop Camus could only triumph over his obsession for solitude.

Madame de Blanc de Mions had an impulsive heart and scrupulous spirit. This was her weak point. "She had a constant need of being reassured, for, because of her scrupulosity she was greatly tormented." She heaped worry upon worry; she posed innumerable odd questions to her director; for example, she asked if she had the right as a devout person to follow the style of powdering her hair. "Oh, my goodness," answered the Saint, "let her powder her head plentifully; pheasants powder their plumage to keep off the lice." Then, on another occasion, "You must not torture your spirit in the midst of cobwebs"; or again, "You must not be so caviling, nor amuse yourself trying to find replies to questions our

Lord has not asked." Briefly, the wise, alert director continued to encourage her, for nothing is more disheartening than
the struggle against scruples, or even against any weak point.

Here is another type of unregulated attachment. The
Countess Le-Loup was one of those absorbing women who
dominate their entourage. She exhibited an extreme and
overpowering passion for her daughter, Mme de Dalet, and
never thought she was sufficiently repaid for the tender care
lavished upon her. The bishop often discoursed on this theme
of an excessive maternal love: "Love, if it is not directed toward God, can be too great; and when it is too great, it is
dangerous. It disturbs the soul because it is a passion and the
mistress of passions. It excites and disturbs the spirit, because
it is an agitation and finding fault with the rules, it upsets the
whole economy of our affections. Now, we must not think,
Madame, that the love of mothers toward their children cannot also be unregulated; thus it acts the more freely because
it seems permissible, having the passport of natural inclination and the excuse of a mother's goodness of heart."

Madame de Veyssilieu was pursued by the fear of death.
This caused her a constant apprehension which almost paralyzed her. Her illness, her *enfantements,* tortured her spirit
more than her body. The cruelty of separations obsessed her.
Francis de Sales wrote to her: "Do not read books or visit
places in which death, judgment and hell are referred to. You
have resolved to live in a Christian fashion and do not need
to be pushed toward it by motives of fright and terror." But
he did counsel other persons to read such books.

The wife of President Brulart of Grenoble, after many
years of fruitless efforts, had no courage left to struggle
against her temptations. "Our enemies," Francis told her,
"can be repelled, but not killed." Madame de Travernay
stopped praying because she lacked the time to meditate.
"You must measure the length of your prayers by the quantity of your duties," he told her, "and since it pleased our
Lord to put you in the sort of life in which you perpetually

have distractions, you must become accustomed to making short prayers, but you must also make them so habitual that you never put them aside except for a great necessity."

Francis de Sales stubbornly combated imaginary evils: "It will be sufficient to accept the trials which from time to time come to us without our anticipating them in our imagination." And to Madame de Grandmaison: "The greatest portion of our trials are imaginary rather than real." Imagination weakens most suffering souls.

It is interesting to note which weak points the holy bishop considered the most important. They are those of persons who, in one way or another, exercise authority; for example, (1) the authority of the priest, (2) the authority of the abbess, (3) conjugal authority, and (4) maternal authority. For St. Francis de Sales, bishop and father, the priest was the sacrament of Jesus Christ; let us say that in regard to priests, he had the same ideas as his contemporaries, such as Cardinal de Bérulle, St. Vincent de Paul, J. J. Olier, and so forth. There were, however, several factors favoring his love and veneration for the priests: (1) he did not speak, as the others did, of the priesthood in general, but called priests his sons whom he directed as individuals; (2) the Protestant heresies which he had combated so ardently had infested the priests first of all; it had calumniated them, persecuted them, and through them, had turned the faithful from the true faith; (3) he was convinced that everything in the Church depended on the integrity of the priests' teaching and good example; (4) he had the instrument of the *Exercises,* the power of which he himself as well as hundreds of priests and religious had tried out; (5) the habits which he had formed in his youth and especially under the direction of Father Possevin were those of St. Ignatius in the elections of the thirty-days' retreat; (6) his writings, which have been published in the great collection of the Visitation of Annecy, contain two long opuscula (nos. xxiii and xxiv), in which we can read with what assiduous and minute care he worked for the sanctity of his priests. To give proofs of these points would require several volumes, rather than just a few remarks.

Perhaps MM. de Bérulle and Olier penned the admirable thoughts preserved in their works without directly quoting their friend and model, but inspired by him. In the seventeenth century the priesthood was glorified more than at any time. Francis de Sales worked very hard to make saints of his priests. In Savoy the clergy still lives today the sacerdotal ideal which St. Francis de Sales, with God's grace, inculcated into their souls, as well as the methods for reform of self which he taught them during his episcopate. The influence of a saint such as Francis de Sales was exercised actively during three centuries. Thus God willed it.

A religious superior does more harm by his "weak point" than does a mediocre religious. That is why St. Francis de Sales, with the help of the Jesuit Fathers and according to the principles of St. Ignatius, concerned himself very deeply with the affairs of the *Abbesses Réformatrices* who consulted him. Henri Bremond composed a long chapter entitled: "The Great Abbesses Who Reformed Convents from 1570 to 1670." He cites the most famous and adds: "I omitted a large number of them; in truth, there are too many" *Histoire*, II.

St. Francis de Sales collaborated very closely with the Jesuit Fathers to propagate meditation, methods of prayer, regularity, austerity, the true spirit of the Gospel. Let us cite only two situations in which he directed an abbess according to the demands of the *Exercises:* Marie de Beauvilliers, Abbess of the Abbey of Montmartre, and Rose Bourgeois, Abbess of Puits-l'Orbe, in the jurisdiction of Auxois. He attacks their "weak spot."

Marie de Beauvilliers, called the "abbess of abbesses," enjoyed an extraordinary prestige at that time in Paris and in all France. Important ladies, religious, and priests often came to the holy hill to be encouraged by the heroic abbess or ask advice of her." She asked Francis de Sales for directives, and he answered this young woman who was "a little imperious, stiff, inhuman," with prudence and independence. He declared immediately that this abbess "who directs the whole spiritual general staff (*état-major*) of Paris" must not be her own director.

"Above all, I *beseech* you [the word is emphatic], make use of the help of some spiritual persons." And to bring out her "weak points" he adds: "For I will say to you with the liberty of spirit which I ought to use everywhere: *your sex needs to be led,* and it never succeeds in any undertaking save by submission; not that it does not often have as much light as the other, but because God has so appointed." Could anyone speak more frankly and more clearly? Madame de Beauvilliers, imperious and accustomed to flattery, must have been surprised.

But another fault of Mme de Beauvilliers compromised in some measure the work of the Holy Spirit. Her will acted without nuances, without adaptation, in short, without psychology. St. Ignatius in his "annotations" had insisted on the indispensable duty of the director to apportion every spiritual exercise to the varied dispositions and capacities of souls. Did she know this? St. Francis de Sales taught it to her forcefully. She had no need to lead her reform like a regiment in battle array; by vigorously imposing her will on all the religious at any cost, without distinction, she risked accidents and setbacks. Some, indeed, were young and inexperienced; others were old and accustomed to the past; some were of robust health and were enterprising; others were sickly or needed much care. An unconsidered resolution, destroying the whole fabric, and constructing a new one with sensitive elements which had lost their suppleness, could legitimately be criticized. "I only beg you, Madame, . . . that because the gate is narrow and hard to pass, you would take the trouble and patience to lead all your Sisters through it, *one after the other;* for to want them to pass in a flock and a crowd, I think cannot well be done; some do not go so quickly as others.

You must have regard for the old ones; they cannot so easily accommodate themselves; they are not flexible because the nerves of their spirits, like those of their bodies, are already contracted" (*Correspondence*, II, 171).

Excessive zeal, indiscretion, eagerness for good on the part of the superior and her directors—they had only wished to break the indolent and stubborn *arrière-garde*. In any case, for young or old, why these military allures, this inflexible severity, this tumultuous ardor? To do things thus, we excite ourselves rather than act; we trouble others along with ourselves.

"The care which you should bring to this holy work ought to be sweet, gracious, compassionate, simple and gentle. Your age, it seems to me, and your own disposition require it; for rigor is not becoming in the young. And, believe me, Madame, the most perfect care is that which approaches nearest to the care which God has of us, that is, a care full of tranquility and quietness, and even in its highest activity without emotion" (Letter to the Abbess of Montmartre). St. Francis analyzed her correctly and touched her sensitive point. Did he convince the abbess to struggle against her authoritarian tendency and to correct herself entirely from her fault? We do not know.

Another great abbess, Madame Bourgeois of Puits-l'Orbe, was also enough to make her poor director lose courage. At one and the same time she was confined to her bed because of a lame leg and was unable to pray: two things which in a superior seemed to be a true misfortune for the community. St. Francis restored her peace with his ordinary gentleness: "Do not be distressed if sometimes, or even very often, you are not consoled by your meditations. Persevere gently, humbly, patiently, without forcing your mind, and read a book when it is fatigued; read a little, then meditate; then read a little again and again meditate until the end of your half-hour. St. Teresa did this in the beginning and found it a good plan; I, too, have tried it and found it helpful. Take it as a rule that the grace of meditation cannot be gained by any effort of the mind, but by a meek and loving perseverance abounding in humility" (Letter CCXLI). As for the pain in her afflicted limb which the "lancet must open," she should imitate Jesus, who on the Cross gave the greatest service to his Father.

One of the most serious and gravest faults of the temperament of Madame de Chantal was her spiritual excess, assaults of manifold desires for good works. Her holy director calms her by letters of admirable finesse. "Is there, perhaps, a multitude of desires which cause obstructions to your spirit? I also have been ill with this sickness." These souls are always cheered by the thought that their director has passed through the same sufferings. "The bird attached to his perch knows that he is attached and feels the restraint of his detention and imprisonment only when he wishes to fly; and yet, before he had wings he knew his inability only by his attempts to fly; and yet, for a remedy, then, my dear daughter, since you do not yet have wings to fly, and since your inability puts a damper on your efforts, do not fight against yourself, do not strain yourself to fly; have patience and you will have wings like the dove. I fear infinitely that you have a little too much ardor for prayer, that you harass yourself and multiply your desires a little too vigorously." Marveling at the trouble that this bishop, burdened with work and consultations, too hurried to respond at leisure to St. Jane de Chantal, we do not dare deprive the reader of the lights he gave her, despite the length of this quotation.

You see the beauty of the lights, the sweetness of the resolutions; it seems to us that almost, almost you are grasping them, and the nearness of the blessings arouses in you an unbounded appetite for them. This appetite presses you and makes you leap forward, but to no purpose, for the Master holds you attached to the perch, or rather, you have not yet your wings. Nevertheless you are becoming thin because of the constant restlessness of your heart, and you are continually weakening your strength. We must make efforts, but moderate ones, without struggling, without getting heated over them.

Examining well your procedure in this situation, perhaps you will see that you are binding your spirit too closely to the desire of this sovereign taste which brings a feeling of strength, constancy and resolution to the soul. You have the strength, for what else is strength than to wish rather to die than to offend or to quit the faith? Courage, now! Stop, do not force yourself; you will find that you will feel better and your wings will more readily become stronger. This agitation is a defect in you, this unrest cannot be satisfied, for it is a lack of resignation. You are resigned, it is true, but resigned with a *but*, for you would rather have this and that, and you struggle to have it. A simple desire is not contrary to resignation, but a whole panting of the heart, a flapping of the wings, agitation of the will, a multiplication of projects—all this is undoubtedly a lack of resignation. . . . Do you know what you must do? You must make a resolution not to fly, since you do not yet have your wings.

All his life, Francis de Sales pointed out to Madame de Chantal her faults to be corrected, even though she had the great wings of the seraphim.

In marriage, the demon, in order to disrupt conjugal union, introduces himself through the weak point of the husband or of the wife. St. Francis de Sales is one of those among a thousand novelists and realists who are able to show this clearly. A single fault leads to misunderstanding, to disorder, to divorce. St. Francis did not content himself by simply preaching the indissolubility of marriage; he fortified it by fidelity and assured fidelity by the constant struggle against those habits opposed to friendship and against jealousy. Devotion, that is, glowing charity, is necessary for union. "Man without devotion," he wrote, "that is, without solid virtue, is a wild animal, fierce and brutal, and husbands must wish their wives to be devout, for without devotion woman is exceedingly fragile and subject to diminish or tarnish her virtue."

He said the same things about maternal love and the education of the children who depend on this love. All their life, parent's bad habits, despite their many virtues, can create an unlimited series of sufferings for their children. Therefore he energetically combated a Jansenistic education in which he saw the source of a life condemned to unhappiness.

From these few examples—which really should be multiplied—we elicit the capital importance that St. Francis attached to the method called "the particular examen" by St. Ignatius. This Ignatian terminology has become very widespread. But it has an aspect perhaps a little too juridical, and seems to concentrate the spiritual life—if it is poorly understood—on focusing continual attention on self and one's own virtues. St. Francis de Sales recommends the examen without using the term itself. He shows first of all that a single fault, a single quality or attachment, an unregulated habit, brings with it an increasing multitude of faults, mediocrities, injuries, especially in the exercise of authority. His analyses are psychological, true, precise, and we are convinced of the seriousness of our fault. The Saint recommends three important helps for the struggle: *effort, perseverance,* and *patience.* This is the particular examen well made. And of these three virtues, perhaps he esteems patience, that is, meekness, moderation, the "little by little" as the most efficacious. But let us note once more that it is an error to tell souls to fight against their "predominant fault," for we are often mistaken. The "weak point" could easily be a dominant quality.

12 *The Angel of Light*

BY CONFIDENT LOYALTY to St. Ignatius' rules for the second week concerning the discernment of spirits, St. Francis saved many souls from the illusions of the demon transformed into an "angel of light." He saved them not only from sadness, discouragement, despair, but also from false idealism, from the prayer of Quietism, from Jansenistic errors, from apostolates contrary to the thought of the Church, from apparent and masked virtues, from rationalizing, from impulsive or tenacious zeal. He enlightened a number of religious, priests, apostolic workers, and nuns too prone to throw themselves into the new or to attach themselves to the routine. Bremond says:

Even before he wrote his *Introduction to the Devout Life* he had acquired extraordinary lights on the action of the Holy Spirit. All historians unanimously concur that "the heavenly group" of mystical souls of the seventeenth century were to receive him, to open their ranks to him, to tell him their secrets; one would have thought that they had known him for a long time, that they had been waiting for him. This was one of the great joys, one of the most animated aspects of his whole life. These groups included doctors of the Sorbonne—Asseline, Gallemant, Duval, the future chancellor Marillac; religious including the Carthusian, Beaucousin, and many others; women and young girls of the world, princesses, servants, a new Teresa, Mme Acarie *l'Humanisme dévot,* p. 96.

Bremond sees him in this first period as *discreet, modest, open, confiding.* He had an excellent education—the best possible—but he was not yet the doctor who regulated, taught, solved problems:

Mme Acarie, who had discovered him, tried to make him pass beyond the ordinary barriers. She presented questions to him which led to very personal problems; she showed herself ready for confidences. He pretended not to understand. . . . Nor did he seem less discreet with Madame de Beauvilliers, with Asseline, with Bérulle—in short, with everyone. In the parlors of convents, when discussing reform, in the salon of Mme Acarie, when the future Carmelites were beginning their path to sanctity, Francis de Sales was as a student . . . His position permitted him to approach both the directors and the directed. . . . He multiplied his experiences. He did not let himself be dazzled by anything at all. . . . He limited his contact with others, retaining only what pleased him. He judged all with as much penetration as benevolence. He later said that Bérulle "haunted" him, that he wished to be like Bérulle. He meant that he wanted to be as holy as he, not exactly like him. He knew the strength and the weaknesses of each one he met. . . . Doctor Asseline, one of the lights of Mme Acarie's group, had too scholastic a mind, was too formalistic, trenchant, and curious about useless things. . . . Much later, in a very private note, he pointed out his small sins to him: "be, then, less of an intellectual"—he expressed it more gently than that— "and more affectionate." He observed from close hand the "angel of light" (Cf. *Œuvres*, XV, 116–120).

What does the expression "angel of light" really mean? St. Ignatius defines it clearly: "The characteristic of the evil angel who disguises himself as an angel of light is to enter into the feelings of the pious soul and then drag it after him. Thus, he proposes holy and good thoughts in harmony with the dispositions of such and such a just soul, then little by little he tries to seduce the soul by attracting it into his secret snares and perverse intentions."

Hence, every soul attached to its own thoughts, its own desires, its own projects, its own affections, its own will, its own consolations, its own lights, because it sees them and believes them good and salutary, fruitful, profitable, and/or necessary, is exposed to following a false light which is given by the demon. It is a danger risked by many souls who accept reluctantly the proofs of faith and obedience. They always say: "He doesn't understand me." St. Francis de Sales directed many generous souls who took the wrong road without knowing it, imagining they were doing well and walking in a straight path; the holy director pointed out their error and turned them away from it.

Let us take two out of thousands of examples of this: Madame de Chantal and Angélique Arnaud. St. Jane de Chantal never had any but the highest desires for greater and greater perfection, ever more and more pure, for herself and the souls in her charge. She was born under the star of heroism; nothing but a leap forward could satisfy her; nothing was sufficiently difficult for her; no accomplishment was sufficiently rapid. However, when she put herself under the direction of St. Francis de Sales—and even that she did without hesitation, without delay because she knew she had to renounce her own will—an event which may seem strange took place, namely, the angel who was leading her towards the spiritual summits was the demon transformed into an angel of light. Madame de Chantal suspected him a little. Harassed by good inspirations, having already led a life of charity toward the poor beyond her means, having made a vow of chastity after the death of her husband without consulting anyone, she felt that there were some precipices in her ascent of the mountain and that she needed a guide. What disturbed her further was the irresistible sublimity of her prayer. She was invaded at one and the same time by thoughts of God without love, by a heavenly sweetness, and yet sometimes by a love of God which sent forth flames. What did these phenomena mean? Madame Acarie experienced the same problem.

St. Ignatius tells us very clearly that even if the demon can make himself into an angel of light, he can also be unmasked by the Holy Spirit. That is why it is important to recall the prayer which St. Jane de Chantal asserts she made "with unequaled force and insistence": "My God, I beg you, give me a holy man to guide me spiritually, one who is truly a saint and your servant, who will teach me your will and all that you desire of me, and I promise and swear to you that I shall do all that he shall tell me in your place." This prayer includes, perhaps, a grain of presumption; nevertheless the door by which the demon wished to enter, that is, to make her a saint *by herself* is definitely closed and bolted. The deceiving angel will try to lead her elsewhere. He proposes to confide in a director, in accordance with her prayer to God.

A priest whom she had met at Dijon seemed excellent to her because he corresponded to all her desires of high perfection. Now this director was to do the work of the demon. He permitted this fiery soul a host of proud austerities which exhausted her physically; he imposed on her at the same time complicated meditations which dulled her spirit. This condition lasted for two years. Madame de Chantal realized that she was suffering from an illusion, but remained faithful to it. This fidelity is what St. Ignatius calls "the chains and nets" (*retia et catenae*) of the demon. Should she break the promise she had unfortunately made of not revealing her soul to anyone but her director?

Having been invited to Dijon by President Frémyot to hear the Lenten preacher, Francis de Sales, she learned little by little how the soul is led by the Holy Spirit. Very soon it seemed to her that Francis de Sales was the holy and wise priest whom God was sending her. She saw him and heard him preach; she met him at the women's meetings, and Msgr. de Bourges introduced them to more personal relationships. But she did not yield to her former error, that of acceding to the natural, even violent need of opening her heart and her conscience to a director. The Holy Spirit, by means of a racking problem of conscience, forced her to consult the preacher in the absence of her director. She conferred with him at the home of Msgr. de Bourges. And the consolation that she experienced at receiving the light of God was so pure, so vibrant, so certain, that the Holy Spirit severed all the other bonds and promises which were tormenting her. She wished to make her confession. Francis, with his extraordinary ability to discern spirits, that is, to understand how the natural is mingled with the supernatural, refused. However, by the lights that saints often have, he clearly saw how necessary it was to lead her to sanctity.

Surprisingly, Francis advised her at that time to be faithful to her director, a recommendation which seemed to cast her back "into the shadows." Soon, however, Francis sent her this note: "It seems to me that God has sent me to you for your soul's sake; I become more and more certain of it hourly.

That is all I can tell you now." How many directors should take Francis de Sales as a model, to avoid confusing the good with the evil spirit! How many ought not be in such haste to undertake the direction of a soul favored by God!

The demon, the "angel of light," is not discouraged by his setbacks. That would be to forget that the more generous and enterprising souls are, the more occasions they offer him for leading them astray. The direction of a saint, even by one so enlightened as Francis, becomes unquestionably necessary. "He that thinketh himself to stand, let him take heed lest he fall" (1 Cor. 10:12).

St. Jane de Chantal, reassured and once more at peace, soon fell again into anxiety. Her vow of fidelity to her former director tortured her to the point of completely depriving her of sleep and appetite. The demon insisted on the vow. The director continued to insist that she keep this pretended vow and forbade her all correspondence. St. Francis then showed himself so respectful of the conscience of St. Chantal that he praised her for her obedience. But he added a counsel which gave her peace: "St. Teresa, having made a vow of obedience to Father Gracián, nevertheless consulted some enlightened persons. You see, then, that having one spiritual director does not preclude confidence in and communication with another, provided that the promised obedience remains firm."

His letter is one of those which would seem to have been written by Jesus himself. It assured her that the bond which attached him to her soul was the strongest of bonds, that of charity; and that she would find peace in charity. "Obey your first director in freedom as a daughter and make use of me charitably and frankly. Guard against pressures, melancholy, scruples. You would not for anything in the world wish to offend God; that is enough to cause you to live happily."

The established peace in the soul of St. Chantal was then banished once more by her reflections. St. Francis continually sought in prayer to know the divine will. Finally, he wished to see her again when she made the pilgrimage in honor of

St. Claude, and after interrogating her at length about her conscience, he concluded firmly: "Truly it is God's will that I take charge of your spiritual conduct and that you follow my directives. These vows (those that were disturbing her) only destroy your peace of conscience. Do not be surprised that I have delayed so long in making a resolution concerning you. I wanted to be sure of God's will and that I would do nothing in this matter except by his hand."

The conquered enemy then changed his tactics and suggested to St. Jane de Chantal that the spiritual direction of St. Francis was not in accord with her zeal and courage. The angel of light said that she was closer to sanctity than Francis would let her believe. The facility that she experienced in prayer, her magnanimity, the attractions of virtue, the freedom of her soul—were not all these signs of more than mediocrity?

In a long letter which followed their separation at Saint-Claude, Francis no longer used the austere language she expected, but insisted on liberty of spirit, on the necessity of doing nothing through force, of acting only from love, from interior sweetness and a great meekness, yielding to all that was not sin or danger of sin. He reminded her that the most mortified saints, like Cardinal Borromeo, on occasion, for the salvation of a soul, knew how to make a truce with their austerities.

An iron will, tensed to the extreme, like that of Mme de Chantal, questioned if it was truly the Holy Spirit who was leading her. Nevertheless, the consolations that she felt in the depth of her soul were accompanied by such peace and certitude (the indubitable sign pointed out by St. Ignatius), that she abandoned herself more and more confidently to her holy director. Several months passed by in this confidence; but the angel of light was still waiting. The frequent dilemmas in the life of a married woman responsible for several children tortured her conscience.

Among the problems that their education posed was that of

their future. Madame de Chantal thought she was doing well by directing one of her daughters, Françon, into the cloistered life of a religious. St. Francis detected a trick of the evil spirit in this decision. He thought it a "great sacrilege" to place in a convent a girl "who had no desire for it." As a widow, she found it increasingly difficult to maintain her social position in the world with children difficult to rear. Always torn by conflicting desires, she then believed that entrance into the Carmel recently founded at Dijon was the God-inspired solution to all her problems. This idea seemed all the more providential because her frequent visits to Carmel had given her a great veneration and friendship for the prioress, Anne de Jésus, who was very close to St. Teresa and a "pillar of Carmel." Despite all the favorable appearances, Francis saw this as a temptation of the angel of light and forbade her to pursue this attractive plan. So, there was Madame de Chantal, once again uncertain of her future. The Carmelites also were very disappointed.

One day in May, 1607, important in the lives of two saints of the Visitation, Francis, who for a long time had been allowing an inspiration of God to ripen, asked Madame de Chantal if she was ready in obedience to enter the Poor Clares; after this he suggested that she become a nursing sister in the hospital at Beaune. She was perfectly indifferent. The Saint then revealed to her that she was to found a religious congregation at Annecy, later known as the "Visitation." But this project frightened Madame de Chantal because all her possessions were in France, not in Savoy, at Annecy, and especially because this institute was proposed as a gathering of simple and weak persons.

We must read the life of Madame de Chantal in order to understand clearly the subtle art of the demon. For example, she had offered her life to God in order to save a niece of Francis de Sales who had been confided to her care and who was at the point of death. The director blamed her excessive zeal and told her that it was the will of God that she keep her peace. Their relationships were not troubled, however. His aim now was to break the multiple and, so to speak, the holy bonds attaching her heart to friends and family. Because the departure to Savoy seemed contrary to French loyalty, M. Frémyot, the president of Dijon in Burgundy, began to lament with "such tenderly paternal remonstrances" that Madame de Chantal, overcome by filial affection, began to retract. Finally, the will of God triumphed over all, and M. Frémyot gave his consent because—it is good to note this— he was persuaded that the bishop of Geneva had "the spirit of God."

Given what she was and the conditions of life in which she found herself in the world and in France, Madame de Chantal could not fulfill the plan of her director to found the Visitation without walking day by day over a mined terrain, to use a modern expression—mined by the demon. We shall not recount this perpetual struggle between the good and the evil spirit, since we are not writing the life of the Visitandines and their holy mother. We shall say only that even after the trials of foundation, St. Chantal was not shielded from the terrible sufferings of the mystical purification. The demon, it seems, wished to avenge her obedience, and at the same time God wished to give her a sign of the highest mystical union.

We cannot count the number of souls that St. Francis de Sales directed according to the rules of discernment of spirits of the second week of the *Exercises*. However, there was one who was much talked about during the seventeenth century, the abbess Angélique Arnaud, of Port-Royal. If Francis de Sales had not died at the moment when the question of Mère Angélique's entrance to the Visitation was posed, perhaps the history of Jansenism and of Port-Royal would have had a different development and a different outcome. But God's designs are impenetrable. What happened between St. Francis de Sales and Port-Royal clearly shows the importance of St. Ignatius' rules for direction.

It seemed that the young abbess Angélique, sent to reform the convent of Maubuisson, which everyone knew had fallen into a decadence of piety and even into scandalous customs, had the spirit of God. By her example, her words, and her authority, she imposed on the members the true religious spirit: regularity, prayer, silence, mortification, poverty. But the demon, like a poison, insinuates himself into every life that is not purely of God. The authority and the very perfection of Mère Angélique were not ruled entirely by the spirit of God, for pride, self-love, domination, could serve the demon of hidden ruses. Francis de Sales, summoned several times to Maubuisson by Mère Angélique, did not allow himself to be blinded by the general admiration for the work of the prioress. His relations with her were of a rare quality. The mother prioress herself declared in her writings that she had an immeasurable veneration for this Saint and confidence in him, and Francis de Sales, on his part, knew how to recognize the good grain—much superior to that which he saw elsewhere—as well as the weeds; and the terrain where the good grain fell demanded that the rocks and thorns be removed and that the good land be cultivated. What became of the decision indicated in the early directives of St. Francis, the decision of a rupture with Port-Royal and entrance to the Visitation, where the spirit was opposed not only to Jansenism but to the rigorous justice of Mère Angélique? The loss of numerous letters does not permit us to quote the words of the Abbess and the Saint. In 1621, Mère de Chantal wrote these lines to St. Francis which dashed their hopes for a solemn defeat of the transformed demon, after long and luminous conversations:

"Here are some letters from my friend at Port-Royal; truly she deserves compassion for her desires for holiness increase in the midst of her unspeakable contradictions. Finally, say what we will, and make such judgments as we will, we will only throw oil on the fire of her holy desire. And if she is to put aside her intentions, it is you alone who can help her do it, for, as she wrote me yesterday, it is only on your word that she will leave all with entire peace. She also told me that, for a reason she can't explain, she feels that God is calling her to the Visitation." St. Jane proposes a few more suggestions to encourage *Monseigneur* to receive her friend, and asks for a prompt reply. "I cannot keep from adding that since God has given her so strongly the spirit of this institute [the Visitation], I believe he desires to increase in this way his glory in the whole institute. I felt that I had to tell you at this time how she feels about it all, and I beg you, my true Father, to let us have news concerning the above as soon as possible."

When we compare the difficulties which St. Francis encountered in giving Mère Angélique the spirit of truth, humility, charity and sweetness characteristic of the heart of Jesus, to those of St. Chantal in following her vocation to found the Visitation, we see clearly that the demon, transformed into an angel of light, had a combat position much stronger at Port-Royal than he had in the soul of the holy Baroness. Indeed, it was necessary to "lay low the mountains." Mère Angélique, like the keystone in an architectural construction, was engaged in a determined vocation. She had an ambitious goal, not easily renounced when one is young and capable. She was the superior of a very important house, a charge which pleased her, and no one likes to disappoint his hopes. Behind her, like a fortress, the Arnaud family gave her invincible support. The religious of Maubuisson and the persons of the world attached to the Arnaud family and to this convent had as little intention as an army to let themselves be overcome. In short, there was so strong a conspiracy about this proposed "reform" that it seemed impossible to touch it without immediately arousing a revolt. On the contrary, St. Jane de Chantal seemed free to dispose of her life, despite her marriage, her children, her fortune and her family.

But these obstacles were not the strongest ones for the demon, for they were exterior. Interiorly, there was the spirit of Port-Royal, so opposed to the spirit of the Visitation that we cannot imagine how Port-Royal could become a Visitation, or vice versa.

The tight linking of stern and rigid virtues was in perfect accord with the character and design of the reformer. To renounce them was considered a weakness, a defeat, even a betrayal. Francis de Sales, like St. Paul, loved only Jesus Crucified; he considered as diabolical, so to speak, everything that did not reflect "Jesus meek and humble of heart." When we read the all too few extant letters exchanged by Mère Angélique and St. Francis, we see that he consistently counseled her to practice the virtues—more difficult for her than we may think—of humility, patience, sweetness, meekness. And he repeated under more and more insistent forms: "To humble yourself, to become lowly, is to advance with the Crucified Spouse. . . . Note that this abasement, this humility, this scorn of self must be practiced gently, with constancy and not only suavely but gaily and joyously."

Henry-Coüannier wrote very fittingly:

We can say that Francis de Sales radiated suavity, while Mère Angélique, overflowing with good desires, with enthusiasm for the good, with rigor toward herself, with authority, with tenacity, with intelligence, was not at all suave. She knew it and was desolated by the fact; she wanted to become sweet. Completely surrounded with success, respect, youthful glory, and avid to direct, organize, dominate—so virile herself, she admired that gentle and meek man who had an almost feminine sweetness even to the point of feeling like a small girl in his presence—humble, confiding, obedient. She took such complacency in these feelings which would have aided her, she thought, to receive from him some day the perfection she dreamed of. And he whom this "extraordinary heart" astonished, who saw the human marvel that could be made of this woman, did not cease to preach to her affectionately the sweetness, the moderation that she needed (Page 404).

Francis de Sales had been so powerful and, we might say, so clever that it seemed that Port-Royal was going to lose its most holy and influential member and that the Visitation would soon have with Mme de Chantal two foundresses such as few religious institutes have ever had at their beginning. And yet, unperceived, the demon was very near winning his game against St. Francis, who deemed the entrance of the abbess to the Visitation to be contrary to the inspirations of the Holy Spirit. Could the Saint maintain his interior decision to resist these latest attacks, the strongest of all? How could he resist yielding to the will of Mère Angélique, who never withdrew in the face of difficulties and who wished to do everything possible to enter the new community of the Visitandines? We say that he loved and admired that soul as much or almost as much as Madame de Chantal and that the very close spiritual bond which had united them seemed almost indissoluble. How could he refrain, finally, from yielding to Mère de Chantal, who cherished for her friend Mère Angélique so strong an affection that he would have had, so to speak, to enter into mortal combat? On the character and the virtues of this abbess, Mère de Chantal based an unbounded hope for the foundation of the Visitation and the lofty spiritual perfection of its first recruits. She ardently wished Mère Angélique as an associate.

A final opponent to which he could hardly refuse to yield was the highly favorable opinion of Rome. For a petition, signed by a council of theologians, had been addressed to the Pope requesting that the abbess be released from the strict vows of Cîteaux and be permitted to live according to a less severe rule. Thus we see that when the demon moves all human powers to arrive at his ends, it takes no less than a saint to confront him with the strength of the Holy Spirit.

A disconcerting development proved that Francis was right. The reply from Rome was delayed longer than had been expected. Madame de Chantal had to leave Paris. The bishop of Geneva died at Lyon very unexpectedly. Madame de Port-Royal remained seven or eight years without a director. She went from abbey to abbey, active, enterprising, admired, obeyed, persevering in the line of austere reform. Then she met M. de Saint-Cyran who took possession of her spirit. She became, under this new director, the great "Mistress of Jansenism" as she was later called. Thus ended the struggle between St. Francis and Port-Royal.

The illusion proper to the angel of light is dissipated only by obedience or by his own delaying and disastrous effects. Madame de Chantal and Mère Angélique were not the only ones whom the extraordinary Saint drected toward the light in these times of fervor when everyone was ardently interested in the mystical life. Among these fervent and devout women who composed the elite Catholic society around the great director of consciences, the *Annals of the Visitation* cite several names: Mme de Sainte-Beuve, foundress of the Ursulines; Mme de Lamoignon, the Countess of Soissons converted from Protestantism; the Countess de Joigny, the first associate of Saint Vincent de Paul; the Duchess of Noailles; the Duchess de Vendôme; the Marquise de Verneuil. When reading these names—and they are only a few among many others—we realize that women of such varied accomplishments consulted the Bishop of Geneva to good purpose and not simply in order to flatter themselves at having him for a director, as the piquant words of LaBruyère would suggest. They all wished, in their own way, to pray, to advance in virtue and to conduct themselves in truth and in love. Naturally capable of great and numerous enterprises, they were God's chosen instruments, but at the same time hearts easy for the demon to turn to generous illusions. To guide them, Francis de Sales needed complete independence, an extraordinary perspicacity. We see, then, that the rules for discernment of spirits were effective in Francis de Sales in regard to all those who had the grace to make use of them.

From this brief study we cannot help but draw a twofold conclusion: (1) that St. Ignatius' rules for the discernment of spirits acquired a supplementary authority of great weight from the fact that St. Francis de Sales, so universally praised as a doctor in the Church, had studied them, loved them, and faithfully applied them all his life with a success never equalled in the history of spirituality. Again, it is through him, by his comments, by his counsels, that we can judge more exactly and more profoundly the inspirations of their author, St. Ignatius, recognized by so many signs. (2) The second conclusion is that the choice of a director of conscience must be made not only on the reputation of a saint, doctor and scholar (as St. Teresa of Avila so strongly recommended) but on the wisdom that he shows in conducting souls according to the rules for the discernment of spirits. And this choice is more necessary if one belongs to an institute derived from St. Ignatius himself.

PART THREE

Charity

13 Charity, the Perfection and Beatitude of God

In order to study more deeply the spirituality of St. Francis, we must know its underlying theology.

No one, in speaking of the saints, can ever say that this or that saint was most beloved by God. But if St. Ignatius surpassed his sons and his disciples in love, it is certain that he found in St. Francis one of those who succeeded in revealing the depths of his inflamed heart. In the same way, without exaggerating the comparison, the Son of God, who received everything from his Father, revealed it to the world. "No one knows the Father except the Son."

St. Ignatius was nourished by his love of God as a flame lives by its fire. His concise journal can be compared to the soliloquies of St. Augustine and to certain pages of St. Bernard's *Canticle of Canticles*. He spoke soberly of his love of God in the *Exercises* and his letters, so soberly even that some persons committed the folly of accusing him of having sought the glory of man more than that of God (anthropocentrism), and the will of man more than that of God (voluntarism).

St. Ignatius expounds straightforwardly the manner in which man should love God. Briefly, he names as principal means: praise, honor, service, utilization of all creatures, interior and exterior, to procure his glory. More precisely and concretely he engages us to follow the Incarnate Word, to participate in his filial spirit toward the Father, his zeal even to crucifixion, his resurrection and union in the Holy Trinity.

We can affirm, without fear of criticism, that the theological virtue of charity was the essential, central, unique subject of the spirituality of St. Francis de Sales, the object of his apostolate, of his works and of his writings. But beyond the text of the *Exercises* of St. Ignatius, he invites us by faith to

133

contemplate love, *as it is in God himself.* And he spoke of it with such an effusion of devotion that one might believe that there was for him on this earth only one happiness, that of mystical contemplation (*Treatise*, III, ix).

Nevertheless, he proposes to find this happiness in the theological virtue of *faith.* This happiness is incomparably superior, he says, to the joy of all the philosophers in the discovery of the truth. Oh, how can we express how greatly numerous souls need it! The consolation of the faith is perhaps what they lack most. "When our soul, raised above its natural lights, begins to see the sacred truths of the faith—Oh, God! Theotimus, what a delight! The whole soul is thrilled with pleasure, possessing her heavenly spouse whom she finds sweeter than the honey of all human knowledge." God has placed his step among creatures, but we see "only the feet of God . . . in comparison to that, faith is a view of the face of his divine Majesty which we do not yet see in the full light of his glory, but nevertheless we see it in the first dawn of day." He recalls the ravishment of Jacob after the night-struggle with the Angel: "Jacob cried out, however: 'I have seen the Lord face to face.'"

Like Jacob, St. Francis cries out: "O how delightful is the holy light of the faith, through which we know with unequalled certitude not only the history of the origin of creatures and of their true use, but also that of the eternal birth of the great and sovereign divine *Word* to whom and through whom all was made, and who with the Father and the Holy Spirit is one God, adorable and blessed, world without end. Amen." "Was he not filled with ardor while he was speaking to us on the way?"

Faith in love is for St. Francis the foundation of the *Exercises;* for no other foundation of virtue—of all virtue—than love, which is God himself, exists. Faith will be transformed into vision in eternity; it is already a certain possession of God in obscurity. "If the divine truths proposed in the obscure light of faith are so sweet, O God, what will it be when

we contemplate them in the brightness of the noon of glory?"
We would not presume to lead a holy life in the midst of so
many obstacles, like those God proposes to us, without being
certain of seeing God as he promised to his children.

When "our understanding will see actually present what it
believed here below, oh, then, my dear Theotimus, what a
delight! what ecstasies! what great admiration! what love and
sweetness! In this excess of sweetness, we shall declare that
never would we have been able to think of seeing such delightful truths. We believed all that was announced to us of
your glory, O great City of God, but we were not able to conceive the infinite greatness of your delights" (*Treatise*, III,
ix).

The Christian life must be, above all, a thirst for God
which gives the faith. Otherwise the passions which cannot
make us happy will cause us to die of despair. Perhaps we do
not meditate sufficiently on this capital truth, before undertaking the awesome task which St. Ignatius proposes for us,
following the Gospel. Did not our Lord begin his preaching
by the beatitudes? "O admirable yet lovable unrest of the
human heart! Remain on this earth always without repose or
tranquility, my soul, until you have met the fresh waters of
everlasting life and the holy divinity which alone can elimi-
nate your weakness and increase your desire." The Psalmist
gives us the deer as an example, which fatigued by the
hounds, "no longer has wind nor legs." Imagine, says St.
Francis, how avidly he thrusts himself into the water that he
was seeking, how ardently he hastens to press himself into
this element; he seems willing to melt and change himself
into water in order to enjoy its freshness more fully."

But what does faith teach us so beautiful and so good that
we find such happiness in it here below? It reveals to us that
God is love, that he is Trinity and that he who says "Trinity"
says "love of three Persons." This revelation dominates all
others; all truth is only a radiance of that first truth. That is
why it is the source not only of all God's creation, but of all

that is in him, of all his perfections. For St. Francis there is absolutely nothing more important for meditation. For the spiritual life is love, participation in the divine life, in the life of the Trinity, then in the love of the Trinity. It is with the Son and in the Holy Spirit that we say Father, receiving him from him and giving to him the love that he gives to his "well-beloved" and that he receives from him. This love is at once infinite, immutable and unique.

"The eternal Father, seeing the infinite goodness and beauty of his essence so vividly, so essentially and so substantially expressed in his Son, and the Son seeing reciprocally that his own essence, goodness and beauty have their origin in his Father as source and fountain—would it be possible that this divine Father and his Son would not love each other with an infinite love, since the will by which they love each other is infinite in one and in the other?"

And let no one say that these relationships of love interest only the theologians who have found in them material for long abstract treatises. They captivate all souls, since these latter have been created, redeemed and preserved eternally, living only to participate each in its own fashion in this infinite love. We must rejoice in this knowledge. Faith teaches us also that this love, before raising up creatures, has this marvelous and extraordinary essence of not being composed of several sighs, unions and liaisons, but of being eternally and infinitely continuous. And all this exists in the Trinity and also by grace for us. The divine love of the eternal Father toward his Son is accomplished in a single sigh, emitted reciprocally by the Father and the Son, who, in this fashion, remain united and linked together. We call this breath the Holy Spirit, the third Person who with the Father and the Son is one only God.

Our union with God and among ourselves is a foreshadowing of the infinite and unchangeable love, the third Person of the Trinity. The consolations of the faith here on earth resemble torrents from the highest mountains, for this infinite and unchangeable love must be contemplated as the fullness of perfection. Although his being is without multiplicity, we conceive in God several perfections which we call wisdom, justice, goodness, mercy, power, gift of self, and so forth. In him, they are not distinguished from love. Wisdom is the wisdom of infinite love, justice is the justice of infinite love, and so it is with all his attributes. This consequence, a necessity of divine life, we deduce from a first truth. Whatever God does, whatever happens, God cannot refrain from loving, for the Holy Spirit cannot be separated from the Father and the Son. It is unthinkable that God would not love in time and eternity what he is (Father and Son), what he created, and what he does. To think thus would be to deny God, the true God in his spirit or in his heart.

Everywhere there is being, there is not merely presence, power, justice, goodness, mercy, and so forth. There is above all another aspect of being, of love: love of God. Creatures cannot be created nor preserved, heaped with blessings for any reason but love. What man does not love, God loves, at least as his creatures. To exist and not to be loved by God is unimaginable. God's love is free and disinterested. It is not imposed by reason, by thought, by some possible good; that is why an absence of liberty, often the defect of liberty, often the defect of the human creature, indicates an absence of God's love. Clearly God cannot constrain the liberty of man whom he has created to his own image because this constraint would be contrary to his love.

That is also why God is not limited, paralyzed, prevented from acting by any adversary or by any obstacle; his love is unchangeable, infinite and all-powerful. Not illness, death, nor annihilation, not even sin weakens God's love. Did not Jesus himself, the Incarnate Word, show this? Sin is the greatest obstacle to love; therefore it is impossible in God and in his activity. But love does not fear sins, even of unlimited number, because then it is called mercy. Mercy is goodness victorious over everything, even over sin. Justice often appears to us as a repelling of unworthy creatures, but these are unworthy only if they reject, repel, deny mercy. God has given to the angels and to men liberty for their salvation and even their merits. The greatest sinner approaches love whenever he wishes.

All these considerations are found in the contemplations of St. Francis de Sales. From the very beginning of his *Treatise*, he places providence in first place among the perfections of God. He sees it in God, and not just in creation. The spectacle of God's love in the care that he takes of creatures is for Francis an enchantment comparable to that of the psalms of David. But the contemplation of God in his source is superlative joy.

"Sovereign providence is nothing else but the act by which God wishes to furnish to men and angels the means necessary or useful for them to arrive at their end." The view of the universe is not so pacifying as that of providential love in God. "This providence, dear Theotimus, touches everything, reigns over everything, and reduces all to his glory. However, there are certain fortuitous cases and so-called accidents; but they are not fortuitous nor unforeseen except to us, and they are unquestionably known to the heavenly providence which foresees them and destines them to the public good of the universe." For God, multiple causes which produce different effects contribute a good which we did not forsee but which, for all eternity, was destined to manifest his love. St. Francis quotes "Joseph of old" who declared to his brothers: "You had wicked designs on me, but God has turned them to good."

He admires especially in God the wisdom which permits him to respond to the outbursts of his infinite love; he resolves in effect to "be engrafted and implanted in the divinity in order to become only one person." "So that as eternally there is only one essential communication in God, by which the Father communicated all his infinite and indivisible divinity to the Son by producing him, and the Father and the Son together producing the Holy Spirit communicates to him also their own unique divinity, so this same sovereign sweetness was so perfectly communicated externally to a creature that the created nature and the divinity, each retaining its own properties, so joined together that they were one same person" (*Treatise*, II, iv).

God is infinitely happy. Happiness never enters into him, but it flows from him as from an inexhaustible spring. All that exists receives an excess of felicity from him; whether angel or man, the creature can be happy only by living in the "will of the Lord," just as it can be present at the wedding of the Son only by entering into the festive hall.

But what produces beatitude in the Trinity? It is not omnipotence, supreme majesty, perfect justice, nor any particular attribute. It is, and can only be, love. The Father without infinite love, the Son without infinite love, are inconceivable. And if the love were interrupted, changing, God would cease to be happy.

Every act of power contributes to his beatitude because it is an act of love. Thus it is with all his acts of justice, of goodness, of mercy, of wisdom. Every creature, no matter how small, is a reflection of his beatitude, because love alone is creator. There is no grace given to man which is not for God an expression of his happiness. And this truth is proportionately more certain as God is determined only by the love he bears toward his Son; the divine providence produces all things "natural as well as supernatural" *in favor of the Savior.*

14 *Charity, the Perfection and Beatitude of Man*

NO MORE THAN St. Ignatius did St. Francis de Sales scorn human nature, as do some spiritual writers, even though they are not Jansenists. Francis de Sales saw the equality and unity of the infinite in the persons of the Trinity. In creation, he saw first of all a hierarchy of values. At the lowest degree of God's work, creatures are beautiful and good: *vidit Deus quod esset bonum*. Lifeless nature is less beautiful than living nature; the latter less beautiful than human nature. Human nature is made up of forces which tend to dominate the will. Above the will there is love. Human love yields infinitely to charity. And charity is the virtue par excellence produced by the Holy Spirit who inhabits the Christian soul. This hierarchy has great importance in spirituality. That is why St. Francis de Sales began his *Treatise on the Love of God* by speaking of the beauty which God has established in creation. He quotes St. Denis: "God, like sovereign beauty, is the author of beautiful harmony, of beautiful luster, and of the charm which is in all things. He causes the distributions and variations of his radiance by which all things are rendered beautiful to burst forth in the form of light. He wishes to establish beauty so that there would be harmony, clarity and charm." St. Francis, like St. Ignatius, loved to see God in all things, and especially in nature.

At a time when many souls are given to pessimism we think it useful to remind the reader that Francis de Sales took delight in comparing the beauty of flowers, birds, doves, bees, stars, and so forth. We can count not by tens but by hundreds the designs, portraits and charming accounts with which he illustrated his theological and spiritual teachings. Msgr. Camus recalls:

140

When I went to visit him, he, knowing that I was wearied by preaching, went to the trouble to entertain me either by a boat ride on the beautiful lake of Annecy or by delightful walks in the fine gardens on its banks. He did not refuse similar recreations which I offered him when he came to see me, . . . drawing many spiritual elevations from them. If any one pointed out to him any beautiful plants, he would say, "We are the fields which God cultivates." If any one showed him rare and exquisite pictures, he would say, "Nothing is so beautiful as the soul which is made in the image of God." At the sight of fountains he would say, "When will fountains of living water spring up in our hearts, leading us to life eternal?" At the sight of rivers, "When shall we go to God as these rivers go to the sea?" Thus he saw God in all things and all things in God, or, to express it better, he saw only one thing—God (IV, 24).

When he went to the Abbey of Talloires to preside at the transferring of relics to the Benedictines, he could not resist the charm of the site: "What a delightful spot!" he cried out. "If our Lord considered it suitable, I would leave the burdens of the day and the heat to our coadjutor and I would choose this place to live and take a little repose." And as he was leaving, he gave orders to the prior to build him five or six cells in this place to which he could retire at leisure. "When we are there," he added, "we shall serve God with our breviary, our Rosary and our pen. We shall enjoy a holy leisure to trace out for the glory of God and the instruction of souls whatever I have revolved in my mind for more than thirty years. There, great and beautiful thoughts will fall thick and fast like the snows in winter. Oh! who will give me the wings of the dove to fly to that sacred desert and to breathe a little in the shadow of the Cross. There I shall await the moment of my passage to eternity, *expectabo donec veniat immutatio mea*" (Camus, IV, 6).

"Doves, unlike other birds," he observed, "murmur with their beaks closed tightly, rolling their voices in their throat and breasts, emitting nothing but a certain resonant, echo-like sound; and this little murmuring serves them both as an expression of grief and a declaration of love" (*Treatise*, VI, 12). "Young swallows, on the contrary, open their beaks very wide in their chirping," and this is remarked by way of commentary on the words of the suffering Ezechias: "Like a swallow I utter shrill cries; I moan like a dove" (Is. 38:14).

He also noted: "The stars are marvelously beautiful to see, and they send forth beautiful rays. But if you have ever noticed, it is by their brilliance, flashes and sparks that they produce their rays, as if they were bringing forth the moon with an effort, at various intervals." In the same way, the saints die of love, after many "strong movements, many assaults, strong obstacles, many languors, much agony." In the same chapter he compares divine love to great rivers which churn and leap, roaring mightily over rough and rocky shallows where reefs prevent the smooth onward movement of the waters, but which flow gently and effortlessly once they find themselves on the plain. So it is with divine love, according as souls resist or accept it. And still another comparison comes to him in regard to the difficulties, oppositions and contradictions which love meets: "Thorns, according to popular belief, are not only different from but even the opposite of flowers, and it seems as if our affairs would progress better if there were none in the world. . . . But still, since they are here, the good husbandman finds a use for them, making hedges and fences around his fields and young trees to protect them from the cattle."

All St. Francis' writings bring out the delight and joy he experienced in regarding nature. And his sermons pleased his hearers when he appealed to their memories: "Have you ever had a dry and searing summer, seeing your gardens with their mouths agape, so to speak, opening their throats to receive the rain?" (*Sermon for Pentecost,* 1593). Bossuet and Bourdaloue had lost that special art of captivating their "Christian hearers." Nature seemed a stranger to the truth they were preaching.

St. Francis de Sales had much greater admiration for the human soul, even apart from the splendor which grace gave to it, than he had for nature. His *Treatise on the Love of God* opens with a chapter on the beauty of the soul. But what ravished him still more than the diverse faculties that it received from God at birth is its harmony, more marvelous than the order seen in the infinitely great and the infinitely small things of inanimate creation.

St. Francis de Sales, intending to speak to us of love, particularly admires that faculty of the soul called the will, that sovereign faculty which the various spiritual powers obey submissively. His thought, as anti-Jansenistic as possible, is also conformed to the supernatural order in which God willed the collaboration of the freedom of man with the gratuitous mercy of God. It agrees perfectly with that of St. Ignatius, whose famous maxim summarizes the alliance of the created and the uncreated: "This is the first rule of action: 'Your faith in God must make you act as if all success depended on you and none on God, while persuaded, nevertheless, that God will do all, and you will do nothing.'" It is a mysterious maxim to which Francis was faithful as the following paragraphs will show.

The will, he said, governs the powers of the soul in various ways according to their function, and especially the sensible appetite. There are, already at this level, a real hierarchy and a real abnegation. For just as life governs matter and gives it the power to move by an interior principle and to reproduce life, just so the soul animates the cells of the body, and the will directs and fertilizes the whole soul. One acts well or badly, according to his wish; one merits or one sins. Man, if he does great works, undertakes them only through his will. From this results an abnegation of the inferior activities because of the excellence of the superior principle which perfects and directs them. Nothing is destroyed, and yet all is destroyed under the form of elevation.

For St. Francis the will is mistress of the action. But the

will itself is animated, elevated, directed by love. From this results a certain abnegation of the will and of all activity which is not love (Cf. I, iv). "All passions or affections proceed from love as from their source and root. They are good or evil, vicious or virtuous, depending on whether the love from which they proceed is good or evil." Then he shows how charity through the Holy Spirit is an abnegation of love because it is a superior love. "Therefore in order to make the love of God live and reign in us, we must put to death our self-love, and if we are not able to annihilate it entirely in everything, at least we should weaken it so that even if it lives in us, it no longer reigns there."

But human love, good as it may be, is penetrated by divine love, by charity, as matter is by life, life by the spiritual soul, the soul by the will, and the will by love. And so we arrive at the capital point of the hierarchy of creatures.

Between the force of the will and the power of the Holy Spirit there is an infinite distance, so to speak. Without doubt the will can oppose the Holy Spirit and drive it from the soul. But the question here is of the consenting will, docile, submitted to God. The will cannot change the nature of the faculties, but the Holy Spirit changes it by superelevation. The very personality of man is, so to speak, re-created. By the Holy Spirit we become the Sons of God. Since we are sons of God, our faculties receive a supernatural life which is God's life in us. This life does not spring by extension from the natural life; it is infused, gratuitous, of a divine order, freely given by mercy. Theologians have expounded at length the marvelous excellences of faith, hope and charity; these are the virtues and all the gifts of the Holy Spirit. With an inspired precision and one which comes from divine knowledge, St. Paul has developed in his epistles the extraordinary privileges of charity (1 Cor. 12).

St. Francis loved to recall this teaching. We could say without exaggerating that he was *repletus Spiritu Sancto,* to use the expression of Holy Scripture. Rare are the pages on which he does not speak of charity. He uses the word "love" more often, but it is always a question either of infused charity or of the Holy Spirit who pours it into our hearts. The Christian is a complete and perfect being if he is conducted by the Holy Spirit. By his gifts he possesses in his soul all that permit him to love, to act, to attain his ideal according to the thought and the will of God. Following St. Thomas (*Summa Theologiae*, Ia IIae, 68, 4c), St. Francis asserts that the "gifts" extend to all domains of the virtues, intellectual as well as moral, and to all forms of activity. He concludes that, no matter what the nature, extent and number of our powers, they are all assumed by the inspiration of the Holy Spirit. *Haec dona extendunt se ad omnia.* We praise highly St. Francis' sweetness, goodness, meekness, patience, tenderness —in short, all his virtues—but all the glory we can offer him must revert to one Person only. He lived only in the Holy Spirit, he acted only by "the unction of the Holy Spirit" (to use St. Ignatius' expression) and by the "inspiration of the Holy Spirit" (as St. Thomas expressed it).

The text of St. Thomas should be recalled here because it must be applied to St. Francis: "The Philosopher [Aristotle] in a chapter of the *Bona Fortuna* said that it is not convenient for those moved by divine inspiration to deliberate according to human reason." And the holy Doctor recalls in the same article the word of Isaia: "Morning after morning he opens my ear that I may hear; and I have not rebelled, have not turned back" (50:4, 5).

Many critics of Francis de Sales thought themselves psychologically acute in considering him an extraordinary being among the saints in the order of his affections, in the order of the heart. We must admit that his language, which is not that of our century, gives a basis for this opinion because he spoke so often of "love" rather than of "charity." It is no less certain that he is especially remarkable not in the order of sentiment but in that of charity, and consequently in the gifts of the Holy Spirit. That is why his life and his works oblige us to insist on this capital point. All his asceticism is based on charity; without charity everything is self-love or imperfect love.

But he does not make charity an abstract principle and, so to speak, the key to a moral system. Nor did he make it an idol of spirituality. Charity is inseparable from the Holy Spirit, although it is an activity and not the Spirit himself.

The Holy Spirit exists in us, dwells in us, lives and acts in us. No doubt, between the Holy Spirit and our activity of charity we must not suppress the very act by which we love. Our will does not remain natural, moved from without by the Holy Spirit. It is perfected in a permanent manner by the charity which is our virtue, our supernatural state, and which permits us to love God with a love that is absolutely ours. But that being said, neither our virtues nor our gifts will ever make our soul live if the Holy Spirit does not live in them and in us.

That is why St. Francis de Sales loved—because he lived by the Holy Spirit and was abundantly filled with him. And that is why we must say that he loved all souls equally, yet in a different fashion, as God by a single act is the Father who begets each son of God, yet in an unequal fashion.

The soul whom St. Francis loved perhaps best of all was St. Jane de Chantal. But this love came assuredly and purely from the Holy Spirit. In this same spirit he loved all souls, if not as much as he loved the holy Foundress, at least in an equally perfect manner, and without self-love. All authors exalt love of neighbor as the virtue most characteristic of St. Francis de Sales, and therefore it is not suitable to omit it from a study of this nature.

15 *The Charity of Man Toward God*

ST. IGNATIUS in the *Exercises* gave two principles of exercising true charity toward God: (1) "We must put love in our works more than in our words." By this emphasis he does not deny that we can also put it in words, in prayers, in the whole liturgy. (2) We must put love in our mutual gift. "Love consists in exchanging one with another; in knowing that the lover gives and shares with the beloved what he has or at least a portion of what he has or can do; thus, reciprocally, the beloved for his lover." By these principles he summarizes the *Exercises* from the Foundations to the descent of the Holy Spirit, and he draws his conclusions from it. The exchange demands gratitude and the gift of self in all things, in return for what the Father and Jesus have done for us.

St. Francis used the same principles; he explained them, he illustrated them, enriched them by his admirable considerations and exhortations. He has consecrated a whole treatise to them (*Treatise,* I, xvi). We shall make only a few remarks about them in this chapter, commenting on some remarkable quotations.

(1) St. Ignatius begins the *Exercises* with the end of creation which imposes on us the duty to praise, honor and serve God. He does not expound the reason for which God created us. Now, we have seen that Francis de Sales places this same reason as the foundation of his whole spiritual life: the reason is our love in God and his love for us. God has created us, it is true. But, in creating us, he gave us above every other natural impulse a principal and pressing inclination to love him above all things. Not to love him would be contrary to nature. Original sin (Cf. I, xvi) has not destroyed this inclination. "Though our heart be formed, as it were, under the wings of nature, still at its first glance toward God, at its first knowledge of him, its natural and hitherto dull and imperceptible inclination to love him awakens instantly. Suddenly love appears as a spark from among the ashes, and touching our will, urges it toward the supreme love due to the sovereign and first principle of all things."

(2) Man's love for God begins by the knowledge that gives faith, and continues by the "loving contemplation" of the

charity which unites the three Persons. Because charity is a grace, it is a participation in the love of the Trinity. "Our human heart naturally produces some beginnings of God's love, but to proceed so far as to love him above all things— the true ripeness of the love due to this supreme goodness –this belongs only to those hearts animated and assisted with heavenly grace, in the state of holy charity. "Nature feels the stirrings of this little imperfect love, but it is a love without a will to produce true effects. It is a will sick of the palsy, which sees the healthful pond of holy love but has not sufficient strength to cast itself into it" (*Ibid.*, I, xvii). This remark warns souls that wish to love God as we must love him and that are desolated at not being able to do so, that their first duty is to take cognizance of their nothingness, of their sin, of their weakness, and to pray to God constantly to grant them this grace.

(3) St. Francis then praises the marvelous effects of grace in us. It is a consolation and an encouragement that St. Ignatius did not give in his "Foundations." Book Five of the *Treatise on the Love of God* is devoted entirely to the analysis of the greatness of love. St. Francis distinguishes, indeed, several sorts of love all of which are capable of inebriating our heart: complacency, condolence, well-wishing. This book describes what the Saint experienced in regard to mystical prayer. The love of complacency is a true love which comes from God. The Father, indeed, was infinitely pleased in his Son and the Son in his Father.

Knowing "by faith that the divinity is an incomprehensible abyss of all perfection, sovereignly infinite in excellence and infinitely sovereign in goodness," the soul exclaims, "O how beautiful you are, my Beloved, how beautiful you are! You are wholly desirable; indeed, you are desire itself; such is my well-beloved, he is the friend of my heart, O daughters of Jerusalem." What St. Francis especially wished to make manifest is the purity of the love of complacency. "We are pleased by the divine pleasure infinitely more than by our own." This love made the saints pronounce with such sweetness that God is God. "Know that the Lord is God," they said. "O God, my God, my God, you are my God. . . . O God, how happy is the soul who takes its pleasure in knowing and realizing that God is God and that his goodness is an infinite goodness. . . . The soul which contemplates the infinite treasures of divine perfections in her well-beloved considers herself too happy and rich in this, that by complacency love makes her mistress of all the perfections and contentments of this dear Spouse."

This love of complacency has no egotistical return to self. It is totally disinterested. St. Francis emphasizes the desire to belong to God more and more and encourages forgetfulness of self, the complete gift of self. "Now in this complacency we satiate our soul with delights in such a way that we do not cease to wish to be satiated, and relishing the divine goodness we still desire to relish it." That enables us to understand slightly the happiness of eternity.

The blessed have constant repose in their movements and movement in their repose; only God has repose without movement, because he is sovereignly pure and substantial act. . . . In short, Theotimus, the soul which is exercising the love of complacency cries out continually in her sacred silence: "It is sufficient for me that God is God, that his goodness is infinite, that his perfection is immense. Whether I die or whether I live matters little to me since my well-beloved lives eternally an all-triumphant life." Death itself cannot disturb a heart which knows that its sovereign love lives. It suffices a loving heart that the object of his love is enjoying eternal happiness, seeing that it lives more in him whom it loves than in him whom it animates; that it lives not itself, but its well-beloved lives in it.

This love of complacency is so elevated, so disinterested that it raised up the soul of Francis when he was crushed by the temptation to despair. God permitted this horrible rending of his heart so as to develop in him pure complacency in no creature but in God alone. That is why it is good to recall this at this point of our analysis.

His love of God attained a purity free from any mixture of self-love, though it may not have reached the very highest point. This kind of purity is achieved only through the trials of darkness and dereliction. We find it described in the book of Job and in numerous psalms; Jesus in his agony in the Garden suffered it in divinized form. The dereliction of St. Francis had consisted in the fear of eternal damnation. Jansenism taught that God found his glory in the condemnation of one part of humanity to eternal misfortune. Two great schools of theology discussed openly the problem of predestination. St. Francis de Sales was one of those who had been crushed by these teachings in which an attempt was made to clarify the obscurities of God's will in the destiny of man, the sinner. But what tormented him was not the obligation to take part in a school and an intellectual solution, but to repel the diabolical temptation which racked his own heart.

Those who have not been tortured by the obsession of despair cannot imagine in what abyss of sorrow this young man, so well-balanced, so wise, so optimistic by temperament, could be buried. It is a fact, nevertheless, that this *idée fixe* rapidly ruined his health and would have killed him if a sort of miracle had not saved him.

"This trial," wrote Msgr. Camus, "experienced in 1586–87, according to Jean Gard, made such an impression on him that he was unable to sleep and could neither eat nor drink. He wasted away visibly and fell into languor. He remained in this state of anguish for a month and spent days and nights in mournful groans; at night he 'watered his couch with tears.'" (Cf. *Œuvres*, XXII, 14 ff.)

Father Liuima wrote: "This was the overwhelming distress of a soul stripped and groaning at the horror of being separated from his love. It was not the torments of hell which afflicted him, but the thought that in hell one does not love

God, and he could not function with this thought of not loving God" (I, 3).

If his body suffered mortal anguish, this anguish was caused by his soul, now submerged by a "deep and watery mud." In the abyss of despair, there was no longer a drop of fresh water to soothe his burning. In the face of his imagined immutable decree of reprobation Francis prayed with a purified love which attained the peaks of disinterestedness.

Ah! Whatever it may be, Lord, at least, let me love you in this life if I cannot love you in the eternal, since no one praises you in hell (*Œuvres*, XXII, 19).

You who are always Judge and merciful Father, I shall love you, Lord, at least in this life. If it is not granted to me to love you in the eternal life, at least I shall love you here, O my God, and I shall always hope in your mercy. I shall always repeat your praises, in spite of the fact that the angel of Satan does not cease to inspire me to the contrary. O Lord Jesus, you will always be my hope and my salvation in the land of the living. If because I deserve to be cursed among the cursed who do not see your sweet face, grant me at least not to be among those who curse your Holy Name (*Ibid.*).

Francis' process of beatification reports to us the testimonies of several important persons concerning the violence of that crisis of despair and the power of prayer and love which triumphed over it. The Benedictine, Claude-Louis Nicolas de Quoex, prior of the Abbey of Talloires, testified the following:

Every day he grew weaker, and because of his helpless weeping, he seemed in agony, spilling his tears day and night and redoubling his sobs. He wearied the air with his lamentations, knocked at heaven with redoubled blows, and tried to touch the heart of God in order that he might either be delivered from all temptation, or, comforted by him, might courageously resist in the faith, and that finally the immutable hope he had placed in divine mercy would not be in vain. In his discouragement . . . he was heard groaning and crying out to the Lord and repeating ardent ejaculatory prayers from the various psalms of the Prophet-King (*Ibid.*, 16, 17).

The same process of beatification preserved the testimony of the wife of President Amelot:

Renouncing everything that concerned his particular interest, he resigned his soul and his intensions purely and entirely into the hands of divine providence. Without wishing to endanger his own salvation further, he resolved and protested that henceforth he would comport himself in the service of God and of virtue with as much affection as if he had infallible assurances of being saved. He declared that if God was to be more honored by his condemnation than by his salvation, he would prefer to be in hell to fulfill the divine will rather than be among the elect contrary to these eternal decrees (*Ibid.*, 18, 19).

And St. Chantal, who was the closest confidante of the Saint, asserted: "He always had in the depth of his spirit this resolution to love and serve God with all his strength during his life, the more affectionately and faithfully as it seemed to him that he would not have the power to do so for eternity" (*Ibid.*, 19).

St. Francis wrote in his notebook:

If I knew that I was damned (God forbid that that should happen!) by that will which the Thomists place in God in order that God may show his justice, struck with stupor and raising my eyes toward the supreme Judge, willingly would I say with the Prophet: "Should not my soul be submitted to God? Amen, Father, because it seemed good to you, may your will be done." And I would say it so many times in the bitterness of my heart, until God, changing my life and my sentence, would answer me: "Have confidence, my son; I will not the death of the sinner but rather that he be converted and live" (*Ibid.*, 65).

Henceforth he was to be faithful in conforming himself to the will of God in all details and under the most touching circumstances, all for the good pleasure of God. It was necessary to recall this terrible crisis of his youth to divine where the purity of his love of complacency became lost in God.

Certain authors allow themselves to be surprised that St. Ignatius did not, in his *Exercises,* begin by proposing to the retreatant the love of complacency. Nevertheless the phrase "to praise God," by which he indicates the end of creation, is without doubt a manner of expressing this love. The love of compassion and that of benevolence, to which St. Francis de Sales attached great importance, are the principal ends of the third and fourth Weeks of the *Exercises.* St. Ignatius is content to refer to compassion as grace to ask for and as principal fruit of the meditations on the Passion. We must "engage all our strength and all our ardor to arouse in ourselves grief, sadness and tears."

The *Treatise on the Love of God* discusses the love of compassion or the "love of condolence" in the fourth and fifth chapters of Book Five. Here the Saint defined it and showed its perfection and efficacy. By it, he said, "the complacency of love is still better declared," that is, we manage to forget ourselves more completely, to cease thinking of our own sufferings, to take to ourselves those of Jesus Christ only. This is evidently a grace which all the saints have sought and obtained, without any exception. By compassion, condolence, or commiseration, we participate in the grief of the one whom our soul loves, "drawing the grief that he suffers into our own heart." Nothing shows its perfection better than if we consider "how love draws all these pains and these torments, works, sufferings, griefs, wounds, passion, the cross and even the death of our Redeemer into the heart of his holy Mother; even the thorns which pierce his head pierced also the soul of this most sweet Mother; she had the same miseries as her Son by commiseration, the same dolors by condolence, the same passions by compassion."

Man is egotistical; he often flees the sorrows of others. Condolence would give him a mother's heart, for the mother suffers with her ailing son, feverish, wounded, tortured, dead, as much as, and frequently more than, her son himself. We see every day and in all times examples of compassion. Jesus, noted St. Francis, ardently desires that we love him as his Mother did. Hence the importance of our devotion to the Seven Sorrows and to the hymn *Stabat Mater*. The Church has us ask through Mary for the great grace of self-forgetfulness by bearing the sufferings of another, Jesus. "This was the love which attracted the stigmata to the loving, seraphic St. Francis of Assisi and the Lord's glowing wounds to the loving, angelic St. Catherine of Siena."

But let us never forget that compassion has a double home. It existed first of all in the soul and the heart of Jesus Christ. He became flesh "for our sins"; and from the beginning of his Incarnation until his death, the sins of the world made this innocent Person suffer, the Word Incarnate, impressing on his whole being the stigmata of our redemption. Compassion, in its extreme violence, made Christ die; the perfection of disinterested love is found in the Passion and on the Cross. That is why the grace which we ask through the Passion of Jesus, by his Blood poured out, and each day by the Sacrifice of the Mass, is the grace of a response, of an exchange, of a communion, and not only a human pity. The love of compassion of Jesus for us sinners solves the almost insoluble problem of suffering. For if we suffer it is because Jesus had compassion on our misery and wished to communicate to us his justice, his redemption, his resemblance to the Son in the eyes of the Father.

The love of benevolence is another form, perhaps even more elevated, of the forgetfulness of self. St. Francis here reveals the sublimity of his heart. Whoever does not know the page which we are about to quote does not know St. Francis very well.

What do we call benevolence? In God it is the complacency that he takes in his creatures, providing for them all possible good even in eternity and averting from them all the evil that threatens them. In man "the love of benevolence which we bear to God is nothing else than an approbation and a perseverance in the complacency which we have in him."

We cannot, with a true desire, wish any good to God, because his goodness is infinitely more perfect than we can either wish or think. Desire is only for a future good, and no good is future to God, since all good is present to him. The presence of good in his divine Majesty is nothing but the divinity itself. Not being able, then, to cherish any absolute desire for God, we foster imaginary and conditional ones, such as: I say to the Lord, "You are my God. Apart from you I have no good." (Ps. 15:2).

Being full of your own infinite goodness, you have no need of my goods, nor of anything whatever. But if, by imagining an impossibility, I could think you had need of anything, I would never cease to wish it for you, even though it cost me my life, my being, and everything in the world. And if, since you are what you are and what you can only be, if it were possible that you could receive any increase of good—O God! how I desire that you should have it! I would desire, O eternal Lord, to see my whole heart convert into a wish, and my life into a sigh, to desire such a good for you! . . . O holy lover of my soul . . . I delight with all my heart in this supreme degree of goodness of yours to which nothing can be added, neither by desire nor yet by thought. O infinite Divinity, O divine Infinity! If such a desire were possible, my soul would be that desire and nothing else, so intensely would it desire for you what it is infinitely pleased to know that it cannot desire. It realizes that its inability to form this desire proceeds from the infinity of your perfection which outstrips all desire and thought. O my God! how dearly I love the impossibility of being able to desire any good for you, since this lack flows from the incomprehensible immensity of your abundance. This fullness is so sovereignly infinite that an infinite desire would be infinitely satiated by the infinity of your goodness, which would convert it into an infinite complacency. . . . "Ah, Lord, I am Augustine and thou art God, but still, if that which neither is nor can be were, that I were God and thou Augustine, I would, changing my condition with thee, become Augustine so that thou mightest be God!"

There is yet another kind of benevolence towards God which operates when, realizing that we cannot exalt him in himself, we strive to do it in ourselves, that is, we attempt to increase still more and more the complacency we take in his goodness. And then, Theotimus, we desire not this complacency for the pleasure it yields us, but purely because this pleasure is in God . . . in imitation of the most holy Queen and Mother of love, whose holy soul continually magnified and exalted God. And so that it might be known that this magnifying was present because of the complacency which she took in the divine goodness, she declares that her spirit exultingly rejoiced in God her Savior (*Œuvres*, V, vi).

This love of benevolence seems to detach us from everything, including ourselves, in a manner opposed not only to jealousy in regard to the persons who seem more gifted than we but even to every surge of generosity which increases us in our own eyes and in the eyes of all those to whom we do good. We have no need, then, of thanks, attention, esteem of anything at all. God alone suffices for us. Father Claude de la Colombière wrote: "Every day I feel more devotion for St. Francis de Sales." Why? Because he developed the teaching that "there is no peace except in the perfect forgetfulness of self; we must resolve to forget even our spiritual interests in order to seek nothing but the glory of God." Summarizing, at the end of his retreat, the lights that it had pleased God to give him during those eight days, he wrote: "The most frequent feeling I had was a desire to let myself go and to forget myself entirely." With St. Francis de Sales, "the soul finds itself stable in such a serenity that merely the words 'confidence, humility, complete yielding without reserve, God's will, Holy Rule,' never present themselves to my mind without light, peace, liberty, sweetness and love entering there at the same time." And his constantly renewed act of offering is expressed thus: "Sacred Heart of Jesus, teach me perfect forgetfulness of myself, since it is the only way by which I can enter into you."

This love of benevolence not only makes us praise God with our whole soul but it makes us call all creatures to his praise, as did St. Francis of Assisi in his *Canticle to the Sun.*

Our model is our Mother, Mother of Jesus above all the elect, the seraphim, the cherubim, the nine choirs of angels; her *Magnificat* is the incomparable praise which, like the dawn, announces the infinite praise of Jesus. Mary's love of benevolence constantly animates the heart of the Spouse of Christ Jesus [the Church]; she sings over all the earth the psalms, her Canticle of Canticles, and celebrates Holy Mass, which is perfect adoration and total thanksgiving.

The soul "invites the Savior to praise and glorify his eternal Father with all the benedictions which his filial love can furnish him and then the spirit arrives in a place of silence, for we no longer are able to do anything but wonder." And St. Francis terminates his fifth book with this astonishing and admirable elevation:

So, while by benevolence we are drawing nearer to the divinity to intone and listen to his praises, we become more and more conscious of how far God is above all praise, and in the end we understand that except by himself he cannot be praised according to his merits. Perceiving this, we cry aloud, "Glory be to the Father and to the Son and to the Holy Ghost." And so that all may know that it is not the glory of created praise that we wish him by this ejaculation, but the essential and eternal glory that is in himself, by himself, and that truly is himself, we add: "As it was in the beginning, is now and ever shall be, world without end, Amen." Thus we give expression to our desire that God should be glorified forever with the glory which he had before all creatures in his infinite eternity and eternal infinity.

It is very desirable that the retreatants making the *Exercises* follow St. Francis de Sales in the ways of love and persuade themselves that the Ignatian principle, "true love proves itself by acts," encompasses all forms of divine love. Is not the zeal of the apostles, when it is pure, one of the effects of charity? "It is this holy desire [to glorify God]," wrote St. Francis, "which caused so many sermons to be preached, which caused Xavier, Berzées, and Anthony to undergo such sufferings, also a multitude of Jesuits, Capuchins, and religious ecclesiastics of all sorts, in India, Japan, South America, in order to make known, acknowledged and adored the holy name of Jesus in many nations. This great desire brought forth countless books of devotion, erected innumerable churches, altars, convents, monasteries. In a word, it is this consuming passion that makes so many servants of God watch, labor and die, victims of the flames of zeal which consume and devour them" (V, ix).

Ignatius' love of benevolence gave to his sons their motto: *Ad majorem Dei gloriam.* St. Francis also repeated this motto very often; we cannot prove this statement, however, without wearying the reader. It meant for him all that we have said about his love of God.

16 *The Good Pleasure of God*

"CHARITY" has several synonyms: love of God, God's will, the good pleasure of God, indifference of man. These expressions form part of the ascetical language of St. Ignatius and St. Francis de Sales. There is no pure love of God without conformity to the will of God and without indifference.

St. Ignatius wrote his *Exercises* with the purpose of converting souls to a total renunciation of their own will so as to choose in all things the will of God. To arrive at this objective requires that we free ourselves from all unregulated affections which turn us away from the path God has chosen for us. It will prove helpful for us to meditate on the three entrances of Jesus into this world. By his Incarnation, the Word declares that he came into the world to accomplish the will of his Father; he enters upon his Passion by an agony in which he constantly repeats that he is suffering in order to do his Father's will, not his own; he dies, placing his spirit in the hands, that is, in the will of the Father. On all the pages of his life, the Son shows and declares that his Father and he have only one will. *Quae placita sunt ei.*

St. Ignatius, wishing this submission of our will to the Father to be practical, insisted on obedience to the Father through the will of the Church and that of superiors. He even made this obedience the characteristic virtue of the Society, a circumstance which has had unlimited consequences on the Society's apostolate.

St. Francis de Sales also strongly recommended obedience according to the suggestions of St. Ignatius. But generally he did not speak much of the will of God as the principal virtue of Christians but, using the language of charity more than that of justice, he emphasized "the good pleasure of God." His *Treatise on the Love of God* includes one of the most important and most beautiful essays in spiritual literature—that on the conformity of our will to God's (Book VIII). This conformity is not that of submission to the Master, to the Leader, to the All-Powerful, but that of docility to the Holy Spirit, that of the Son's love for the Father. That is why he distinguishes what God *ordains* (the commandments) from what he *counsels,* and what he indicates through *inspirations* when he makes known his *good pleasure* through the Church and superiors in his name. In short, this conformity must be practiced with love and not with servile fear, always, everywhere, and in everything. He makes of it—as St. John does in his epistles—a form of love and not merely an obligation of justice.

But take note, Theotimus, that I am not treating here of the obedience due to God because he is our Lord and Master, our Father and Benefactor, for this kind of obedience belongs to the virtue of justice, not to love. I am not speaking of this at present, for even though there were no hell to punish the rebellious, nor any heaven to reward the good, and though we had no obligation or duty to God (an impossible case, scarcely imaginable), still the love of benevolence would move us to render all obedience and submission to God by election and inclination, by a sweet violence of love because of the sovereign goodness, justice and rectitude of his divine will (VIII, ii).

God expresses his will clearly. St. Francis de Sales calls this will the "known will of God." Conformity to this will "consists in our desiring all that divine goodness indicates to us as his intention, believing according to his threats, loving and living according to his commands and admonitions." But God makes us know it *under the form of desire,* like the Lord who invites to a feast, and not as a Master who stuffs food into our throat and forces us to swallow it.

Now, among the "known wills" of God there is that of our salvation. "God has indicated to us in so many ways and through so many means that he wished *all* of us to be saved, that no one could be ignorant of it." A true will of God does not suppress our liberty but acts through grace. St. Francis tells us that this will is charity and produces the happiness of God, which is love. Let us consider this thought:

"One thing I ask of the Lord; this I seek: to dwell in the house of the Lord all the days of my life" (Ps. 26:4). But what is the delight of the sovereign goodness, except to pour out and communicate his perfections? Truly he "found delight in the sons of men" (Prov. 8:31) and in showering his graces upon them. Nothing is so agreeable and delightful to free agents as to do their own will. Our sanctification is the will of God and our salvation his good pleasure, nor is there any difference at all between good pleasure and delight, nor, therefore, between delight and the divine good will. The will God has to benefit man is called *good* (Rom. 12:2) because it is lovable, kind, favorable, agreeable, delectable. It is, as the Greek Fathers, following St. Paul, said, true philanthropy, that is, a benevolence, an entirely loving will towards man.

The whole celestial temple of the triumphant and of the militant Church resounds on every side with the canticles of this sweet love of God for us. And the most sacred body of our Savior, as a most holy temple of his divinity, is all decorated with the marks and tokens of this benevolence, so that when we visit the divine temple, we behold the loving delights which his heart takes in doing us favors.

Let us, then, a thousand times a day, turn our eyes upon this loving will of God and make ours melt into it. Let us devoutly cry out: "O Goodness infinitely sweet, how lovable is your will, how desirable are your favors!" (VIII, iv).

The commandments of God are, then, for St. Francis de Sales completely loving wills and, so to speak, a desire which God gives to himself while attracting men to the road of union with him. St. Francis recommends that we meditate on Psalm 118. Let us try to give an account of this "desire" in the heart of Jesus, a desire which he has tasted and which he tastes each time that he fulfills the good pleasure of the Father, gives us his body to eat, his blood to drink, his own mother as ours, and his spouse the Church to direct us toward beatitude. "Alas," complained St. Francis, "who speaks to us of God's will in this fashion? and who makes us feel the weight of this yoke of justice, contrary to the word of Jesus, 'My yoke is sweet!' "

Many keep the commandments as sick men take medicine, that is, more from fear of dying in a state of damnation than from love of living according to our Savior's pleasure. But as some persons have an aversion for medicine, no matter how pleasant, only because it bears the name of medicine, so there are some souls who abhor commands simply because they are commanded. . . . On the contrary, the loving heart loves the commandments; and the more difficult they are, the sweeter and more agreeable it finds them because thus it pleases the beloved more perfectly and gives him greater honor (VIII, v).

If love commands, even more does it recommend, or *counsel*. By these counsels it seeks the good of the entire Church. That is why the counsels are given in different fashions according to the needs of holy Church. Thus if anyone wishes to ask him why he performs these acts of charity, "he will . . . boldly make answer: The Lord had need of them (Mt. 21:3). All is done for charity and charity for God. All must serve her and she none. Rather, she does not serve her well-beloved because she is not his servant but his spouse, whom she loves" (VIII, vi).

O law of all love and for all love! . . . The Psalmist cried out, "Those who love your law have great peace" (118:165). . . . Truly, that great king whose heart was made according to the heart of God relished the perfect excellence of the divine commandments so greatly that he seemed to be a lover captivated with the beauty of this law as with the chaste spouse and queen of his heart.

The Saint finds in the Bible a comparison which can arouse us to observe the counsels, that is, the desires of the Beloved, with great eagerness:

One day David was in his camp and the Philistine garrison was in Bethlehem. David longed and said, "O that some man would get me a drink of the water from the cistern that is in Bethlehem, near the gate!" And he had no sooner said the word than three valiant men set out, hand and head lowered, to break through the hostile camp, go to the cistern of Bethlehem, draw water, and bring it to David. When he saw the risk which these three knightly men had run to gratify his longing, he would not drink the water obtained at the peril of their blood and life, but poured it out in sacrifice to the eternal God (Cf. 2 Kgs. 23:14–17). Ah, Theotimus, notice the zeal of these knights in the service and satisfaction of their master! They hasten, they break through the ranks of their enemies, they incur a thousand dangers to gratify only one simple desire which their king expresses to them. . . . Noble souls need no other spur to the undertaking of a design than to know that their beloved desires it. "My soul," said one of them, "melted when he spoke" (VIII, viii).

We must have this same ardor in following even ordinary *inspirations*.

How happy are they who keep their hearts open to holy inspirations! . . . Without inspiration our soul would lead an idle, sluggish, and fruitless life, but on receiving the divine rays of inspiration we feel a light mingled with a quickening heat, which illuminates our understanding and which excites and animates our will, giving it the strength to will and to effect the good necessary for eternal salvation. (*Ibid.*)

Souls never lack the means of inspiration, which are infinite. Without them our will could not perfectly observe the commandments nor the counsels.

Truly, souls which are not content with doing what the heavenly Beloved requires from them by his commandments and counsels but also promptly comply with sacred inspirations, are the souls whom the eternal Father has destined to be the spouses of his well-loved Son. . . . When we are at a loss and human help fails us in our perplexities, God then inspires us, and he will not permit us to err as long as we are humbly obedient (*Ibid.*).

Then, under some form or appearance which is manifested to us, the will of God becomes an act of God's love for us, and it is by uniting our human will to his divine will that we give him the testimony of our love for him. Any disposition of our will which would make us prefer creatures to God is contrary to love.

This love of God's will is often called *indifference*. In French the word "indifference" is equivocal. It can mean the lack of interest or the lack of heart in regard to all created things; for St. Ignatius and for St. Francis de Sales it is, on the contrary, a synonym for the love of God. St. Ignatius makes it, so to speak, the foundation of the spiritual life, or at least the foundation of the *Exercises*. Since God has created us, he said, for himself—and not for another than himself nor even for our selves—everything which is not God but was created by God has the same end: to praise, honor and serve God. The consequence is immediate; we must not turn creatures aside from their end nor utilize them for any other end than praise, honor and service of the Creator and Lord of all things. Two loves are therefore impossible. We cannot love anything at all, not even our own being, contrary to God nor outside of God, nor in any other manner than God himself. Alone, absolutely alone, love of God for God must make us love creatures and self. Indifference is, then, not scorn for creatures and self but as intense a love as possible for all creation, flowing from the love of God and returning to God without any reservation. That is the thought of St. Ignatius. Like St. Ignatius, St. Francis de Sales considered indifference as a fundamental virtue. But he speaks of it in all his works and with much more insistence, it seems, than does St. Ignatius.

St. Francis made St. Ignatius' thought understood, not only through analyses and examples, but also by comparisons.

> The indifferent heart is like a ball of wax in the hand of its God, receiving with equal readiness all the impressions of the divine pleasure. It is a heart without choice, equally disposed for everything, its will having no other object than the will of its God, and placing its affection not upon the things that God wills but upon the will of the God who wills them. . . . To conclude, God's will is the sovereign object of the indifferent soul; wherever she sees it she runs after the odor of its perfumes, ever directing her course where it appears, considering nothing else. She is conducted by the divine will as by a beloved chain; any way it goes, she follows it (*Treatise,* IX, iii).

But St. Francis, while repeating almost the same words of St. Ignatius, extends to all things the particular objects pointed out by him. He said: "Indifference is to be practiced in things belonging to the natural life, such as health, sickness, beauty, deformity, weakness, strength; in the affairs of the spiritual life, such as dryness, consolation, relish, aridity; in actions, in sufferings—briefly, in all sorts of events" (IX, v). St. Ignatius had not spoken of spiritual things.

Is it not surprising that we must be indifferent even "in things belonging to the service of God"? Indeed, it is truly necessary. "Yes, Theotimus, because in order to exercise us in this holy indifference God often inspires us with very high designs, which we will not yet have accomplished. But then, as we boldly, courageously and constantly begin and pursue the work as far as we can, we are sweetly and quietly to acquiesce in such results of our enterprise as it pleases God to send us" (IX, vi). St. Francis cites several examples, among them this one:

St. Ignatius of Loyola, having with much difficulty established the Society of Jesus, from which he saw so many fair fruits and foresaw many more in the time to come, yet had the nobility of soul to promise himself that if he should see it dissolve (which would be the bitterest pain that could befall him), within half an hour afterwards he would rest tranquil in the will of God. . . . Oh, how blessed are such souls, bold and strong in the undertakings God proposes to them, and withal, tractable and facile in giving them over when God so disposes! These are marks of a most perfect indifference, to leave off doing a good when God pleases and to return from half way when God's will, which is our guide, ordains it (*Ibid.*).

Let us advance another step on this road. Can we be indifferent in regard to the virtues which we must practice? Is there a contradiction in wishing and not wishing to be virtuous? St. Ignatius does not speak of it. St. Francis de Sales responds: "It belongs to us diligently to cultivate our heart, and therefore we must faithfully attend to it, but as for a plentiful crop or harvest, let us leave that care to our Lord and Master." Thus do the laborers. This is also the case of the souls in purgatory who detest their sins and who lovingly await their deliverance. When we have committed sin, we must unite ourselves purely to the will of god, whether he punishes us or not. "We must ever adore, love and praise God's avenging and punishing justice as we love his mercy, since both are daughters of his goodness. . . . We should therefore submit ourselves to the divine will, and kiss the right hand of his mercy and the left hand of his justice with equal love and reverence." Let us, then, not speak of the universality of indifference. Let us not speak of the *purity* of indifference, for

our hearts . . . formed and exercised little by little in holy love are imperceptibly changed. Instead of loving God in order to please God, they begin to love him for pleasure they take in the exercises of holy love; and instead of falling in love with God they fall in love with the love they bear him and are attracted to their own affections. They no longer take pleasure in God, but in the pleasure they find in his love (IX, vii).

It would be necessary, then, in order to be truly indifferent, to renounce even the happiness of loving God by loving him. It often happens that we are discouraged when that sweetness ceases. It is then, when we are experiencing no consolation, "that we are to show an invincible courage towards our Savior, serving him purely for the love of his will, not only without pleasure but amid this deluge of sorrows, horrors, distresses and assaults, as did his glorious Mother and St. John on the day of his Passion."

Then the will is as dead. St. Francis de Sales called this spiritual death by a name which has remained famous: the *loving death of the will*. It is not sufficient, then, to make our will indifferent; we must make it die. He had already spoken of the death of the intelligence by *blind obedience* which he had praised highly, like the ancient monks and St. Ignatius. As St. Francis defines it, the intelligence is totally sacrificed by blind obedience. He attributes three properties to this obedience:

The first is that it never looks at the face of superiors, but only at their authority; the second, that it never informs itself of the reasons nor the motives which the superiors have in commanding such or such a thing, letting it be sufficient for him to know that they have commanded it; and the third, that it does not seek the means necessary to do what is commanded, assuring itself that God, by whose inspiration they have given us the command will also give him the power to accomplish it, and instead of asking how it will do it, will begin to do it.

Evidently, all these matters demand practical explanations and directives. St. Francis does not ignore this fact and develops his subject in two long, admirable Conferences (X and

XI). But he in no way diminishes his ideal of obedience as he has just defined it.

"The loving death of the will," as the name indicates, is radical. And in the *Treatise on the Love of God* he insists very strongly on this death to self which requires the total sacrifice of the will and all its desires. "It is true, our will can no more die than our soul, yet it sometimes goes out of the limits of its ordinary life to live wholly in the divine will. This takes place when it neither wills nor cares to desire anything at all, but gives itself over totally and without reserve to the good pleasure of divine providence, so mingling and saturating itself with this good pleasure that in itself it is seen no more, but is all hidden with Jesus Christ in God, where it lives, not it, but the will of God lives in it."

The comparison that he chose is *à propos:* "And just as he who is on board a ship does not move by his own motion but is moved by that of the vessel, so the heart that embarks on the divine will." He gives another charming example of the child who lives in the arms of his mother and who knows only to will and to love nothing else than the breast and face of his dear mother." "The will that dies to itself to live in that of God is without any personal volition, . . . quite annihilated to itself and cemented into God's."

Another example of Francis' imagery—a small masterpiece —makes us admire the abandonment of Jesus in the arms of his Mother Mary; delighted at his contemplation, our Saint cried out:

O divine child of Mary! Permit my poor soul these outbursts of love. O most amiable little Babe, go, then—or rather, do not go, but remain thus holily fastened to your mother's sweet breast. Always go with her and never without her while you are still a child! Thus should we, too, be, . . . not permitting our thoughts to wander aimlessly in wishing and willing things, but leaving God to exercise our will for us as he pleases, casting all our solicitude upon him, because he cares for us, as the holy Apostle says (1 Pt. 5:7). And note that he says: "all your anxiety"—that is, what concerns events as well as what pertains to only willing or not willing, for "he cares for" the issue of our affairs, willing what is best for us.

It seems that in discussing the death of the will as the effect and sign of true love we can add nothing further. And yet, Francis de Sales in a subtle and accurate analysis describes the activity of the will which lives in God:

It is very difficult to express exactly this extreme indifference of the human will, when it is dead to self and absorbed in the will of God. For, it seems to me, we should not say that it acquiesces to that of God because acquiescence is an act of the soul which declares its consent. Nor should we say that it accepts or receives, because accepting and receiving are in a certain sense passive actions, by which we embrace and accept what happens. It is not correct, either, to say that the will permits, since even permitting is an act of will in that it does not act and yet lets action be done. It seems to me, then, that the soul thus indifferent and willing nothing, letting God will what pleases him, should be said to be in a simple and general state of waiting; since waiting, though voluntary, is not acting, but a simple disposition to receive whatever shall happen. As soon as the events come and are received, the waiting changes into consent or acquiescence, but before they happen, the soul is truly indifferent to all it shall please the divine will to ordain (*Treatise*, IX, xiv).

This loving death to the will is so perfect and necessary that almost all St. Francis' letters recommend it as the best solution to all problems and all spiritual difficulties.

17 *Charity and Love of Self*

PERFECTION suppresses imperfection without destroying whatever good there may be within it. The "more" excludes the "less." Childhood suppresses infancy; adolescence suppresses childhood; adulthood suppresses adolescence. In the same way we find that the virtue of abnegation is born. Love begets abnegation; charity suppresses self-love. We should be careful, then, not to define abnegation as a purely negative and destructive virtue. It is positive, the fruit of love, and although it seems to precede charity, in reality, it follows it. We could say that it is not distinct from the love of God. The Holy Spirit, by dwelling in souls and by infusing charity into them, does not leave love to nature alone. When the Spirit acts, love ceases to be self-love and becomes charity. This transformation is what St. Francis de Sales, like St. Ignatius, calls abnegation. There are here two opposing formulas: the first, to love God *and* all things; the second, to love God *in* all things. The first divides love and multiplies it into an infinity of objects under the dependence of God. The second preserves its unity in the unique Spirit and unique charity. St. Ignatius and St. Francis teach the same doctrine, namely, that we must love God: what he is, what he loves, what he wishes and what he does. We must love only God, love him exclusively in all things. We must love him by rejecting as evil or as not existing whatever he does not love, does not wish, does not do.

It is, then, necessary to renounce, to combat all that is opposed to the love of God and therefore to *our* love of God. Abnegation means, then, a love of God and at the same time a renunciation, a detachment, a refusal. Following the example of Jesus Christ, all the saints have demanded abnegation. In the Gospel, the law proclaimed by Jesus Christ is a law of renunciation in order to be free to follow Jesus. We must leave all—all and everything—not only our goods and our family, but our soul and our self. St. Francis de Sales understood, explained, and preached the love of God crucified in Jesus Christ, and this love is abnegation. "We do not give sufficient attention to the fact that under the pen of the Saint 'devotion' is synonymous with 'perfection,' and 'perfection' synonymous with 'pure love' in the crucifying sense that the greatest mystics give to this word" (Bremond, I, 105). "Most demanding in regard to himself, the saint is also exacting with others, even in the smallest details." In his directives to St. Jane de Chantal he wrote: "Cut, slice, prune, . . . you need the shears and the knife" (*Œuvres*, XIV, 103).

St. Ignatius taught the same doctrine, but in a different style. "Receive, O Lord, all my liberty, my memory, my understanding, my whole will. . . . I restore to you all that you have given me. I ask only your love and your grace; with these I shall be sufficiently rich and will desire nothing else." This prayer could easily have been signed "Francis de Sales."

Was this same abnegation of love at the basis of the soul and the heart of St. Jane de Chantal? She wrote to her holy director:

It is true, I have an extreme desire and, it seems to me, a firm resolution to remain in my self-renunciation, thanks to the grace of God, and I hope that he will continue to aid me. I feel that my spirit is entirely free, and that it enjoys a certain infinite and profound consolation at seeing itself thus in the hands of God. . . . I must say this to you, that if I were to let my heart go, it would seek to reclothe itself with the affections and desires that it seems our Lord is willing to give it. But I do not yield to this desire, with the result that these propositions are seen only from a distance. In the end, it seems to me that I must no longer think anything, desire nor will anything except what our Lord makes me think, love, and will, as my higher faculties will command me. As for my baser instincts, I am correct in disregarding them (*Sa vie et ses œuvres*, IV, 112).

The following day the Saint answered her: "O my Jesus, what a blessing and consolation to my soul to know that you are quite stripped of self before God! . . . It is the end of the Transfiguration, my dear mother, to see no longer Moses, nor Elias, but only Jesus, . . . for we must have our affection united so absolutely and so simply to God that nothing may cling to us" (*Œuvres*, XVII, 216). The purpose of all this detachment is attachment to God alone: *amorem solum mihi dones et dives sum satis.* We could perhaps believe that the spiritual blessings, the virtues, the sweetness of the presence of God are not included in these garments which we must cast off without giving them too much attention. This is not the opinion of St. Francis:

Let us say that this evening you should renounce all the virtues, wishing them only in the measure which God will give them to you, and not willing to have any care for acquiring them except in proportion as his goodness will employ you for that, according to his good pleasure. Our Lord loves you, Mother, and he wishes you to be completely his. No longer permit any arms but his to bear you up, do not rest on any other breast but his and that of his providence. Do not look elsewhere; focus your attention on him alone. Hold your will united to his in all things that it may please him to act with you and in you, through you and for you, and in all things outside you, that nothing may divide you two. Think no longer of the friendship nor of the unity which God has made between us; not of your children, your body, your soul, nor of anything whatever, for you have given all over to God. Clothe yourself with our Lord crucified (*Ibid.*, 218).

Did St. Jane understand this last expression of his demands? Not immediately.

Alas, Father, today I remembered that one time you told me to despoil myself and I answered, "I do not know of what I can despoil myself further!" Then you told me, "Have I not often told you, my daughter, that I would despoil you of everything?" Oh, God, how easy it is to put off the things around us, but to put off our skin, our flesh, our bones and to penetrate into the intimate marrow, is a great thing but difficult, even impossible without the grace of God. The only glory, then, is due to him and may it be given to him forever (*Ibid.*, 410).

Shall we believe that St. Francis asked more of her? Yes, he wished her to detach herself from all complacency in the *mystical presence of Christ.* She wrote to him: "It seems that our Lord, throughout these past days, has withdrawn a little that small sweetness and suavity which the sentiment of his

dear presence gives." Francis wished for her only complacency in the good pleasure of God. He answered: "Take
courage, for if he has stripped you of the consolations and
sentiments of his presence, it is so that his very presence may
no longer hold your heart, but only himself and his pleasure;
as he said to Magdalen, wishing to embrace him and cling to
his feet, 'Do not touch me, but go, tell all to Simon Peter.'"

Can we think for an instant that the direction given to St.
Jane de Chantal is exceptional and that it is not the same for
all souls? Whether one is with the Visitandines, at Carmel, at
Port-Royal, or in the world makes little difference; the law of
true charity is that of abnegation; the way to go to God is
that of renunciation, of Jesus dying on the Cross.

That is why the Abbess of Maubuisson, Angélique Arnaud,
by renouncing herself had to show that she followed the good
road and possessed the Holy Spirit. Unfortunately, she could
not sustain her observance of the counsels of St. Francis until
the end. He wrote to her: "I see clearly this ant's nest of inclinations which self-love breeds and pours forth over your
heart, my dear daughter, and I am well aware that the nature
of your mind—subtle, delicate, fertile—contributes toward
this."

On the occasion of a participation by the Abbess in the literary life of the times, he wrote: "One thing only have I to
say to you, my dear daughter, on your writing to me that you
nourish your pride by little arts in conversation and in letters.
In conversation, indeed, affectation sometimes enters so imperceptibly that one scarcely notices it at all; but still, if one
does perceive it, the style should be altered immediately. In
letters this is certainly a little less—rather, much less—to be
tolerated for we can see better what we are doing. If we perceive a notable affectation we must punish the hand that
wrote it, making it write another letter in another fashion." He
also combats her taste for corporal austerities. "Through the
lines of St. Francis de Sales the character of the young abbess
is clearly portrayed: imperious, absolute, but deeply gener-

ous, ardent in her desire to belong wholly to God" (Cognet, *La Mère Angélique et saint François de Sales*, 115).

These few extracts from letters would suffice if we imagined that the holy director contented himself in blaming her frequent seizures of pride and self-love. But he forced himself to pursue the effort and victory of true love, according to his habits and his principles, by sweetness. Let us read again this charming letter:

Truly, I know you well, and you always have in your heart an invariable resolution to live completely for God. But I also know that this natural activity makes you feel a great variety of attacks. O my daughter, I pray you, do not believe that the work we have undertaken in you can be finished so soon. Cherry trees bear their fruits early because their fruits are only cherries, lasting but a short time; but the palm, the prince of trees, does not bear fruit for a hundred years after it has been planted—or so they say. A mediocre life can be acquired in a brief year, but the perfection toward which we are aiming, my dear daughter, can come only after many years of effort, ordinarily speaking (Dec. 16, 1619).

These words could only encourage Mère Angélique to perseverance in her struggle for obedience. Unfortunately, the death of the director left her to herself, and then to Saint-Cyran. It is not useless to quote St. Francis again, for these letters can do good to many souls. "Ah, yes, my daughter, I see your entanglements in those thoughts of vanity; the fertility and at the same time the subtlety of your mind lend a hand to these suggestions." According to an agreement made between her and the saint, the latter wrote to St. Jane de Chantal:

Her natural impetuosity is the cause of all her trouble for it animates her vivacity and her vivacity animates her impetuosity. However, tell her for me that her principal care must be to hold her spirit in modesty, sweetness and tranquility. To do that she must temper all her exterior actions, her deportment, her gait, her countenance, her hands, and, when she speaks, her tongue and her language. She should find nothing strange in this because to train a young horse to the saddle and bridle is not the work of a single day, but of several years.

That suggestions of the soul may come from movements of the body is a fact which passes for a modern discovery, yet it was known in the sixteenth century. Let us terminate this chapter with a letter which is, more than all others, perhaps, typical of the Saint.

Accustom yourself to speak softly and slowly and walk in a more sedate manner. Do all that you do gently and quietly and you will see that in three or four years [Francis did not suffer from any illusions] you will have regulated this hasty impetuousness. But remember to act thus gently and speak softly on occasions when impetuosity is not urging you and when there is no danger of it, as, for example, when you are going to bed, getting up, sitting down, eating, when you are speaking with Sister Marie or Sister Anne. In short, in all and everywhere, never dispense yourself (*Œuvres,* IX, 124).

This advice strongly resembles the particular examen of St. Ignatius. Sometimes the Holy Spirit spreads charity in hearts suddenly and superabundantly, as on the apostles at Pentecost. But most often he communicates it drop by drop, so to speak, according to the dispositions, the efforts, and the progress of souls.

18 *Love of Neighbor*

"IT IS MY RESOLVE to love nothing at all but God, and all souls for him" (*Œuvres,* XX, 216). Love of neighbor is love of God just as that of God is for all men. St. Francis de Sales recognizes especially the purity and universality of that love. For him, friendship is a foreshadowing of the love which unites all souls in heaven:

O how good it is to love on earth as we love in heaven, and to learn to cherish each other in this world as we shall do eternally in the other. . . . If our mutual and reciprocal communication is made in charity, devotion, and Christian perfection, O God, how precious will our soul be! It will be excellent because it tends toward God, excellent because its bond is God, excellent because it will last eternally in God (*Ibid.*, III, 203).

If we love outside of God, we "run the risk of not loving purely nor constantly, nor equally; but there, in God—in the heart of the Savior—who will not love him?" And here is an even more precise statement: If we love in God, then even the "natural love of kinsmen, companions, acquaintances, love begotten of similarity, compatibility, sympathy and grace will be purified and will reduce to perfect obedience the all pure love of the divine good pleasure. Certainly, the greatest good and the happiness of souls who aspire to perfection is to have no desire to be loved by creatures except by this love of charity" (*Ibid.*, VI, 219–220).

Msgr. Camus quoted Francis as saying: "As long as love of neighbor is limited to nature, there will be no goodness, no beauty. As soon as it is exposed to the sun of God's love and sanctified by his Spirit, who is charity, it will be seen in its perfection" (X, 35).

An author who has made a special study of St. Francis de Sales, wrote this very accurate description: "His attitude toward Madame de Chantal is the prototype and the summation of his love toward souls and his friendship for them which is solely according to God and in God" (Liuima, p. 271). Since it comes from the Holy Spirit, it is the same toward all souls. This is one of the lessons to be drawn from his correspondence with the Baroness de Chantal. A letter on the choice of her spiritual director written at Annecy, June 24, 1604, reveals to us how much St. Francis loved his "Philothea": "I am not able to express either the quality or the greatness of this affection which I have for your spiritual service; I tell you that I think it is from God, and for that reason I cherish it fondly, and every day I see it increase notably." He does not say that he forces himself to increase it.

I must die to you in order to cut off the road to all the replies which can form in our heart. I have never heard that there was any liaison between us which bore any obligation except that of charity and true Christian friendship, the bond of which St. Paul called the bond of perfection. Truly it is indissoluble and is never loosened. All other bonds are temporal, even that of obedience which can be broken by death and many other occurrences, but that of charity increases with time and takes new strength by its duration. It is exempt from severance by death, the scythe which cuts off all but charity (*Œuvres*, XII, 284–85).

The reason for this is evident: it is united to the Holy Spirit who "diffuses" it, as St. Paul says. Francis de Sales felt himself constrained to rely on the divine character of his love:

Here is, my good Sister—and please permit me to call you by this name which is that by which the apostles and the first Christians expressed the intimate love they bore each other—here is our bond, here our chains, which the more they bind and press us the more they give us ease and liberty. Their force is nothing but sweetness, their violence, suavity; nothing else is so pliable, nothing else so firm as that. Consider me, then, closely united to you, and know that this is not contrary to any other bond, whether it be the bond of a vow or even of marriage (*Ibid.*).

And another time he repeated this thought, perhaps expressing it even better. He said that he felt an "extraordinary sweetness" of completely pure and spiritual affection. Indeed, he

loves that love incomparably. It is strong, unyielding, and without measure or reserve, yet sweet, facile, completely pure, completely tranquil; in short, . . . all in God. . . . God who sees the depths of my heart knows that there is nothing in this love except what is his and according to his will. Thanks to his grace, I desire to be nothing to anyone and that no one be anything to me, except in him. I wish not only to keep this unique affection, but to cherish it very tenderly (*Ibid.*, XIII, 295).

He speaks repeatedly of unity to St. Jane ("our union, our one single heart," "the one soul of our one life and the one life of our one soul"). But he constantly reiterates: "God has established for us a most invariable and indissoluble unity; may he be eternally blessed!" Spiritual men realize that all these words are explained by the gifts of the Holy Spirit. Nor is there any question here of self-delusion. He is not deluding himself when he writes: "I shall not speak to you of the greatness of my heart in your regard, but I shall tell you that it dwells far above every comparison. This affection is whiter than the snow, purer than the sun. Lord God, what a consolation it will be for us in heaven to love each other in that full sea of charity since these tiny rivulets bring us such joy" (*Œuvres,* XIII, 84). How can we fail to perceive in this manner of speaking that he is thinking of the effusions of the Holy Spirit?

We must now ask ourselves *why* Francis de Sales gives testimony of so great affection for Madame de Chantal, a love "purer than the snow." For what he says on this subject is true equally for all the souls which are entrusted to him. He loves her because he "sees God in all things"—but also to cause her to increase in perfection of the love of God and all other spiritual blessings. The following remark enlightens us: "Each affection has its particular difference from all others; that which I have for you has a certain special quality which consoles me infinitely and, to express it freely, is extremely profitable for me" (*Ibid.,* 354). There is no doubt that every affection leads him to union with God. "My affection is not satisfied, for it is insatiable in its desire to render to my God the duty I have towards you. I say 'to God,' my daughter, because every day I am more confirmed in the belief that it is God who imposes this duty upon me; that is why I cherish it so incomparably" (p. 309). And he prays much for her with this intention, often repeating to her: "I shall never cease to pray our good God that it will please him to accomplish in you his holy work, that is, the good desire and the good design of arriving at the perfection of the Christian life."

According to a law of reciprocity or of spiritual communion, when through charity one gives the Holy Spirit, one receives him at the same time. St. Francis de Sales often experienced this; but especially with Mother de Chantal, who had been very helpful to him in the composition of certain passages of the *Treatise on the Love of God.*

The Holy Spirit gave him assurance of his presence by the eternal duration of his friendships. "I have received the note with your good wishes, and I keep it and examine it carefully as an instrument of our alliance, completely founded in God. It will last for all eternity, thanks to the mercy of him who is its author" (*Ibid.,* XII, p. 341).

It is not surprising, then, since the Holy Spirit diffused charity into his heart, and, as the substantial bond of the Trinity, unites souls by the bond of grace, that Francis de Sales loved all men—saints or not, sinners or not—whether they caused him suffering or sweetness, in the same manner.

To the Abbess of Puits l'Orbe, he wrote: "I beg you by the heart of our Lord to believe without any doubt whatever that I am entirely and irrevocably at the service of your soul, and that I will apply myself to this service to the full extent of my powers and with all the fidelity that you could ever wish. God wills it, as I know full well; more I cannot say. On this firm foundation, I will employ my spirit and my prayers in thinking out all that will be useful and necessary for making a thorough reformation of your whole monastery" (*Ibid.,* 368).

If there ever was a soul, which although healthy required that one should write to her with prudence and reserve, it was indeed Mère Angélique of Port-Royal. Thus, some time after 1653, she wrote to her nephew: "The holy prelate was of great help to me and I am willing to say that he honored me as much with his affection and his confidence as Madame de Chantal" (Cognet, p. 104). "I continued, as long as I lived,

to write to him my dispositions and he took the trouble to answer me with great care and extreme kindness" (*Ibid.*, 106).
"Believe me, my dear daughter, my soul is consoled by writing to you, so true is it that God wishes my soul to care for yours, to cherish it and to be perfectly yours. . . . In short, my heart turns at every moment in your direction and does not cease to expand with wishes for your advancement to the pure and courageous, but humble and meek, divine love" (*Ibid.*, 109).

Let us not be surprised that St. Francis writes with candor to Mother de Chantal herself: "Oh, how it annoys me not to be able to write to my dear daughter Madame de Port-Royal, nor to Mesdemoiselle Arnaud and Le Maître. But there is no means. However, there will be soon. These girls are truly at the center of my heart." These religious were not Visitandines. On August 4 he wrote again: "Alas, I shall not write to my dear daughter of Port-Royal, nor to Mlle Le Maître, but I shall pray God that he will console them with the abundance of his holy love" (*Ibid.*, 122, 125).

The universality of his charity equals its purity. There is no soul about who we can say: "Francis de Sales did not love her and repulsed her." This universality and this abundance of charity is a sign that the gifts of the Holy Spirit had their total dominion over him. Those who did not write to him had easy access to the priest. "Meek and humble of heart," he listened patiently and put at ease as much as possible all the children, the poor, the importunate, the quarrelsome, the malcontents, and, we must add, even thieves, who did not go away empty-handed. It is the mystery of goodness to serve and not be served: *Non veni ministrari sed ministrare.* But his predilection pushed him especially toward priests, his priests. Monsignor Camus was very moved by this.

I have often heard him repeat this beautiful sentence: In the prison of holy love there are no criminals; all the inmates (he was speaking here of priests) are voluntary. Based on this principle he never made any command except under the form of advice and request. The words of St. Peter were held by him in special veneration: "Feed my flock," not by constraint, but freely and voluntarily. He could not approve of those absolute spirits who wished to be obeyed willy-nilly and who demanded that everyone yield to their dominion. He wished that in the matter of spiritual government we should conduct ourselves in relation to souls in the same manner as God and the angels—by inspirations, insinuations, remonstrances, solicitations (VII, v).

According to the *Exercises* of St. Ignatius, the Holy Spirit acts in this manner. Sometimes Francis' enemies criticized his benignity. The Abbé d'Abondance said of him one day: "Francis de Sales will go to paradise, but as for the Bishop of Geneva, I am not so sure, because he does not sufficiently chastise the people of his Church." The Saint began to laugh. "You do not wish us to have penitents? The priests in these regions, thanks be to God, very rarely commit any crime which deserves death or prison. Would it not be better to make them weep over their sins and make a good general confession than simply to punish them and thus make them more hypocritical than virtuous?"

He wished his priests to be merciful toward all sinners. "Remember that the poor penitents at the beginning of their confession call you *Father,* and truly you must have a paternal heart toward them, receiving them with an extreme love, patiently supporting their rusticity, ignorance, weakness, slowness and other imperfections. . . . Thus, although the prodigal son returned home completely stripped, filthy and smelly from living among the swine, his father nevertheless embraced him because he was his father, and the hearts of fathers are very tender toward their sons" (*Œuvres,* XXIII, 281).

The bishop gave the example and his dignity did not prevent him from being paternal in this manner, for he had, as they say, the fullness of the Holy Spirit. He wrote to Msgr. Camus, irritated by his parishioners: "Monsignor, we must

suffer much from our children while they are young. . . .
The four words of the great Apostle must serve you as a
motto: *opportune, importune, in omni patientia et doctrina.*"
He placed patience first because it is most necessary and because without it learning is of no use. "Let us continue to cultivate well, for there is no earth so unresponsive that the love
of the laborer does not fertilize it" (*Ibid.,* XV, 28).

In his opinion, preaching also must be "meek and humble
of heart." He habitually had a slight aversion toward those
preachers who shout and thunder on every occasion, even
when the subject does not require it. He used to say: "I love
preaching which refers more to love of neighbor than to in-
dignation, even to the Huguenots, whom we must treat with
a great compassion, not flattering them, but weeping with
them." "In discussions with heretics," testifies M. G. Rolland,
"he did not conduct himself in a manner to anger or confuse
them. He was often censured by Catholics for treating his
adversaries too gently. He answered that he had to seek their
salvation and not their confusion. In the pulpit he avoided
the words 'heretic' and 'Huguenot.'" A piquant anecdote is
narrated for us by Father de la Rivière:

One time, when speaking from the pulpit about Calvin, the word
punais ("stinker") escaped his lips, at which all his auditors made
the sign of the Cross, since they had never before heard him use
such terms; but he pronounced that epithet with so modest and
so gracious an intonation that each could easily judge that holy
affection or the salvation of souls, and not passion or contempt
had snatched this word from his unthinking lips.

The ears crowded together in a beautiful wheat field are
the image of the acts of charity which fill the life of St.
Francis de Sales. Just as the wheat harvester cannot gather in
all the grains but lets a great number of them fall to the
earth, so the authors of Saint Francis' life could not assemble
a half or even perhaps a tenth of the abundance of charity
which makes his glory in the Church and in heaven. We shall
return to this subject of charity when we speak of his zeal.

19 *Love for the Incarnate Word*

ST. IGNATIUS' DEVOTION to the Incarnate Word, to Jesus in Palestine, born of the Virgin Mary, is as ardent as his extraordinary cult of the Holy Trinity. We never weary of talking about the well-known details of St. Ignatius' voyage to Palestine. In his desire to see the land where Jesus lived, he lost his appetite and could not sleep. According to the documents assembled by the historians, the emotions of the pilgrim from Spain were so strong that tears almost blinded him when he first caught sight of the sacred shore. Impregnated by his prolonged contemplations of the *Life of Christ* by Ludolph of Saxony, he had no difficulty in being mentally present, as the Carthusian recommended in his Introduction, at the discourses and actions of the Lord Jesus as if he heard them with his own ears and saw them with his own eyes, meditating on all that was said or that happened as if it was happening for the first time at the very moment of his prayer.

The *Exercises* and the counsels of meditation of St. Francis de Sales agree in advising us to look and to hear in a concrete fashion the scenes of the Gospel. St. Peter Canisius, reviewing the biography of Ignatius by Ribadeneyra, wrote:

Perhaps it would be possible to add a point which comes to me from Master Favre, namely, the state of spirit in which Ignatius visited the holy places and with what tender piety, what burning love of God and what torrents of tears he contemplated, as if he had them under his eyes, the mysteries of the life and the passion of Christ. An ardent desire to spend the rest of his days in this land seized him (MHSI, I, 714).

Historians have recounted in detail the sojourn of Ignatius in Jerusalem, and especially his visits to the places where Jesus suffered his Passion. When we read the details of Ignatius' loving search for the least traces of Christ's passage, whether they be engraved on the rock or on the earth, his

182

concern with the width, the length, the depth of each trace preserved or recalled, for example (to quote only one), "on which side was found Jesus' right foot and on which the left, on the Mount of Olives," it is with infinite regret that we omit them here and send our readers to books which recount them. Later, Ignatius, writing the *Exercises,* was to ask the retreatant to spend a whole week in contemplating the scenes of the Passion as he himself had contemplated them in Palestine. His love for Jesus, like that of St. Paul, was always a love for Jesus Crucified. But all the scenes of the life of Christ, of the Nativity, of the Ascension, were contemplated by his soul with enraptured adoration and ardent passion.

St. Francis de Sales, whose soul resembled very much that of St. Ignatius, bore a most lively interest in all that struck his senses, his imagination, his heart, his tenderness for the humanity of Jesus, for men and for all God's creatures. He would probably have made the pilgrimage to Jerusalem in the same way as Ignatius. And he would have drawn the same fruits from it, especially an extraordinary love for Jesus Crucified.

We can think that "the very illustrious and virtuous knight" whose pilgrimage is recounted in the *Treatise on the Love of God* is the image of Ignatius Loyola or of Francis himself. To reproduce his account is to reveal his devotion to the Word Incarnate.

Once upon a time, then, a very illustrious and virtuous knight went beyond the seas to Palestine to visit the holy places in which our Lord had accomplished his Redemption. In order to begin this holy exercise properly, he worthily confessed and communicated before starting out. First he went to the town of Nazareth where the angel had announced the Incarnation to the most holy Virgin, and where the adorable conception of the eternal Word had taken place. There this good pilgrim contemplated the heavenly goodness which had deigned to take human flesh in order to save men from perdition. Then he proceeded to Bethlehem, to the place of the Nativity, and no one can say how many tears he shed there, contemplating the tears with which the Son of God, the Virgin's little Infant, had bedewed that holy stable, kissing and kissing again a hundred times that sacred earth, and venerating the dust which had received the infancy of the divine Babe.

From Bethlehem he went to Bethabara, and advanced as far as the little town of Bethania. Remembering that our Lord had unclothed himself to be baptized, he also disrobed and as he entered into the Jordan and bathed in it, drinking its waters, it seemed to him that he saw his Savior receiving baptism from the hand of his precursor, and the Holy Spirit descending upon him in the form of a dove, with the heavens still opened, while from them the voice of the eternal Father seemed to come, saying: "This is my beloved Son in whom I am well pleased."

From Bethania he went into the desert, and there with the eyes of the Spirit he saw the Savior fasting, fighting, and conquering the enemy; then he saw the angels ministering to him. From there he went up to Mount Tabor where he saw the Savior transfigured, then to Mount Sion where he seemed to see our Lord still on hs knees in the supper room, washing the disciples' feet and afterwards distributing to them his divine body in the sacred Eucharist. He passed the torrent of Cedron, and went to the Garden of Gethsemani, where his heart melted into tears of a most loving sorrow. He represented to himself his dear Savior sweating blood in that extreme agony which he suffered there, to be soon afterwards bound fast with cords and led into Jerusalem.

He followed in the footprints of his beloved, and, in imagination, saw him dragged hither and thither, to Annas, to Caiphas, to Pilate, to Herod, scourged, blindfolded, spat upon, crowned with thorns, presented to the people, condemned to death, loaded with his cross. While carrying it he experienced the pitiful meeting with his mother all steeped in grief and with the daughters of Jerusalem who wept over him. At last this devout pilgrim ascended Mount Calvary. In spirit he saw the cross laid upon the earth, and our Savior stripped naked, thrown down and nailed hands and feet upon it, most cruelly. He watched, then, how they raised the cross and the Crucified into the air, and the blood streaming from all parts of this racked, divine body. He regarded the dear holy Virgin, transpierced with the sword of sorrow. Then he turned his eyes to the crucified Savior whose seven words he heard with a matchless love. At last he saw him dying, then dead, then receiving the lance-stroke and showing his divine heart through the open wound. Then he watched the Savior taken down from the cross and carried to the sepulchre, whither he followed him, shedding a sea of tears on the places moistened with the blood of the Redeemer. And so he entered into the sepulchre and buried his heart by the body of his divine Master.

Then, rising again with him, he went to Emmaus, and saw all that passed between the Lord and the two disciples. At last he returned to Mount Olivet where the mystery of the Ascension took place, and there he saw the last marks and vestiges of the feet of the divine Savior. Prostrating himself before these holy feet, and kissing them a thousand times with signs of an infinite love, he began to gather up in himself all the strength of his affections as an archer draws his bowstring when he wishes to shoot his arrow, then rising, he turned his eyes and his hands to heaven, and said: "O Jesus, my sweet Jesus! I know no more where to seek and follow you on earth. Ah! Jesus, Jesus, my love, grant then to this heart that it may follow you to paradise."

With these ardent words he instantly discharged his soul into heaven, a sacred arrow which as an archer of God he directed into the center of his holy target. But his companions and servants who saw this poor lover fall suddenly as if dead, amazed at this accident, ran instantly for a doctor, who, on his arrival, found that the knight had really passed away. To make a safe judgment on the causes of so unexpected a death, he inquired of what temperament, manners, and feelings the deceased might be. He learned that he was of a very sweet, very amiable, wondrously devout disposition, most ardent in his love for God.

Thereupon the doctor said: "There is no doubt, then, that his heart has broken with excess fervor of love." And in order to confirm his decision, he had him opened and found that glorious heart burst open, with this sacred text engraved upon it: "Jesus, my Love!" Love, then, performed the office of death in this heart, separating the soul from the body, with no other cause concurring. St. Bernardine of Siena, a very wise and very holy doctor, recounts this story in his first sermon on the Ascenion (XII, vii).

In the heart of Francis de Sales, there is no doubt that the love of Christ Jesus was the principal and overflowing source of his words, his writings, and all his human activity. Of all the mysteries, the one that dominated his mind and his heart most was the Passion. In Book Five, chapter five of the *Treatise,* he expressed sentiments of "condolence and complacency in the Passion of our Lord," which all the pages of his books and of his correspondence re-echo. The first book St. Francis ever wrote was called *The Standard of the Cross.* This was a title evidently beloved by St. Ignatius, since the first Bull (that of Paul III) which approved the Society asserts that this Order "wished to fight under the standard of the Cross." And since that time the Society has not ceased to repeat this same expression.

When I see my Savior on the Mount of Olives with his soul sorrowful even unto death—Ah, Lord Jesus, I say, what force except love, can have brought the sorrows of death into the soul of life? This love, exciting commiseration, thereby drew our miseries into your sovereign heart. How can a devout soul, seeing this abyss of heaviness and distress in the divine lover, fail to experience a holy, loving sorrow? . . . How could a faithful lover behold such torments in the one she loves more than life itself without swooning away and becoming pale and wasted with grief? . . . Alas, he suffers insupportable pains, this well-beloved divine love. This grieves me and makes me faint with anguish; but he takes pleasure in suffering, he loves his torments and dies with joy though dying with pain for me. Therefore . . . not only do I grieve with him, but I glorify myself in him (*Treatise,* V, v).

Francis then cites the example of St. Francis of Assisi whose love drew upon him the stigmata, and the example of St. Catherine of Siena who suffered "the burning wounds of the Savior." And he speaks of them as a soul who desires to feel the same "loving condolence." Neither St. John of the Cross, whom he had probably not even read, nor St. Teresa of Avila seems to have given more burning accents to their love of Christ.

We would like to note here that the person who pours forth this burning love is the *Word Incarnate suffering in his humanity*. This truth is to be kept in mind at all times, because it was not only in the seventeenth century that souls were tempted by an intellectual mysticism which did not take into account the humanity of Jesus. It is always necessary to react against certain illusions. Carmel itself cherished the doctrine of Jesus' humanity, faithful to the Christological spirituality of St. Teresa of Avila. The first French prioress of the Carmel of the Incarnation, the venerable Madeleine de Saint-Joseph, complained of the great number of deluded persons who forget "the holy person of our Lord Jesus Christ under the pretext of more elevated things," to follow erring ways. Some imperfect souls seem to be attached to the delights of the world and the distractions of the century, and, following bad advice, imagine that they are retired into the bosom of the eternal Father, thinking they are plunged to the depths of the divine essence. They consider themselves annihilated to self and so completely purified of all the things of the world that they no longer touch the earth except by the tip of one toe. They neglect the mysteries and examples of the Son of God, and without working at the abnegation which is the first degree of Christianity, think they have arrived at the peak of perfection. St. Teresa (1515–1582), beatified during the lifetime of St. Francis, on April 24, 1614, affirmed in her autobiography (XXII and XXIII) that it is a great mistake to put aside even in prayer the humanity of Christ. Pope Piux X praised this capital point in the Teresian doctrine, where it is said that we must concern ourselves with the humanity of Christ (March 7, 1914).

The *Interior Mansion* refutes all objection by the principle that "one becomes a saint with a saint." The humanity of the Word is the perfect image of the Father. It is the road leading to the Father, the light by which to see him, the source for receiving the divine life. St. Bernard attached himself with delight to this humanity; St. Anthony of Padua loved the mysteries of the infancy; St. Francis of Assisi was inebriated with those of the crib and of the passion.

If the Trinity was the first cause of the Redemption, the humanity of Christ—that is, his love, his heart, his intelligence, his words, his actions, his suffering, then his Church, his priesthood, his sacraments—were the totally unique instrument. Our sanctification comes wholly from Christ through his humanity. St. Ignatius made this truth the very substance, so to speak, of the *Exercises*. St. Francis de Sales gives us immense consolation by his luminous and enthusiastic development of the gift and the human acts of the Incarnate Word. We owe him much gratitude for having shown us so beautifully that all the wealth of our poor, sinful souls is in Jesus Christ. Our heart, he said, invites not only all creatures and the Virgin Mary, "Mother of honor and of beautiful love," to praise God for his benefits, but it also invites

our Savior to praise and glorify his eternal Father with all the benedictions which a Son's love can furnish him. And then, Theotimus, the spirit comes to a place of silence, for we can no longer do anything but wonder and admire. O what a canticle is this of the Son to his Father! O how fair this well-beloved is among the children of men! O how sweet is his voice, as issuing from the lips upon which the fulness of grace was poured! All the others are perfumed, but he is perfume itself; the others are anointed, but he is balm poured out . . . (*Treatise*, VI, xi).

From these considerations, Francis de Sales passes to the contemplation of the heart of Jesus:

Truly, Theotimus, divine love, seated in our Savior's heart as upon a royal throne, beholds by the cleft of his pierced side all the hearts of the sons of men. This heart, the King of hearts, keeps his eyes ever fixed upon hearts. . . . This heart of divine love continually sees our hearts clearly and regards them with the eyes of his love, but we do not see him clearly; we only half-see him. For, O God! if we could see him as he is, we should die for love of him . . . as he himself died for us while he was mortal and as he would die again if he were not immortal. O, when we hear this divine heart singing with a voice of infinite sweetness the canticle of praise to the divinity, what joy, Theotimus, what thrusts our hearts send up to heaven that we may hear it forever! (*Ibid.*, V, xii).

20 *The Heart of Jesus*

JUST AS PASSIONATELY as St. Paul, St. Ignatius and St. Francis de Sales loved Jesus Christ and his humanity, crucified and risen again. It would not be suitable, nor is it possible, to say which Saint gives witness to the greatest love for Jesus. We know that St. Ignatius received from heaven an extraordinary devotion to the Name of Jesus—to his soul, his body, his blood, his pierced side, his holy wounds—all dear to his heart, as the prayer *Anima Christi* demonstrates.

St. Francis de Sales had the same devotion, especially to the Heart of Jesus. We have not a great deal to say of St. Ignatius' devotion that has not already been thoroughly discussed by others in regard to his spirituality. As for St. Francis, it is important even in this brief study to recall facts which are not too well known. First of all let us call to mind that the extensive knowledge that Francis had of the mystical schools, his close relations with the souls of mystics of his epoch, his personal supernatural lights, his graces as Founder of the Visitation and Father of the future canonized saint, Margaret Mary, all initiated him to this devotion which he advocated because of its depth and importance to the interior life. He had read the writings of the mystical authors who had preceded him, but he did not copy them like a schoolboy; he kept his own judgment on the matter of spirituality. But there is no doubt that his reading was affective and contemplative.

He loved the Flemish school of spirituality, the wealth

of which the French writers had admired and then imitated in their own writings. St. Francis de Sales is one of the precursors who gave a taste of it to the spiritual elite of the seventeenth century. The Rhineland mystics, with Eckhart, Tauler and Suso, and the Flemish mystics with the "modern devotion" of Ruysbroeck (1293–1381) and Gerard Groot (1340–1384) completed the formation which St. Francis de Sales received from St. Ignatius and the *Exercises.*

The "modern devotion" was a treasure, for it had assimilated in a very happy fashion all the medieval tradition. In it, the whole doctrine and all the traditions of the past are blended into a piety at once practical and contemplative, in no way scorning the exterior cult but placing the accent rather on the intimate relationships of the soul with God. In France, the influence of this devotion was felt in the reform of numerous monasteries, in the sanctification of the clergy, and in a very strong current of austerity in the Christian life. We know that St. Francis de Sales favored this influence all the more because the doctrine corresponded with his ideas. It was characterized by a practical mysticism, based on complete and humble resignation to the will of God, on the intimate knowledge of the life of Jesus, the source of all virtue and the model of all sanctity. The great masters, like St. Augustine, St. Bernard, St. Bonaventure, Blessed Henry Suso, and the spiritual schools like those of the Carthusians and the Victorines formed the basis of this school. The influence of the Flemish spirituality, spread throughout countries other than France, owed its strength to authors familiar to St. Francis, such as John Ruysbroeck, Thomas à Kempis, John Monbaer, John Tauler, Master Eckhart, Ludolph of Saxony. It is difficult to pick out the borrowings made by the Saint from the writings of these mystics of the Netherlands and the Rhineland; any comparison would be useless here.

Nevertheless we would like to call attention to the fact that devotion to the Heart of Jesus which should, according to his views, produce an interior disciple through intense love for

Jesus, was very fervent in the mystics of these schools. It was particularly in the ardent effusions of St. Bernard, in the *Mystical Vine* of St. Bonaventure, in the glowing writings of St. Mechtilde and St. Gertrude, in the revelations of Richard of Saint Victor, of Gueric and William of Saint-Thierry, that he found the flames of love for the Heart of Jesus for which his soul experienced so consuming a need. St. Mechtilde and St. Gertrude seemed to live again in the first religious of the Visitation.

The works of the Spanish school, the authors of which are so famous today, appeared only later in France. The Carmelites, on their introduction into Paris, made them better known. Like Cardinal de Bérulle, St. Francis de Sales drank deeply of them. He loved to recall Peter Alcántara, John of Avila, St. Teresa, Louis of Granada, and, as we shall show, the numerous books of the Society of Jesus, all very devout in regard to the Heart of Jesus.

The Italian mystics of the sixteenth century were still more familiar to the Saint of Savoy. The venerable Mother Claire-Marie of the Passion, foundress of the Carmelites of Regina Coeli, who died in 1575, recounts that her soul was attracted one day "with a delicious force, into the sacred side of Jesus Christ and even to his heart. . . . I understood that this divine heart was full of love so pure that I had no words to express it. I saw my soul as if plunged into that heart. . . . And feeling myself thus engulfed by that heart of Jesus Christ, I knew clearly and with an inexplicable joy that this place . . . was a most eminent place." St. Francis loved this saint of his own country whose language he spoke so easily. He found consolation in this account of St. Catherine de Ricci (1552–1590) no doubt because of the touching action of the Blessed Virgin from whom he had received an unshakable confidence in the love of Jesus.

"O my Son," said Mary one day to Jesus, "here I am presenting to you our dear virgin Catherine who is begging a favor from your tenderness. She seeks the grace to change her heart of flesh into a completely celestial heart so that she may be more worthy of you, by making her heart like to yours."

The response was the sort that delighted St. Francis:

"O my Mother," answered Jesus, "I have never refused you anything, and is not your heart the natural path to my heart? It will be done as you have asked.—And you, my dear daughter Catherine, remember that from this instant forward you no longer belong to yourself but that you are mine. I will purify your heart of all affection which is not mine and I will fill it with my love alone."

Could not such an anecdote also have been told of St. Francis de Sales?

St. Magdalen of Pazzi (1566–1607) had said of St. Aloysius Gonzaga, a contemporary of St. Francis de Sales who died in 1591, a word which was dear to the Saint whose youth had many points in common with that of the pure Mantuan: "Oh, how beloved he was on earth! . . . He hurled his arrows to the heart of the Word. . . . Now that he is in heaven, he understands and enjoys the acts of love and union which he practiced on earth."

Of all the Italian mystics, the Saint that Francis preferred above all others to study, imitate and quote was St. Catherine of Siena (1347–1381). She had a special attraction for his soul. Their temperaments seemed of equal "fire." She said of herself: "My nature is fiery," and St. Francis, in his turn, did not fear to affirm that there was no one more filled with love than he. Their love of Jesus Christ, of the holy Church, of the redemptive blood of the holy Virgin, and for souls, was strongly similar. The life of St. Catherine is too filled with ecstasies and testimonies of love for us to give even a small idea of it. There are very few lives in which the Heart of Jesus has manifested the power of his love as much as in that of this poor young girl who wore the habit of the Third Order of Saint Dominic as a sign of the gift of herself to the Church. St. Francis de Sales noticed, among other manifestations of

Christ's love for her, that Catherine had asked the Heart of Jesus the following question: "Sweet immaculate Lamb, you had already died on the Cross when your side was pierced by the lance. Why, then, did you decide that it should be struck and eternally wounded?" Has not every soul meditating on the blow of the centurion's lance asked the same question? But Jesus answered St. Catherine: "For several reasons. Here is one: I had an infinite desire for the salvation of men; my finite sufferings and sorrows could not manifest this unbounded desire. Therefore I wished my heart to be opened. By that you would know its intimate secrets and that it loved you more than a finite wound could show."

St. Francis de Sales knew thoroughly this life of Catherine of Siena which we can only encourage our readers to peruse. In his *Treatise on the Love of God,* among the saints who "died for divine love" he cites in the first place St. Catherine of Siena, then St. Francis of Assisi, his patron, then the "little" Stanislaus Kostka, St. Charles and several hundred others. The Saint then adds this thought which recurs so often in the works of souls totally consecrated to the Heart of Jesus:

So, my dear Theotimus, when the fervor of holy love is great, it makes so many assaults on the heart, so often wounds it, causes so many languors in it, melts it so habitually and puts it so frequently into ecstasies and raptures, that by this means the soul that is almost entirely occupied in God, not being able to afford sufficient assistance to nature . . . his animal and vital spirits begin little by little to fail, his life is shortened, and death occurs. Oh God! Theotimus how happy this death is! (*Treatise,* VII, x)

His close relationships with the fervent souls of the seventeenth century also led Francis to the Heart of Jesus. He had the most intimate spiritual relationships with the souls most favored by God in his times, and with all the religious orders. Let us list some of the best known names: Cardinal de Bérulle, M. Olier, Marie de l'Incarnation, Louise de Marillac, Blessed Armella. The religious congregations who called upon him and followed his directives were Carthusians, Franciscans, Benedictines, Ursulines, Carmelites, and at times even Port-Royal, into which he managed to insert a few seeds of true devotion.

Francis de Sales was the soul of this movement and he absorbed not only the experiences of the mystical life but also many lights on devotion to the Sacred Heart. In order to realize fully this mystical invasion, we should read the first chapter of Father Hamon's book, *Histoire de la dévotion au Sacré Cœur*. The title *"Mystical Invasion"* is not exaggerated. But neither is it exaggerated to affirm (and even the most ardent Bérullians, such as Henri Bremond, agree) that the most venerated saint, the most enlightened theologian, the most learned counselor, the most sought-after director, in short, the uncontested master of this fervent period was the Bishop of Geneva, St. Francis de Sales. He did not allow himself to be influenced by mystical exaggerations. He proved this incontestably during the rest of his life. But he did encourage devotion to the Sacred Heart because he recognized its excellent fruits and because he found it most efficacious for asceticism as well as for mysticism, an incomparable power for the fervor of religious orders and against Jansenism.

But among the influential directors of the sixteenth and seventeenth centuries we must also include the Fathers of the Society of Jesus. St. Francis was totally in agreement with them and directed souls in the same paths. These relationships, of which we already noted the frequency, duration, and spiritual depths, had originated at the *Collège de Clermont* where he was the favored child of the Fathers. They continued at Padua where Father Possevin had impressed on his confiding soul a very ardent and solidly theological devotion to the Sacred Heart as well as devotion to the Blessed Virgin. Let us recall here these dates and relationships. St. Francis died at Lyon on December 28, 1622, in full glory, at the age when all his gifts were fully recognized. He had openly manifested his love for the Heart of Jesus. It is not difficult to recognize from the twenty years of his sacerdotal ministry that this love had become the source of his direction, his preaching and of his *Treatise on the Love of God.* He had found in St. Ignatius what no one denies today: that if the writings of the Saint did not contain the expression of the devotion to the Sacred Heart (can we find it more explicitly in St. John of the Cross?) nevertheless it is in the logic of his *Spiritual Exercises,* much more in the very form that most of his meditations take. The whole interior life of the Founder of the Society breathes forth an intensely Christocentric piety, a loving conformity of life and a constant union of heart with Jesus. His predilection for the *Anima Christi,* his extraordinary cult for the Eucharist, his fidelity in wearing on his person the famous image of "Our Lady of the Sacred Heart"—all are evidences of his devotion to the Heart of Jesus. Peter Favre (1506–1546), with the same ardent piety that is so remarkable in his compatriot of Savoy, Francis de Sales, speaks of his contemplation of the wounds of the Savior in several passages of his *Mémorial.*

July, 1543. At another time . . . I was meditating with some profit on the five wounds of Christ, inspired by the sight of a crucifix. I was contemplating the wounds of the hands and the feet, and it seemed to me that they were inviting me especially to progress in works and desires for good, so that our work would be done with fervor and would be translated into acts, so that we would be full of zeal and that without fear of enduring long marches and journeys on foot, we would live in such a manner that our hands and our feet would bear the marks of our works, as St. Paul said of his whole body: "I bear the marks of the Lord Jesus in my body" (Gal. 6:17).

We shall recall these words when we see what asceticism and virtues he was seeking for the Society of Jesus, and, in the case of St. Francis, devotion to the Sacred Heart. The following part of this note in the *Mémorial* is even more remarkable:

I noticed that the wound in the side was made after the death of Christ. After all was accomplished and all the merits of Christ were accumulated, at the very end, his blood flowed for us mingled with water (Jn. 19:30), diffusing all the riches of his merits and teaching us that if we did not die we would not be able to taste these interior gifts which accomplished the salvation of hearts. It was before his death that this first source of treasures—his hands and his feet—were opened to us, and, after his death, his right side and his heart.

Here the Blessed Peter Favre repeats one of his favorite ideas (*Mémorial*, pp. 379–80): that it is necessary to go from the exterior to the interior, from the flowers and the fruits to the roots. Elsewhere he notes the significance of this wound of the heart for the sake of sinners. His reflections are repeated later by St. Francis de Sales.

I noticed also a devotion which the crucifix and the other images preserved at the church of the Holy Cross at Mainz had inspired in me, but especially this crucifix . . . that penetrated me with a thought which never left me, so to speak: such goodness for the sinner who offends him! After his death he also gave his blood for the poor blind Longinus who profited from it and saw the light. And I noted constantly: when I was so destitute because of my ingratitude and so many sins against my Lord, he responded to my blows only by shedding his blood and by granting me the grace to profit over and over from his sacrifice.

Peter Favre also, raising himself to an apostolic point of view, saw the Heart of Jesus, "meek and humble" for all sinners. It is this heart which is the prime source for all grace.

Thus in this world where so many faults and so many blasphemies against Christ, his saints, and his Church are committed, his divine goodness does not cease to multiply the marks of love toward all the culpable. It lets them strike with such blows that finally, giving us in turn a most forceful blow (and there are many souls for whom no other remedies are effective), we finally realize our cruelty and find the innocent Blood that can cure us. Meditating on the blood of the Lord Jesus Christ, Lamb without stain, I realized the great power of this Christian sweetness which Christ had taught us by his word and by the perfection of his life. Nothing triumphs better over cruelty, anger, total baseness than this sweetness which, refusing to resist all blows and receiving everyone with benevolence and cordiality, permits the one who strikes him to do all that he wishes. In the end (if not always) his heart will be broken and will be softened at the sight of your patience and profound goodness.

This page, and others like it, seem to have been taken from the works of St. Francis de Sales, Favre's childhood comrade and very dear friend. But they acquire an even greater value from the fact that Peter Favre was, so to speak, plunged into the spiritual current of the *devotio moderna* that we spoke of before.

We cannot omit the fact that Favre spent at least a year (1543–44) in Cologne, where the monasteries were enthusiastically publishing the works of Denis the Carthusian, Lansperge, Tauler, Ruysbroeck, Suso. In his *Mémorial,* Favre cites only a few works. But it is remarkable that those which he prefers as his familiar works are those of the great devotées of the Sacred Heart: St. Gertrude, St. Brigid, Lansperge, the *Imitation of Christ,* the *Vita Christi* of Ludolph of Saxony, and so forth.

Other Jesuits had also exercised a great influence on St. Francis de Sales. Father Letierce, S.J., gives us their names and a portion of their works: Francis Borgia, Báltasar Alvarez, Suárez, Salmerón, Tolet, Maldonatus, Lugo, Cornelius a Lapide, Ribadeneyra, and so forth. But the closest to Francis de Sales is Peter Canisius (1521–1597). His name will suffice. They cultivated and preached the same doctrine. No historian has spoken or could speak of St. Peter Canisius without recalling the capital fact of his vision of the Heart of Jesus on the day of his perpetual vows. We must not forget that it was St. Ignatius himself who accepted his solemn profession. While he was praying at the tomb of the holy Apostles Peter and Paul in the Vatican basilica, Jesus appeared to him and opened his heart to him, from which he drank the waters as from a divine spring.

My soul was lying on the earth, deformed, impure, cowardly . . . . You, then, Lord opened to me the heart of your holy body and it seemed that I saw it there before me. You ordered me to drink from this spring, inviting me to draw my salvation therefrom, O my Savior. And I, I desired ardently that those waves of faith, hope and charity which were flowing from it should burst over me. I asked you to purify me entirely and to embellish me. Finally, after I had reached your sweetest Heart and dared to cast myself into it, you promised me a garment woven from the three virtues most capable of protecting my soul: peace, love, and perseverance. Fortified by this garment, I trusted that nothing was lacking to me and that all contributed to your glory (O. Braunsberger, *Bi. Petri Canisii Epist. et Acta* [Fribourg, 1896], I, 54 ff.).

"The great Saint," adds our biographer, "recommends in his exhortations to his brothers in religion 'to unite their will to that of the Heart of Jesus, . . . to devote themselves unreservedly for souls, since the divine Redeemer has given them to drink the blood of his heart.' He invites them to 'make their nest in the cleft of the rock, to take refuge in all their temptations in the lovable Heart of Jesus, to unite their thanks to those of the Sacred Heart.'"

In the manuscript copies of St. Mechtilde we find the "prayer to greet the Heart of Jesus in the morning" and other prayers to the Sacred Heart for the moment of retiring, and still another for the beginning of work. This is because Canisius continued to be inspired by the work of his spiritual masters, the Carthusians of Cologne, especially Lansperge, as well as by the learned and pious Van Esche, all of whom were fervently devoted to the Sacred Heart. But in this there was especially an apostolic echo of the great mystical favor, received at Rome in 1549, and from his contacts with Ignatius and Favre, to whom Canisius acknowledged that he was most indebted for his spiritual life. We know with what admiration Francis de Sales followed Canisius in his catechetics and entertained close relationships with him.

Among the testimonies of St. Francis de Sales' devotion to the Sacred Heart, we must cite the history of the Visitation, because this Congregation was inspired, and is still inspired, by his spirituality. Among the most privileged, let us not forget St. Margaret Mary. The fact that she had been sent by the Heart of Jesus into the Visitation while she was humanly attracted by other congregations, seems to be a sign that the spirituality that she would receive from the Visitandines and that she herself in turn was to give them, was favorable to fulfilling the mission which had been confided to her: the spirituality of St. Francis de Sales. Certain authors would deny this mission to the Visitation, because they do not know the essentials of her vocation and put it under the spiritual dependency of Bérulle or St. Teresa of Avila. They make it Carmelite. Why would they not make Father de la Colombière a disciple of de Bérulle or of St. John of the Cross? Our Lord confided the direction of his *confidante*, the well-beloved of his Heart, to his "perfect friend," the blessed Claude de la Colombière, son of St. Ignatius and deeply attached to St. Francis de Sales.

Monsignor Gauthey, who had deeper insight into the soul of Margaret Mary than any other of her biographers wrote: "St Margaret Mary is incomparable as mistress of the spiritual life. Nurtured by the Salesian traditions, she shares the force of St. Jane de Chantal and the sweetness of St. Francis de Sales" (*Vie et œuvres*, II, 17). And they tell that St. Francis de Sales (and not Bérulle nor St. Teresa nor any other saint) appeared to her to reproach her for certain faults committed against humility and charity.

Blessed Claude de la Colombière, a saint whose Ignatian formation is evident, had even before his priestly ordination a deep devotion to St. Francis de Sales. When the Visitation at Avignon celebrated the canonization of Francis de Sales by a double solemn octave, it was Blessed Claude, in preference to several other more famous speakers, who was chosen to honor him with a panegyric considered a masterpeice. Marie-Béatrice d'Este, the duchess of York, had received from Father de la Colombière, in England, a great devotion to St. Francis de Sales and to the Heart of Jesus. She would have liked to become a Visitandine. Having come to France, she was staying at the palace d'Ainay, near the Visitation of Bellecour. She wrote:

This morning we received Holy Communion at the convent of the dear Sisters where the heart of St. Francis de Sales is kept. . . . I felt an immense consolation on seeing his relics. And, close to that sweetest heart, I dared to place mine and to confide it to his entirely. . . . It is in the wound of the "holy side of Jesus" (a devotion very dear to St. Francis de Sales) that he continually gives a *rendezvous* to the Visitandines of Modène.

In his spiritual notes, made in London, Blessed Claude wrote: "Every day I feel greater devotion to St. Francis de Sales" (IV, 123). In a letter to Mère de Saumaise in 1689, St. Margaret Mary described the vision of the Heart of Jesus in which the Blessed Virgin told the Saint and St. Francis de Sales, present on either side of her, that the Society of Jesus, represented at that time by Claude de la Colombière, was charged by the Sacred Heart to make known the value and usefulness of this devotion.

He [Jesus] made me see this devotion of his adorable heart as a beautiful tree which had been destined from all eternity to take its seed and its roots in the midst of our institute, then to extend its branches into the houses which compose it, so that each of them could gather the fruits at its pleasure and according to its taste, although with unequal abundance, . . . fruits of life and of eternal salvation which must renew us in the primitive spirit of our vocation. It seems to me that never was the accidental glory of our holy Father and Founder so greatly augmented as it was by this means, but he wished the daughters of the Visitation to distribute the fruits of his holy tree with abundance to all those who desire to eat of it, without fear that it will ever fail them. Thus he hopes to give his life over and over again to many persons by this means.

Accustomed to "resting on the heart of Jesus Christ" where "his repose could not be interrupted by the greatest occupation" (*Vie de la Mère Clément de la Visitation de Sainte-Marie*, p. 457), Francis speaks of it often in his works, and with what ardor of love! He sees in the "pierced bosom of the Savior" the point of departure for all the redemptive graces. In the early days of the foundation, he designated this sacred side as the domicile for Madame de Chantal during the time of Lent, and then for always. His whole desire is that "night and day" in the heart of his dear daughter, as on an altar, God "makes glow and gleam the fire of his holy love." Never did he see so clearly how much she is his daughter, and he insists: "I say that I see it in the heart of our Lord. . . . How many desires I have that we may be one day annihilated to ourselves to live completely in God and that our life may be hidden with Jesus Christ in God. . . . Oh, when will he live completely in us? I shall pray ardently for that, and I shall pray to the royal heart of the Savior."

Mother de Chantal, always the echo of her blessed Father, let fall words like this: "My very dear Sisters, become truly humble, meek, and simple, so that by this means your . . . heart may be truly a heart of Jesus." "May the meek Jesus fill your heart with the pure love of his own." "This violence that God now requires of you, my dear daughter, finally will ravish his divine heart, and win you his holy paradise."

That is why, in 1638, more than thirty years before the revelations of Paray, Mère Clément could write: "Our holy Founder has set up an institute in the Church to honor the adorable Heart of Jesus Christ and the two virtues dearest to him furnish the foundation of the rules and constitutions of the Visitation." These lines remained at Melun in the secret of the intimate notes of this truly saintly soul, when in 1643 the doctors of the Sorbonne approved a collection of meditations for the annual retreat of the religious of Sainte-Marie. At the desire of St. Jane de Chantal, they were sent to Paris by Mother H. A. Lhuiller, whose vocation Francis de Sales had directed. We cannot read this passage without astonishment:

Consider that not only our dear Savior showed us his love through every work of our redemption with all the Christians, but that he obliges us especially, we of the Visitation, by the gifts and favors he has given to our Congregation, and to each of us in particular, gifts of his heart—or to say it better, of the virtues which reside in it, since he has founded our dear institute on these two principles: Learn of me for I am meek and humble of heart. That is the share of his treasures which has fallen to us and the epitome of all his blessings together. . . . It is very sweet, O my dear soul, that this benign Jesus has chosen us to become, if we wish, "daughters of his heart." Why, O my Savior, have you not favored someone else in your Church? What have we done for your goodness that you have destined for us in these last centuries this treasure of all eternity?

That is not all. A few days after the first Mother of the Visitation made her oblation, God gave to Francis de Sales during the night a thought that he hastened to communicate to Mother de Chantal:

Our house of the Visitation is sufficiently noble and influential to have its own coat of arms, its own blazon, its own motto and rallying cry. I have thought, then, my dear Mother, if you are in agreement, that we must take for our coat of arms a single heart pierced with two arrows, enclosed with a crown of thorns. This poor heart will serve as the enclave of a cross which will surmount it and be engraved with the sacred names of Jesus and Mary. . . . Truly, our small congregation is the work of the hearts of Jesus and Mary. The dying Savior gave birth to us through the opening of his Sacred Heart; it is very apt that by careful mortification our heart should remain always surrounded by the crown of thorns which will rest on the head of our Leader while love holds him attached to the throne of his mortal griefs.

It is touching to see with what delicacy God made the holy Founders and most especially St. Francis de Sales intervene in the definitive manifestation of his plans. On January 29, 1686, this great Saint "made me understand very clearly," said the privileged soul of Paray, "the ardent desire he had that the Sacred Heart be known, loved, and honored in his whole Institute." "It is our holy Founder, " she wrote a few months later, "who desires and solicits that this devotion be introduced into his Institute because he knows its effects." "And it is to the Mother of all goodness," she said elsewhere, "that this true friend of the heart of God" addressed his supplications.

Admirable mercy of the divine goodness! The following year, on the same date, the Mother of love appeared again to Margaret Mary and this time "in a very eminent, spacious and admirable place," the divine heart inundated her with his heat and light. St. Francis de Sales was there also with Father Claude de la Colombière and all the daughters of the Visitation, each one holding a heart in her hand and accompanied by her guardian angel: 'Look," said the Queen of Goodness to them, showing them the admirable heart, "this precious treasure is particularly manifested to you by the tender love which my Son has for your Institute which he regards and loves as his dear Benjamin. It is necessary that not only members of this Institute be enriched by this inexhaustible treasure, but rather that they abundantly distribute this precious wealth of their power trying to enrich everyone with it, not fearing that its supply will fail. The more of it they take, the more there will be to take."

Then the Blessed Virgin announced to Father de la Colombière that he also had a "great portion of this precious treasure, for if it is given to the daughters of the Visitation to know it and distribute it to others, it is reserved to the Fathers of his Society to make them see and know its usefulness and value." Finally, the holy Founder invited his daughters to "draw from the source of benedictions those waters of salvation which he himself had already begun to trickle into your souls by the streamlet of your constitutions which have come forth from it."

But much more than all the saints and all the doctors who have been for St. Francis de Sales the models and the promoters of the devotion to the Sacred Heart, the Blessed Virgin has been the supreme and irresistible reason for loving Jesus and especially his divine heart. Consequently we can be certain that there exists none other more convincing. We read in the *Treatise on the Love of God* two moving chapters on the love of "the most Blessed Virgin, Mother of God." The Blessed Virgin, he said,

and her Son had but one soul, one heart, one life, so that this heavenly mother, living, lived not, but her Son lived in her! . . . But the sweet Mother, who loved him more than all others, was more than all others transfixed with the sword of sorrow. The sorrow of the Son at that time was a piercing sword which passed through the heart of the Mother, because that Mother's heart was glued, joined and united to her Son with so perfect a union that nothing could wound the one without inflicting a lively torture upon the other. Now this maternal heart, being thus wounded with love, not only did not seek a cure for its wound, but loved her wound more than all cures, lovingly keeping the shafts of sorrow she had received because of the love which had shot them into her heart. She constantly desired to die of them since her Son died of them, who, as all the Holy Scriptures and the doctors say, died amidst the flames of his charity, a perfect holocaust for all the sins of the world (VII, xiii).

Is it not evident that we have in these few lines the foundation of the devotion of the Sacred Heart such as St. Francis de Sales understood and practiced it?

21 *The Blessed Virgin*

WE WOULD BE greatly surprised if St. Francis de Sales, the beloved son of Madame de Boisy and pupil of the Jesuit Fathers, had not given witness during his youth and even more during his whole life, to a very ardent and filial devotion to our Lady. Many Christians know and recite the prayer attributed to him. Some experts maintain that it is not original with him. Nevertheless it is written in a style which is completely his. We found it engraved in its entirety on the walls of the chapel of Notre Dame d'Etang in Burgundy, a shrine to which St. Francis de Sales surely made pilgrimages.

O sweetest Mary, Mother of God, you are my Mother and Queen. I beg you to accept me for your son and servant because I wish no other Mother and Lady than you. I beg you, then, good, gracious, sweet Mother, be pleased to console me in all anguish and tribulations, spiritual and corporal.

Remember, sweetest Virgin, that you are my Mother and that I am your son, that you are most powerful and that I am a poor, weak creature. Therefore I beg you, sweetest Mother, to govern and defend me in all my ways and actions, for, alas, I am a poor needy beggar who have great need of your holy protection. O most holy Virgin, my sweet Mother, preserve and deliver my body and my soul from all evils and dangers, and make me a sharer of your blessings and virtues, especially of your holy humility, excellent purity, and fervent charity.

Do not tell me, gracious Virgin, that you cannot, for your beloved Son has given you all power in heaven as on earth. Do not tell me that you ought not, for you are the Mother of all human beings, and especially mine. If you cannot, I will excuse you, saying: "It is true that she is my Mother and that she cherishes me as her son, but the poor thing lacks means and ability." If you were not my Mother, naturally I would be patient, saying: "She is rich enough to help me, but, unfortunately, since she is not my Mother, she does not love me." Because, then, sweetest Virgin, you are truly my Mother and because you are truly powerful, how could I excuse you if you did not comfort me and come to my aid and assistance? See, Mother, you are forced to grant me what I ask of you.

Be exalted, then, in heaven and on earth, O glorious Virgin and my dear Mother Mary, for the glory and honor of your Son. Accept me as your child, without regard for my miseries and sins. Deliver my soul and my body from all evil, and grant me all your virtues, especially humility. Present me with all your gifts, blessings and graces that may please the Blessed Trinity, Father, Son and Holy Spirit. Amen.

We can distinguish two parts in St. Francis de Sales' devotion to our Lady: the facts of his life which show his piety and the sweetness of his preaching. The following facts mentioned by his biographers, and especially by Msgr. Francis Trochu, are relatively few because only a handful have been preserved in the tradition. His very birth was, after a fashion, a miracle ascribed to the Blessed Virgin. A prayer to our Lady of Liesse during a solemn pilgrimage drew the benediction of this blessed maternity upon Madame de Boisy. The crowd was honoring the holy kerchief at the chapel of Notre Dame de Liesse, at Annecy (Trochu, p. 22). The privileged child was born prematurely, shortly after the feast of our Lady's Assumption, in the evening of August 21, the anniversary of the promise made to our Lady of Liesse (p. 25). Forty-five years later our Saint himself wrote on November 21, 1614: "Of all my childhood memories, none was so pleasing to me as that of having been taken to the church in my third year, on the day of the Presentation of the Mother of God" (p. 42).

As a student, whenever he took a walk he never failed to make his companions, whom he chose according to his "sweet humor and suavity," enter the church and visit the chapel of our Lady of Compassion. This shrine was situated at the entrance to the cemetery of the public wards, whose poor souls he recommended to the Virgin (p. 85). The students often prayed, also, at the oratory of the Abbaye-aux-Bois to Notre

Dame de Tout-aide, for success in their examinations. But Francis had a preference for the Black Virgin of Saint Etienne-des-Grès, called "Our Lady of Holy Deliverance," and venerated today at Neuilly-sur-Seine (p. 99). He used to say that this was a very quiet place and most suitable for recollection. The image represents the Virgin with the Infant in her arms, the Child holding the globe in one hand and pointing to his Mother with the other (p. 116). In the sixteenth century a royal confraternity of charity for the ransom of persons imprisoned for debt had been formed under the title of "Our Lady of Deliverance."

It was to this Black Virgin that he prayed with extraordinary confidence for six weeks and who finally cured him of the crisis of despair which, as we have already pointed out, made him ill almost to the point of death. No theologian could give him peace, but, through the intercession of our Lady, we are told by St. Jane de Chantal, the sickness fell from him like scales from a leper. In thanksgiving, Francis made to Mary his vow of virginity (p. 131).

When a student at Clermont, Francis was prefect of the Sodality of our Lady, and therefore responsible for promoting devotion to her. In this office he carried on the long tradition of this great center which had fostered many vocations, among them that of the famous Father Etienne Binet, S.J., who was later so beloved by Francis de Sales (p. 118). Of his devotion to our Lady, Father Nicolas Talon reports:

Francis never spoke of the Blessed Virgin without a holy delight, and very often he was obliged to relieve his heart by tears, so filled was he with love for his subject. He was even heard to cry out to her with filial respect, when alone in his room, "Ah, who does not love you, O my dearest Mother! O Queen of hearts and Mother of holy love! I am completely yours for all eternity! May all creatures live and die for love of you!"

If he was surprised at his prayer, one saw only a lovable flush that covered his whole face. . . . Several of his fellow students who saw him at Paris have attested that at sight of him at prayer they felt moved by a special devotion. Especially when he was in the Sodality of our Lady, he regulated his conduct so carefully and manifested a piety so natural that anyone seeing his exterior could not be ignorant of what took place in his heart.

At Padua he continued to invoke our Lady with an affectionate devotion each time that he was obliged to speak in public. And when he left that city, he called the attention of his preceptor, M. Déage, to the fact that among the visits of thanks he first had to make his visit to our Lady. "I am going to thank the Lady who has helped me the most in Padua." And he entered a chapel of our Lady and remained there for two hours.

He entrusted his priesthood to the Blessed Virgin. And as proof of his complete devotion to her, he celebrated his second Mass, December 22, in the college chapel of Notre Dame de Liesse. His mission at Chablais was placed under the protection of Our Lady of Voirons, where there was also a Black Virgin invoked by a great number of pilgrims, but profaned by an apostate and by the Protestants.

When he was appointed bishop, he designated December 8, the feast of the Immaculate Conception of the most holy and most pure Mother of God, as the day of his consecration. On Thursday, November 21, the feast of our Lady's Presentation, Monsignor de Sales went with Father Fourier to the Church of Saint-Maurice de Thorens for the "presentation of his oath to the Sovereign Pontiff. He chose that day because exactly thirty-three years before he said he had been carried as an infant to this church by his good mother to be offered to God and had been blessed by the priest."

He chose Saturday, December 14, to enter his episcopal city "so that the holy Mother of God, Mother of the Sovereign Shepherd, might be his sponsor at the sheepfold of her Son."

He loved to preside at *"le grand jubilé,"* sometimes called *"les grands Pardons,"* at the chapel of Notre-Dame de Liesse. On the bell-tower floated "the standard of the great Pardons," which was the rallying sign for all Savoy. His fervor drew large crowds.

At Saint-Jean d'Aulph he reproached the Curé for leaving his parishioners in ignorance of the mysteries of the life of the Blessed Virgin. And in order to instruct them he composed a "method of saying the Rosary" which soon became customary among them. When he visited the sanctuary of Notre-Dame de Peillonney, he cried out: "I feel a great consolation at seeing so many parishes and so many churches of my diocese dedicated to the Blessed Virgin. When I enter a place consecrated to this Blessed Queen, I confess that I feel a certain thrill in my heart because I am entering the home of my Mother and because truly I am the son of this kind Virgin, the refuge of sinners."

In his opinion the foundation of the Visitation was the homage of his whole heart to the Blessed Virgin. St. Jane de Chantal was to write later: "It was by a special inspiration that this holy man dedicated our Congregation to the Blessed Virgin. Only a few days before our entrance he told me very happily that we would be the daughters of our Lady." On the following July 1 the inspiration was made precise: it was Our Lady of the Visitation who, on the eve of her feat, was chosen as protectress and model of the little group. Mère de Chaugy described it thus: "He chose this mystery because it was a hidden mystery and was not celebrated solemnly in the church like the other feasts. At least it would be celebrated in our Congregation." He found in it "a thousand spiritual specialties which gave it a particular light of the spirit which he desired to establish in his Institute. The devotion to the Blessed Virgin which he inspired in his daughters was so profound that the poor and the sick noticed it and by popular acclaim named them 'the holy Marys.'" A few lines from the primitive constitutions throw light on our subject:

This Congregation has two principal exercises: the one, contemplation and prayer, . . . the other, the service of the poor and the sick. . . . Our Lady of the Visitation was aptly chosen for patron, since in this mystery the most glorious Queen performs her solemn acts of charity toward the neighbor, such as going to visit and serve St. Elizabeth . . . and in addition composed the *Magnificat,* the sweetest, most enlightened, most spiritual and contemplative canticle ever written.

Our Lady's protection of her daughters was all-encompassing. On a Sunday, November 21, while on her way to church, Mlle Aimée de Blonay felt a certain bitterness in her heart at having to make way for the *chatelaine* of the place, even though the land had originally belonged to her ancestors. Engrossed with this thought, she had fallen asleep in the pew and saw in a dream a great number of young girls following the Blessed Virgin into the Temple. She wished to join the group but the holy Virgin refused her, saying: "You are not sufficiently small for me who have chosen to be abject and the last in the house of my God." Then the Queen of Virgins began to ascend fifteen steps, and as she placed her foot on each one, she left a virtue written in large golden characters. The first was humility and the fifteenth, the highest and the end of all, was charity. The vision soon vanished, leaving the young Aimée in great confusion and under an influence of grace which was to last until she died. She did not pass a single day without the memory of this mystical fifteen which was to lead her to God in union with Mary, serving as nourishment for her piety and a spur to more fervent practices.

Every day Francis recited the fifteen decades of the Rosary and spent a whole hour in doing it. At the age of twelve he had made a vow to say at least five decades each day, and he wore his Rosary attached to his belt. He never went to bed, whether it was eleven o'clock or even midnight, unless he had fulfilled his obligation. While reciting it, he loved to meditate on the mysteries which reflected the life and admirable virtues of this glorious Virgin whom he was accustomed to call his Lady and his dear Queen.

His preaching, always gentle, humble and attractive, resembled in some degree the speech of the Blessed Virgin as we are told she talked to the apostles and the other persons around her. Furthermore, his intention was to speak only with her and through her, to make her Son better known and loved. He especially wanted his listeners to give her the greatest homage of veneration, to have for her the confidence of a child for his mother, to imitate her virtues.

Among the tributes he paid her we have the "Dedicatory Prayer" of the *Treatise on the Love of God.* Not in the sixteenth century nor in the following centuries do we find a similar dedication for a book of theology, even mystical theology. It gives the tone of all his preaching and also the meaning of the *Treatise,* which he calls "a little work of love." First of all he greets Mary under her most glorious titles, according to his custom:

Most holy Mother of God, vessel of incomparable election, Queen of love and delight, you are the most lovely, the most loving, and most beloved of all creatures! From all eternity the love of the heavenly Father found its good pleasure in you, determining your chaste heart to the perfection of holy love so that some day you might love his only Son with unique and motherly love.

Then he expresses his dedication in this manner:

O well-beloved Mother of the well-beloved Son . . . I dedicate and consecrate this little work of love to the immense greatness of your love. Ah! I beg you by the heart of your sweet Jesus, King of hearts, . . . animate my heart and all hearts that read this writing by your all-powerful favor with the Holy Spirit, so that henceforth we may offer up in holocaust all our affections to his divine goodness. May we live, die, and live again forever amid the flames of this heavenly fire which our Lord, your Son, so ardently desired to kindle in our hearts that he never ceased to labor and sigh for this until his death, even the death of the cross.

St. Francis always demanded that his readers and hearers render honor, love, confidence and admiration to Mary. Let us recall a few extracts from his *Théologie mariale.* The dogma of the Immaculate Conception was not yet defined by the Sovereign Pontiff. Francis, despite the difficulties raised by several adversaries, taught, as did the Society of Jesus, that Mary was preserved from all sin, original and actual.

I know that the Blessed Virgin, our Lady, was never bitten by this infernal serpent, in as much as it is very clear and manifest that she had no sin, either original or actual. She was privileged and preferred above all other creatures, and this privilege is so great and so singular that there has never been another to receive this grace in the fashion that this glorious, holy Lady and Mistress received it. There has never been nor will there ever be another who dares to pretend or to aspire to so special a blessing, for this grace was due only to her who was destined from all eternity to be the Mother of God.

And thus he [God] first of all destined for his holy Mother a favor worthy of the love of a Son, who being all wise, all mighty and all good wished to prepare a mother to his liking. Therefore he willed his redemption to be applied to her in the manner of a saving remedy, so that sin spreading from generation to generation should not reach her. As a result she was so excellently redeemed that when the time came for the flood of original iniquity to pour its wretched waves over her conception with as much impetuosity as it had done on all other daughters of Adam, when it reached her it did not pass beyond, but stopped. In the same way the Jordan had stopped in the time of Josue, and for the same reason: that river held its stream in reverence for the passage of the Ark of the Covenant; so original sin drew back its waters, revering and dreading the presence of the true Tabernacle of the eternal alliance.

In this way, then, God turned away all captivity from his glorious Mother, giving her the blessing of both states of human nature. She had the innocence the first Adam had lost, and enjoyed marvelously the redemption acquired for her. Wherefore, as a garden of election which was to bring forth the fruit of life, she was made to flourish in all sorts of perfections. The Son of eternal love having thus clothed his Mother in gilded clothing, surrounded her with variety (Ps. 44:10) so that she might be the Queen of his right hand, that is, the first of all the elect to enjoy the delights of God's right hand (Ps. 15:11). This holy Mother, being altogether reserved for her Son, was redeemed by him not only from damnation but from every peril of damnation. He gave her grace and the perfection of grace, so that she went like a lovely dawn which, when beginning to break, increases continually in brightness unto perfect day. Admirable redemption! Masterpiece of the redeemer! And first of all redemptions by which the Son with a truly filial heart presenting his Mother with the blessing of sweetness, preserved her not only from sin, as he did the angels, but also from all danger of sin and from everything that might divert or retard her in the exercise of holy love. And he protests that among all the reasonable creatures he has chosen, this Mother is his one dove, his all perfect one, his dear love (II, vi).

He was convinced that Mary, even in the womb of her mother, St. Anne, enjoyed the perfect use of reason and faith, through which she

knew God and believed all truth, so that, filled with this clarity, she dedicated and consecrated herself completely to the divine Majesty, in a very perfect manner. . . . It is very certain that from the instant of her conception God rendered her all pure, all holy, in an admirable fashion that cannot be sufficiently admired. He had had this thought from all eternity because his thoughts are most lofty and what could never have entered the understanding of men, God had meditated on before all time (Sermon XXXVII, *Œuvres,* IX, 384–85; see also Sermon XVI, XXVI).

This privilege, which today perhaps seems to us excessive, was also discussed by Blessed Claude de la Colombière, who adds that "at the moment of her conception . . . she received the grace of the perfect use of reason and her intellect was adorned with all the lights of wisdom, of all knowledge, natural and moral. This opinion, he preached, has been accepted from the time of the Fathers by the most learned theologians and the whole School today agrees in accepting it."

The privileges of Mary are so exceptional that she merits an honor above every other honor. Francis does not name our Lady unless *honoris causa.*

Let those persons who are afraid that we are giving too much honor to the Virgin, withdraw, for she is worthy of all honor belonging to a creature pure spiritually as well as corporeally. Those who are not illegitimate children of Christianity, but are of the true generation of Jesus Christ, love this lady, honor and praise her in everything and everywhere: *Beatam me dicent omnes generationes.* *"Non habebit Christum in fratrem qui Mariam noluit habere in matrem, et qui non erit frater Christi, sane nec cohaeres"* (Pseudo Aug., Sermon III *De Symbolo*). Then whoever wishes to have the Holy Spirit, let him join with Mary, *qui cum ea non colligit, spargit* (Mt. 12:30). But more about this another time; now you must do this favor for me: help me to sing the praises of this Virgin a little more fully and I, too, shall pray to her to make me more capable. Serve her, honor her, so that he who comes to us through her may receive us through her: *Per te nos suscipiat qui per te ad nos venit* (*Sermon pour la Pentecôte*).

The whole ancient Church, throughout all the places in the world, in a perfect consensus had always greeted the Mother of God in the words of the angel: *Ave Maria gratia plena.* And our more proximate predecessors, following the sacred tone of their ancestors in a devout harmony, sang on every occasion and in all places *Ave Maria,* thinking to make themselves more agreeable to the heavenly King, reverently honoring his Mother, and not knowing where to find a more suitable manner to honor her than by imitating the respect and honors which God himself had decreed for her and fitted to her according to his good pleasure, in honor of the day on which his divine Majesty wished to glorify all mankind in this Virgin, becoming man himself. O holy salutation! O authentic praises! O rich and admirable honors! A great God dictated them, a great angel pronounced them, a great evangelist recorded them, all antiquity practiced them, our ancestors taught them to us (*Œuvres*, VII, Sermon I).

In this holy exercise we mount from step to step by using the creatures which we invite to praise God. We pass from the insensible to the reasonable and intellectual and from the Church militant to the Church triumphant, where we rise through the angels and the saints until above them all we find the most sacred virgin who in a matchless manner praises and magnifies the divinity more highly, holily and delightfully than all other creatures together can ever do (*Treatise*, V, xi).

Not only was she adored with all virtues and graces, but she did not cease augmenting those she had received from the time of her conception. Our Lady could never fall from the first grace which she received from the sovereign Majesty because she always advanced, adhering closely to the divine will and unceasingly meriting new graces. The more she received, the more her soul made itself capable of clinging to God, so that she was united ever more closely and thus strengthened her first union with him. If, then, we can find any change in the most holy Virgin, it was brought about by uniting herself more closely and by increasing as much as possible all virtues, so as to render unchangeable the resolution which she had made to belong completely to God. To do that, she wished to retire to the Temple, not that she had need of it for herself, but to teach us that we, since we are subject to change, must make use of all possible means, interior as well as exterior, to strengthen and preserve our good resolutions. As for her, it was sufficient to persevere in her good purpose that she be given to God from the first moment of her life, without needing to leave the house of her father. She had no fear that exterior objects might divert her, but, like a good mother, she wished to teach us to neglect nothing to assure our vocation.

The Blessed Virgin had the use of reason from the instant of her conception, and at the same instant the divine goodness preserved her from the precipice of original sin into which she would have fallen if his all-powerful hand had not restrained her. In thanksgiving for this grace, she dedicated herself and consecrated herself henceforth so absolutely to his service that the word which she gave to the divine Majesty was irrevocable.

She was never subject to change and could never separate herself from that first union and adhesion she had made of her will with that of God. This favor was granted to no other creature, not even to the angels, for they could change and depart from the grace they had received from the divine Majesty in their creation. Thus she was the model of the virtue of religion.

This lovable child was hardly born before she began to use

her small tongue to sing the praises of the divine Lord and all her other small members to serve him. His divine goodness inspired her to withdraw from the house of her father and mother to go to the Temple and there to serve him more perfectly. This glorious Virgin conducted herself at this early age with so much wisdom and discretion in the house of her parents that she astonished them. They judged from her speech and from her actions that this infant was not like others, but that she had the use of reason. It was necessary to anticipate the normal time and to conduct her to the Temple to serve the Lord with the other girls who were to do the same thing. They took her, then, this little Virgin, at the age of only three years, and partly led and partly carried her to the temple of Jerusalem.

O God, how great were the sighs and bursts of love of this small Virgin—as were her father's and mother's but especially hers— as she was going to the sacrifice, straight to her divine Spouse who had called her and who had inspired in her this withdrawal.

In all things she accomplished perfectly and integrally the will of God:

"Where are you going, glorious Virgin, with your little Babe?"
"I am going to Egypt."
"What makes you go there?"
"The will of God."
"Will it be for a long time?"
"As long as he pleases."
"And when will you return?"
"When God commands it."
"And when you return, will you not be much happier than you are in going?"
"Oh, certainly not!"
"And why?"
"Because I am doing the will of God as much by going there as by staying or returning."
"But when you return, you will go back to your own country?"
"I have no country but that of fulfilling the will of God."

She lived and died for love.

Likewise, Theotimus, the Virgin Mary gathered up in her heart by a very lively and continuous memory, all the most amiable mysteries of the life and death of her Son. She always received the most ardent inspirations that her Son, the Sun of Justice, bestowed on human beings as the strongest noon of his charity. In addition, she held him in a perpetual movement of contemplation, and finally the sacred fire of this divine love consumed her completely, like a holocaust of sweetness, so that she died of it, her soul completely ravished and transported in the arms of the love of her Son. O death lovingly vital! O love vitally mortal!

But this increase in grace was a completely different thing with the Blessed Virgin than it is for us, for, as we see the beautiful dawn of morning increase, not at several attempts or by fits and starts but by a certain continuous dilation and growth which is almost imperceptibly noticeable, so that truly we see it increase in brightness, but so smoothly that no interruption, separation or discontinuation is perceived in its increase, just so the divine love increases at each moment in the virginal heart of our glorious Lady, by sweet, calm and continued increase, without any agitation or violence. Ah, Theotimus, we must not put impetuosity or agitation into this heavenly love of the maternal heart of Mary, for love, of itself, is sweet, gracious, calm, tranquil. If sometimes it makes assaults and gives jolts to the spirit, it is because it finds a resistance there. But when the passages of the soul are open to it, without opposition or contrariness, it progresses peacefully, with an unparalleled sweetness. Thus, then, the holy love used its strength in the virginal heart of the holy Mother without effort or violent impetuosity because it found neither resistance nor any hindrance there. For, as we see mighty rivers make whirlpools and turbulence with great noise in the rocky places, as rocks form banks and reefs which oppose each other and prevent the flow of water, or, on the contrary, when water finds itself on the plain, it runs and floats along effortlessly, just so the divine love, finding in human souls several obstacles and resistances—since, in truth, all of them have some, though in different fashions—it creates violence there, combating evil inclinations, striking the heart, pushing the will by divers agitations and different efforts so as to make a place for itself or at least to overcome these obstacles. But in the

Blessed Virgin everything favored and seconded the course of heavenly love. It progressed and increased, making itself incomparably greater than all other creatures, a progress, nevertheless, infinitely sweet, calm, and tranquil. She did not swoon from love or compassion at the foot of the Cross of her Son; still, at that time she had the most ardent and dolorous access of love that can be imagined. Although this influx of love was extreme, it was equally strong and sweet, powerful and tranquil, active and calm, composed of a sharp yet sweet warmth.

Therefore she is given to us as a model to be imitated.

Our glorious St. Luke regarded her then several times in order to impress deeply on his imagination and still more deeply in his heart the form and traits of the face of this holy Lady so that he could record them more naturally on the picture he was painting of her for the consolation of all mortals.

O my God, how much sweetness this saint received in his interior, gazing on the brow of the blessed Virgin, and not only on her brow but also on her whole blessed face. What virginal modesty he beheld there! If her daughters, no matter how meager their natural goodness might be, show their modesty on their face, blushing at the least word that is spoken to them, O God, what thought would you have, you who saw yourself in the face of this holy Virgin when she was regarded by her painter. How many admirable qualities he discovered in this modest and chaste look! What contentment to consider her who is more beautiful than the sky or than the plain strewn with a variety of flowers, surpassing in beauty both angels and men! But who can imagine the humility with which St. Luke begged her to look at him and the sweetness and simplicity with which our Lady did it? What lights he received from this saintly glance! How his heart remained inflamed with her love! What great knowledge he drew from the eyes of this sweet Virgin as they rested on him! They impressed on his heart so great a love of purity that he persevered in it constantly all through his life and maintained his celibacy until his death.

As we have said, he also received that evenness and strength of spirit which gleamed so singularly in the Blessed Virgin; that is why we have seen all his enterprises accompaned by an admirable constancy and perseverance in good once they have been begun. But over and above this, he also took from this holy Virgin her manner of speaking, for she loved to be the last and always chose the lowest place. This humility she taught very well to her Evangelist. Knowing this, then, and seeing that he was able to satisfy her and follow her intention, still without prejudicing in the least the honor that he owed her nor the esteem which he should have for her, he named her last and entirely apart from all others. In this way he indicated that she was greater than the apostles and disciples, even greater than all angels and men taken together.

What St. Francis de Sales recommended especially was confidence; confidence of a child in his mother; confidence at every instant and in all things; confidence still more at the hour of death and for all eternity.

Honor, revere, and respect with a special love the sacred and glorious Virgin Mary; she is mother of our sovereign Father and therefore our grandmother. Let us have recourse to her, then, and like grandchildren, let us cast ourselves on her bosom with a perfect confidence at every moment, on every occasion. Let us proclaim this sweet Mother; let us invoke her maternal love and let us try to imitate her virtues. Let us have a true filial devotion toward her.

Ordinarily, people of the world imagine that devotion to our Lady consists in wearing a Rosary at one's belt, in reciting countless Hail Mary's. In this they are gravely mistaken, for our dear Mother wishes that we do what her Son commands and considers as done for herself the honor that we give to her Son by keeping his commandments. At the wedding of Cana, Jesus said to his Mother:

"How does this concern of yours involve me?" Ah, Lord, your concern is to change the creature through its Creator, from whom it holds its being and its life. What has the Mother to do with her Son except to join the Son to the Mother from whom he has received his body, that is, his humanity, flesh and blood. These words seem to be very strange, and, indeed, they were misunderstood by some ignorant people who, by wrongly interpreting them, gave rise to three or four heresies. But, O God, who is so bold as to wish to fathom this mystery by his intellect alone, sharp and penetrating though it may be, without having received the necessary lights from on high? Christ's response was so loving that the Blessed Virgin, who knew him so well, felt herself the most obligated mother there ever had been. She showed this when after that, her heart full of holy confidence, she said to those who were serving, "You have heard what my Son has said, yet you who do not understand the language of love may think that he has not heeded me. Do not fear; only do whatever he tells you, for he will look after your need."

From the sermons of St. Francis we could draw many other examples which form, so to speak, a portion of his Marian theology.

PART FOUR

The Virtues

22　The Practice of the Virtues

In St. Francis de Sales we find repeated the teachings of St. Augustine, St. Thomas, St. Bonaventure, St. Francis of Assisi, St. Bernard, St. Ignatius and St. Teresa. And yet he has his own personality, his individual traits, the finesse of his special touch, his own attitude toward all the creatures of God. He differs from all those whom he studies as most of the saints differ from their parents and ancestors. This originality in sanctity is a gift from God who loves infinite variety, who alone is able to multiply differences.

But what appears to us the most original aspect of his writings, one sufficient to place him at the head of the hierarchy of spiritual writers, is his manner of describing and practicing virtue. We could also say it is his manner of looking at Jesus Christ and of understanding the imitation which the Incarnate Word desires in our life.

The Mother of God imitated the incomparable sanctity of her Son. Although she resembled him more than any other creature, to such an extent that we can say that in certain traits Jesus gave her of his beauty, nevertheless it is also true that Christ has infinite perfection and Mary only that of a human mother of her age in Palestine.

On the other hand, those who imitate St. Francis de Sales sometimes produce caricatures: caricatures of sweetness, benignity, loving tenderness, vulgar simplicity, and even of style; caricatures which are recognized as strange and vapid copies. These distortions prompted this study of the virtues as St. Francis de Sales and St. Ignatius understand and recommend them in their direction of souls. We do not follow the immense plan of the *Summa* of St. Thomas, nor that of St. Ignatius, but the few virtues that we discuss have a great importance in the spirit of these two saints.

St. Ignatius, who did not write a *Treatise on the Love of*

223

God and who is not a doctor of dogmatic theology, can still be venerated as a supereminent teacher of the love of God in his creatures. His disciple, St. Francis de Sales, illustrated his doctrine with a supereminent wisdom. He is truly admired as the incomparable Doctor of "theological charity in all things." The dominant Ignatian principle is that true virtue has its source and its perfection in charity. This virtue is also the principal force of action, of conservation, of increase of the Society, so that in all things the love of God must be our principal intention. Love and the desire for all perfection, of the greatest possible glory and praise of Christ our Creator and Lord, may be substituted for the fear of offending God.

This love of God should be the principal bond of union. The feeling toward the Society that we must develop in our novices is not servile fidelity, but love. Toward the superiors, we must have a perfect obedience, but the soul of that obedience in the Society is love. In regard to our superiors, our brothers, our neighbors, the weak, the ailing, the tempted, the virtue of charity dominates all. The virtue which St. Ignatius requires of the Father General, and after him, of all superiors, is charity. But this charity must be, as they say, a "splendor."

Poverty must be loved as a mother. Humiliations of all sorts should be just as passionately sought as worldlings seek honors and riches. Evidently it is the love of God and of Jesus Christ which is the root of all these virtues. Should anyone read Part IX of the Constitutions, he will realize that there does not exist in the virtues—which for St. Ignatius are essential to the vocation to the Society—any human source, any natural exigency, but an all-powerful and unique motivating force—charity.

St. Francis de Sales, with a conviction which has inflamed the souls of all centuries and all countries, followed the same doctrine as St. Ignatius, namely, that charity must be the source of the most perfect virtues and of all consideration of creatures.

He did not say that without charity the virtues of the pagans did not exist. He did not teach that each virtue had any value of its own without charity, nor in charity. He did not say that it was necessary to multiply as much as possible acts of charity apart from the virtues. But, following St. Ignatius, and according to the formulas already borrowed by this Saint from the Second Epistle to the Corinthians (6:4–5), "Let us conduct ourselves in all circumstances as God's ministers, in much patience; in tribulations, in hardships, in distresses, in stripes, in imprisonments, in tumults; in labors, in sleepless nights, in fastings." And St. Paul adds that not only in all sorts of sufferings but also in all virtues he is strengthened as minister of God "in innocence, in knowledge, in long-sufferings; in kindness, in the Holy Spirit, in unaffected love; in the word of truth, in the power of God; with the armor of justice on the right hand and on the left; in honor and dishonor" (6:6–8). By this enumeration the Apostle shows that in all things, good and evil, he seeks only one end: to love and serve God.

These words summarize the twenty-one chapters St. Francis de Sales wrote in the *Treatise on the Love of God* to teach the same idea, namely, "that holy love renders the virtues far more agreeable to God than they are by their own nature. And as he easily sees God in all things, the least among them suggests comparisons with the supernatural life. "If you graft a rose-tree," he said, "and in the cleft of the stalk you put a seed of musk, it will produce roses completely penetrated with the musk. Cleave your heart with holy penance and place the love of God in the cleft; then engraft on this any virtue you like and the results which proceed from it will be perfumed with holiness without need for any care but that."

He gives many other examples: "If you wish to sanctify human virtue and morality as preached by Epictetus or Socrates, let a truly Christian soul, that is, one who loves God, practice it. Thus God will consider him first as a good Abel, then he will consider his offering; so that the offerings take their grace and dignity in the eyes of God from the goodness and piety of him who presents them." His manner of thanking God for his love of us is very remarkable.

O sovereign goodness of our great God, who favors his lovers (that is, those who act through charity) so much that he cherishes their least actions in order to sanctify and ennoble them by giving them the title and the quality of saints. In the contemplation of his beloved Son he wishes to honor his adoptive children, sanctifying all that is good in them: their bones, their hair, their clothing, their sepulchres, and even ghosts of their body; their faith, hope, love, religion—yes, even the sobriety, courtesy and the affability of their hearts.

In these few lines we see how human Francis de Sales is, and how everything human seems to him to be inundated, illuminated and perfumed by the grace of Christ. All his life he tried to persuade his hearers and his correspondents who might complain of their lot of this truth which seems to him basic to spirituality: "Love God in all things"; love his will, his love, his presence, his benefits.

He adds one counsel, however: "All the virtues receive . . . dignity by the presence of holy love; but faith, hope, fear of God, piety, penance and all the other virtues which of themselves tend particularly to God and to his honor receive not only the impression of the divine love, but they depend totally on him, associate themselves with him, follow him and serve him on all occasions." This consideration is not merely theoretical; it ends in a precise directive:

That is why, among all virtuous actions, we must carefully practice those of religion and reverence toward divine things, those of faith, hope and of holy fear of God. We ought often to speak of heavenly things, think and aspire to eternity, frequent churches and sacred services, read spiritual books. The saint nourishes himself by these exercises and sanctifies his simply human acts by their graces and properties.

We cannot omit mentioning the many outstanding reflections on the beauty of the virtues illuminated by charity which St. Francis de Sales develops with such gracious art. It is true that he repeats himself as one loves to sing his favorite melody over and over. However, we extract what seems to be the direction of his thought. For example, in his eyes, charity is so superior that without it the other virtues remain imperfectly developed, like the bees who "are at their birth little wriggly things, without feet, without wings, without form. . . . When they are grown they are formed bees, perfected because they now have what they need to fly and to make honey" (Chap. IX). It is probably the same thought which St. Ignatius expressed by saying that virtues can be "solid and perfect" or not.

It follows that the charity which perfects all the virtues cannot be perfected by any of them,

not even obedience, which is the one which can most perfect others. For again, although love is commanded, and by loving we practice obedience, if, nevertheless, this love does not draw its perfection from obedience but from the goodness of the one who loves, in that degree love is not excellent because it is obedient but because it loves an excellent good. Certainly in loving we obey, as in obeying we love, but if this obedience is so excellently amiable, it is because it tends to the excellence of love, and its perfection depends not on what in loving we obey but on what in obeying we love.

This passage seems worthy of being quoted because it expounds the doctrine of St. Francis on all the virtues. That is why he adds this conclusion: "In the same manner that God is the last end of all that is good, he is its first source—love, the origin of all good affection and its last end and perfection."

Because it can encourage many souls, we recall here a consoling thought to which St. Francis devoted his twelfth chapter, but which we do not find in the writings of St. Ignatius. He believes that Christian sinners who lose grace by their lack of love do not destroy radically and definitively their antecedent life as adopted sons of God. He compares the effect that charity produces in the soul when it is reborn to the renewal of nature in spring after the chill of winter. First of all he quotes Holy Scripture: "Turn and be converted from all your crimes that they may be no cause of guilt for you" (Ez. 18:30), a text which Francis de Sales interprets thus: "That is, your crimes shall be no cause of guilt for you provided that the crimes have already been atoned for."

He also cites the case of Job, the innocent image of the penitent sinner who in the end receives doubly all that he had lost, and that of the prodigal son to whom were restored all his clothing and all the graces, favors and dignities he had lost. He considers the words of the Council of Trent (Sess. VI, *De Justif.*, xvi) very important: those recommendations which "desire the returned penitents to be animated to that sacred love of God eternal, by these words of the Apostle: 'For God is not unjust, that he should forget your work and the love that you have shown in his name' (Heb. 6:10)."

And the Saint adds this commentary: "Now God's justice obliges him to regard first of all the good works of the past, as if he had never forgotten them, otherwise the penitent would not have dared to say to his Master: 'Give me back the joy of your salvation, and a willing spirit sustain in me' (Ps. 50:14)." St. Francis insists on the *joy:* "This joy is nothing else but the wine of celestial love, which rejoices the heart of man."

We can gather much confidence from this chapter on the virtues. Contrasting the virtues with the vices, our holy doctor, flooded with charity, notes here: "Sin is annihilated by holy penance; on the other hand, love, returning to the soul of the penitent, revives the former holy works because they were not abolished, but merely forgotten. . . . By the return of charity we are restored to our rank as children of God, and consequently, made susceptible to immortal glory, God remembers our former good works, and they are immediately made fruitful for us." Consequently, who does not see how important it is to educate youth to habituate themselves for years to fill their souls with virtuous piety? Therefore St.

Francis exalts the mercy of God. "Sin proceeds from our weakness; charity proceeds from the divine power. If 'sin has reigned unto death, so also grace may reign by justice unto life everlasting' (Rom. 5:20); and the mercy of God by which he effaces the sin is always exalted and gloriously triumphs over the rigorous judgment by which God had forgotten the good works which preceded the sin." Finally the Saint affirms that "all theologians say and teach most clearly" that holy works revive by penance "in the sun of grace and charity." He offers a last comparison, that of the slime of the well converted into flames on the return of Israel from captivity, releasing the power and the mercy of God.

From the whole chapter there springs forth an encouragement to practice virtues and an exaltation of the divine mercy through the special virtue of charity. In reading this, how many souls would find the consolation which they need so pressingly!

One last question which St. Francis asked himself and which merits our attention is this: Does charity drive all fear from the heart? Can we have such assurance in charity that we no longer have anything to fear from the justice of God? (Ch. xvi to xxi).

The soul which follows the *Exercises* of St. Ignatius is often divided between fears of various sorts and the impulses of love. St. Ignatius does not treat the question theoretically; he leaves to the director the care of directing the soul in the opposite waves of consolation and desolation.

St. Francis de Sales resolved the problem in the fashion most capable of producing peace. In his *Institute,* St. Ignatius declares (P. IX, c. iii, no. 20), that his Constitutions do not oblige under pain of sin. Much more than that, it is necessary to be free from the fear of offending God and to observe the rules only through love, through the desire to attain the highest perfection and to procure for Christ, our Creator and Lord, the greatest glory. Here it is a question, evidently, not of all fear but of the fear that the theologians call servile. St.

Francis de Sales explains it in a very enlightened fashion. Love which penetrates and perfects all virtue also penetrates fear and produces filial fear, or the "loving fear of spouses." This latter is a gift of the Holy Spirit. "By this sacred fear of the divine spouses the great souls of St. Paul, St. Francis, St. Catherine of Genoa and others were touched. They could say, 'It is now no longer I that live, but Christ lives in me' (Gal. 2:20)."

At the same time that love perfects filial fear, it dissolves servile fear. The Saint compares this fear to a needle which pierces cloth in order to introduce the thread of gold, silk, or silver. The needle comes out when it has done its work. "Perfect charity," said St. John, "casts out fear" (1:4:18). In the meantime, both the heavenly enjoyment of love and the servile fears are to be used so that we may live according to God, as navigators use all the instruments which they carry with them for storms; they are accessories for the repose of holy love. But "although servile and mercenary fear may be greatly useful for this mortal life, it is unworthy of having a place in the eternal, in which there is assurance without fear, peace without defiance, response without care. Nevertheless, the services which these servile and mercenary fears have rendered to love will be rewarded there." Charity will have triumphed over all passions, over all self-love, and will produce the fruits and blessings of the Holy Spirit in unimaginable splendor.

But already in this terrestrial valley where everything still remains imperfect, charity is the source not only of the virtues, but also of the fruits and the blessings of the Spirit of love. When we read the page we are going to quote as a termination of this chapter, we get the impression that the Saint is speaking from experience, not from books; not from association with mystics, but from his personal experience of the life of the Holy Spirit in his own charity.

In a word, holy charity is a virtue, a gift, a fruit and a beatitude. As a virtue, it makes us obedient to the exterior inspirations which

God gives us by his commandments and his counsels. In executing these, we practice all virtues, wherefore love is the virtue of virtues. As a gift, charity makes us docile and tractable to interior inspirations which are, as it were, God's sweet commandments and counsels. We employ the seven gifts of the Holy Ghost to practice these, with the result that charity is the gift of gifts. As a fruit, it gives us an extreme relish and pleasure in the practice of the devout life, which is felt in the twelve fruits of the Holy Spirit, and therefore it is the fruit of fruits. As a beatitude, it makes us consider the affronts, calumnies, revilings and insults which the world heaps upon us as the greatest of favors and singular honors. It makes us forsake, renounce, and reject all other glory except that which comes from the beloved Crucified, for whose glory we rejoice in the abjection, abnegation and annihilation of ourselves, desiring no other marks of majesty than the thorn-crown of the crucified, the scepter of his reed, the role of scorn which was put upon him and the throne of his cross. With these, holy lovers enjoy more contentment, joy, glory and felicity than delighted Solomon on his ivory throne (XI, xix).

After this sort of synthesis of the spiritual life, we must not be surprised that St. Francis de Sales gave the Visitandines and the souls for whom he wrote his *Treatise* charity as their characteristic virtue and, in a more concrete fashion and one most like the charity of our Lord on the Cross, the cult of the Sacred Heart as their principal devotion.

23 *The "Little" Virtues*

IT SEEMS SUITABLE to return to this subject here. The mystical authors were very familiar to St. Francis; yet he recommended them with much reserve and prudence. He restricted this reading not at all because he thought them less enlightened and less holy than others but because, according to the Ignatian formula in the final meditation of the *Exercises*, it seemed to him that the love of God is tried and manifested by actions (*amor debet poni magis in operibus quam in verbis*) and by the total gift of self to God (*ut det et communicet amans amato ea quae habet*). We read in his *Introduction to the Devout Life* the strong expression which defines his thought. The ecstasies, raptures and special gifts

of which certain other books treat, promise to raise the soul to purely intellectual contemplation. . . . Note well, Philothea, that these perfections are not virtues. Rather, they are rewards that God gives for virtues, or small samples of the happiness of the life to come, that God sometimes presents to men to make them enraptured with the whole, which is only to be found in paradise. For all that, we must not aspire to such graces, since they are by no means necessary for serving and loving God well, our only intention. Neither are they graces that can be obtained by labor and industry, since they are passive rather than active, and we may indeed receive but cannot produce them in ourselves. We have engaged ourselves to be good, devout, pious men and women. We must strive hard to achieve this end. If it should please God to elevate us to these angelic perfections, we shall then be good angels also. In the meantime, let us endeavor sincerely, humbly, and devoutly to acquire those little virtues which our Savior has set forth for our care and labor. These are patience, meekness, mortification of heart, humility, obedience, poverty, chastity, tenderness toward our neighbors, bearing with their imperfections, diligence and holy fervor.

St. Francis chose his way, that of the life of Christ; he will never deviate from it, neither for his own sake nor for that of another. A few precise points that he adds here flow from his style of life: "Let us willingly leave these supereminent favors to elevated souls; we do not merit so high a rank in the service of God. We shall be too happy to serve him in his kitchen or in his scullery, or to be his lackeys, his porters, his chamberlains. . . . We must neither rashly despise nor censure anything. Blessing God for the supereminence of others, we must keep ourselves in our lower but safer way . . ." The purpose which Msgr. Jean-Pierre Camus reports in his book, *Esprit du bienheureux François de Sales* (p. 29) is taken from an actual conversation: "I intend to speak only of perfection, and I see very few people who practice it."

He does not hesitate to write to Madame Brulart: "In the house of a prince it is not so great to be the scullery maid in the kitchen as it is to be the valet of the chamber; but in the house of God, the menials are most often the greatest because when they become soiled it is for the love of God, for his will. God's will gives value to our actions, not only to their exterior appearance" (*Œuvres*, XIII, 214).

In April, 1606, he wrote to the same soul: "Let us remain, my dear daughter, a little longer in these low valleys, let us again kiss the feet of the Savior; he will call us to his holy mouth when he pleases." St. Bernard uses almost the same terms to exhort his monks to kiss first of all the feet of the crucifix (*Canticle of Canticles*). Let us quote the same thought once more, this time from a letter to the President Bénigne Frémyot, father of the Baroness de Chantal: "The soul who wishes to go to God must first of all kiss the feet of the Crucified, purge its affections and resolve to retire little by little from the world and its vanities. Then kiss the hands, for new actions should follow changes in affections; and finally the kiss of the mouth, uniting the soul by an ardent love to this Supreme Goodness" (Oct. 7, 1604). Is this not the same method as that of the four Weeks of the *Exercises* of St. Ignatius?

We could multiply texts similar to those we have reported. "We must lose ourselves," they say, "in a certain obscurity (in which all contemplative men are happily lost) in such a way that like treasures hidden in the earth, we cannot ever be found in this abyss. In this obscurity of love our spirit is dead to itself, and the divine manifestation of eternal life is begun."

He permits individual souls already making great progress to read one or the other mystical authors. "You may usefully read the books of Mother Teresa and of St. Catherine, the

Method of Serving God, an abridgement of *Christian Perfection,* or the *Evangelical Pearl."* But his admiration does not go so far that he advises these souls to follow their teaching: "Do not be eager to practice all that is beautiful in the books you read. Make your way very slowly, aspiring after these glorious teachings with moderation and admiration" (*Œuvres,* XIII, 334–35).

One of the books that he recommends most often to those he is directing is the *Spiritual Combat.* "Read and reread the *Spiritual Combat.* This should be your dearest book; it is clear and completely practicable."

We should note that even the admirable books on the mystical life demand very extensive and very attentive reading, therefore he did not advise all his souls to drink from the same springs. At the end of his *Treatise on the Love of God* he returns to his preferred authors: Louis of Granada, St. Bonaventure, Louis de la Puente, Diego de Estrella (*Œuvres,* V, 342).

But what explains his thought with greater force is that he makes no exception for souls called by God to mystical ways. He respects their special vocation, even admires it and directs it. Nevertheless, he recalls to the dearest of all, St. Jane de Chantal, the capital lesson of the little virtues for which our Lord gave the example. "The virtues a widow should practice are humility, scorn of the world and of herself, simplicity. Her spiritual exercises are love of her abjection, service to the poor and the sick; her place is at the foot of the cross, her rank, the last; her glory, to be despised; her crown, her misery; all the 'little' virtues." He proposes the Blessed Virgin as model of humility. "I do not say that we should not hope for the great virtues, the supreme virtues, but I do say that we should practice the little ones without which the great ones are often false and deceiving. . . . Let us learn to suffer willingly abasement and the belittling of our opinions and our thoughts; then we shall learn to suffer martyrdom and

to annihilate ourselves in God, unshakeable in all things"
(*Œuvres*, V, 109–10).

Let us not forget that Jane de Chantal was already accustomed to passive contemplation. Her holy director did not
forget it but he wished it to be based on asceticism. Let us
examine his manner of giving her a lesson: "I do not forbid
elevation of the soul, mental prayer, interior conversation
with God, the perpetual sending of the heart to our Lord; but
do you know what I mean, my daughter? I mean that it is
necessary to be like that valiant woman of whom the Wise
Man said: 'She puts her hands to the distaff, and her fingers
ply the spindle' (Prov. 31:19). Meditate, elevate your spirit,
bear it to God, that is to say, draw God into your spirit; those
are strong things. But with all that do not forget your distaff
and your spindle. Whoever says anything different is deceived
and in error" (*Œuvres*, XIV, 110).

Once more, to Mme Brulart, he insists: "The feeling that
you have of belonging completely to God is not false, but it
requires you to exert yourself a little more in the exercise of
the virtues and to have a special care to acquire those in
which you find yourself most lacking. Reread the *Spiritual
Combat* and pay special attention to the teachings contained
therein; they are very suitable for you. The sentiments of
prayer are good, but we must not so completely satisfy ourselves with them that we do not employ ourselves with them
that we do not employ ourselves diligently to the virtues and
mortifications of the passions" (*Œuvres*, XV, 165).

The *Spiritual Conferences*, which contains the largest portion of the homilies made by the saint to the religious of the
Visitation, are a striking witness to his spiritual preference.
For there were among the Visitandines some Sisters who
took down his words in writing in order to publish them,
souls certainly called to passive contemplation. If their Father sometimes made this subject the theme of his recommendations, they would have been only too happy to note

them down and to make them known. But they have not gathered up a single word which wanders from his tenacious thought that Dom Mackey summarizes in his preface: "To propose the most perfect and most divine model which he could find of a life of consummate sanctity, though common in appearance, he offered the Holy Family at Nazareth for the contemplation of his daughters. It is the humility, the silence of the most Blessed Virgin, and the obedience, the equability of soul, the abnegation of St. Joseph which he recommends to their imitation. According to him, the putative father of the Savior is the 'true religious' par excellence. Our Doctor was pleased to speak of his virtues, to celebrate his praises at a time when his cult was still not very widespread."

In terminating his study of the *Conferences*, Dom Mackey wrote: "What he proposes principally for the imitation of his daughters is the intimate and hidden virtues of the Savior: submission to the will of God, abandonment to his good pleasure, meekness and humility." The *Conferences*, then, seem to be only a sort of commentary on the words of the great Apostle to the Philippians: "Have this mind in you which was also in Christ Jesus" (2:5). And fortunately, Dom Mackey concludes that "the Son of God will reward this humble institute (of the Visitation) by giving it his heart."

To sum up this chapter, no one would blame us for reproducing here a page from the *Conferences* entitled "Why We Should Become Religious":

Well, my dear daughters, we desire to erect within our souls a great building, the dwelling-place of God. First, then, let us consider maturely whether we have sufficient courage and resolution to crucify and annihilate ourselves, or, rather, to permit God to do this for us, so that he may then rebuild us and make us the living temples of his Majesty. I tell you my daughters, that our only aim ought to be to unite ourselves to God, as Jesus Christ united himself to his eternal Father—that is, by his dying on the cross. For I am not now speaking to you of that general union which is effected by baptism, in which Christians unite themselves to God by receiving this divine sacrament, the stamp of Christianity, binding themselves to keep his commandments and those of Holy Church, to perform good works and to practice the virtues of faith, hope and charity. This union is indeed a true one, and may justly hope for paradise. Those who have united themselves by this means to God as to *their* God are not bound to do more; they have attained their end and aim by the general and broad way of the commandments. But for you, my dear daughters, this is not the way. Besides this obligation, which is binding upon you in common with all Christians, God, by a very special act of love, has chosen you to be his dear brides.

You must understand clearly how and what it means to be a religious. It is to be bound to God by the continual mortification of ourselves, and to live only for him. Our heart is surrendered always and wholly to his divine Majesty; our eyes, tongue, hands and all our members serve him continually. That is why religion, as you see, furnishes us with all the means suitable to this end, such as prayer, spiritual reading, silence, the inward secret withdrawal of the heart to rest in God alone, and constant aspirations to our Lord. We cannot possibly arrive at this except by the constant mortification of all our passions, inclinations, dispositions and antipathies. We are therefore obliged to watch over ourselves unceasingly so as to overcome all these. Remember, my dear daughters, that "unless the grain of wheat falls into the ground and dies, it remains alone. But if it dies, it brings forth much fruit" (Jn. 12:24–25). The words of our Lord are quite clear on this subject, since his own sacred lips spoke them. Therefore, you who are aspiring to be novices, and you who are preparing to be professed, search your hearts again and again to see if you have resolution enough to die to yourselves and to live only for God. Weigh the whole matter well; there is still time for consideration before your veils are dyed black. I declare to you, my dear daughters, plainly and most seriously, that those who desire to live according to nature should stay in the world, and only those should enter religion who are determined to live according to grace. Religion is nothing else than a school of renunciation and self-mortification. Therefore it provides you, as you see, with many instruments, both outward and inward, for mortifying yourselves.

"But," you will say to me, "that is not what I was intending at all. I thought that in order to be a good religious it was sufficient to desire to pray well, to have visions and revelations, to see angels in human form, to be rapt in ecstasies, to love reading good books. And then I thought I was so virtuous, so mortified, so humble! Everyone admired me. Was it not being very humble to speak to my companions so nicely about devotional subjects; to tell those who had not heard the sermons all about them; to behave with gentleness to all members of the household, especially when they did not contradict me?" Certainly, my dear daughters, that was all very well for the world, but religion demands that we perform works worthy of our vocation (Eph. 4:1)—that is, that we should die to ourselves in all things, as well in what is good in our opinion as in what is bad and useless. Do you think that the monks of the desert, who enjoyed such a close union with God, arrived at it by following their own inclinations? Certainly not; they mortified themselves in the very holiest things, and though they delighted in singing divine canticles, in reading, praying, and so on, yet they never did these things in order to please themselves. On the contrary, they deprived themselves voluntarily of these pleasures, in order to apply themselves to painful and laborious works.

It is indeed quite true that devout souls receive a thousand sweetnesses and satisfactions amid the mortifications and labors of holy religion, for it is to them chiefly that the Holy Spirit distributes his precious gifts. But still, they must seek in it God alone and the mortifications of their dispositions, passions, and inclinations. If they seek nothing else, they will never find the consolation to which they aspire.

Would we not say that these pages are extracts of works of St. Ignatius Loyola? The expression "religious intentions" chosen by St. Francis replaces the more solemn title of "the standard of Christ" in the *Exercises.* The term can seem pompous to those who do not know how much importance St. Ignatius gave to the virtues inscribed under this famous banner of Jesus in the spiritual combat: poverty, humiliations, humility. All other virtues lead to this abnegation of self. His prayer, *Suscipe, Domine,* permits no reserve in the gift of his faculties. Does not his *Institute* (P. III, c.l. no. 22

and 10) express on all occasions the necessity of this renouncement? We have already pointed out this fact in our
chapter on the love of Jesus. It is of sovereign importance.[1]

24 *Mental Prayer*

For St. Francis de Sales, as for all the saints without exception, mental prayer is recommended as a necessary means for
attaining holiness. We maintain ourselves in grace with God
and, much more important, we do not arrive at the perfection
of the virtues except through prayer. We are not going to attempt to show this necessity here; we accept it as an essential
truth.

It is generally said that there are two forms of prayer: mystical prayer, which is a gratuitous gift of God to certain souls,
and the prayer common to all souls. St. Francis de Sales has
expressed his personal ideas on mystical prayer in two books
of the *Treatise on the Love of God.* Since he did not borrow
his analyses from St. Ignatius, who was careful not to reveal
his own experience (we do not know why), spiritual writers
compare the teaching of St. Francis de Sales with that of other
mystical saints. M. Pierre Serouet made a profound study of
the doctrine which St. Francis de Sales accepted from St.
Teresa of Avila (*Etudes carmélitaines*). We shall not even try

---

[1] "*Magnopere conferet devote, quoad fieri poterit, ea munera obire, in
quibus magis exercetur humilitas et caritas. Et in universo loquendo
quanto aliquis se arctius Deo astrinxerit, et liberaliorem erga summam
Maiestatem se praestiterit; tanto eum in se liberaliorem etiam
experietur . . .*

"*Ab illusionibus daemonis in suis spiritualibus exercitationibus
caveant, et se contra omnes tentationes tueantur; simul rationes sciant
quae adhiberi possint ut eas superent; et ad veras solidasque virtutes
consequendas insistant, sive plures adsint visitationes spirituales, sive
pauciores. Curent vero semper in via divini servitii progressum facere.*"

to give here the conclusions of that study, which is foreign to our subject. But we shall show that for ordinary prayer, St. Francis de Sales gives the same counsels as St. Ignatius.

It will be sufficient to select a few of his counsels to convince souls who have made the *Exercises*. M. Serouet has noted the passages of the works of St. Teresa which seem borrowed from the *Exercises* or inspired by them, and by her Jesuit directors; all her directives in common prayer are Ignatian in origin. St. Francis de Sales states that the intellectual part of the meditation is secondary or preparatory, and that it should stop when the Holy Spirit begins to warm the soul with his love. "You must also know that it sometimes happens that immediately after the preparation you will feel your affections moved toward God. In this case, Philothea, you must yield to the attraction without following the method I have given you. Generally speaking, consideration precedes affections and resolutions. However, when the Holy Spirit gives you the affection before the consideration, you must not then seek the consideration since it is used for no other purpose than to arouse the affections" (*Introduction*, II, iii).

One question presents itself in relation to mental prayer. Do all men have this grace as they do that of the adoptive filiation? St. Francis concedes that not everyone has the gift of mental prayer, but that it is true that almost everyone could have it, even the most unspiritual, provided that he has good directors and that he is willing to work as hard to acquire it as its difficulty merits. St. Ignatius also thinks that every one can be given the method of the *Exercises*.

What about vocal prayer? Francis recommends the *Pater, Ave, Credo*. But it is necessary to say them "driving your thought deeply and exciting your affections by their meanings. Do not hurry in any way to say many of them, but say what you do say wholeheartedly. A single *Pater* said with feeling is better than several recited rapidly and thoughtlessly." He advises us also to say the Rosary in the same manner, as well as the litanies of our Lord, our Lady and the saints, and "all the vocal prayers which are in the manuals and the approved hours." All this recalls almost word for word St. Ignatius' three manners of prayer. And, on his example, he adds this important counsel: "If you have the gift of mental prayer, keep it for the first place, so that if after that . . . you cannot make vocal prayer you do not put yourself to any pain about it. If, when making your vocal prayer you feel your heart drawn to interior or mental prayer, do not refuse to go there, but let your spirit flow gently in that direction, and do not have any care for not having completed the vocal prayers which you proposed for yourself; for mental prayer which you have made in their place is more agreeable to God and more useful to your soul."

St. Teresa herself advises us to make use of a book if that is useful or necessary in order to arrive at mental prayer. St. Ignatius makes prayer proceed from preparation with a book. St. Francis de Sales is of the same opinion.

Should it happen, Philothea, that you feel no relish or comfort in meditation, I urge you not to disturb yourself on that account but sometimes open the door of your heart to vocal prayer. Lament your condition to our Lord, confess your unworthiness, and beseech him to assist you. Kiss his image if you have it at hand, saying to him those words of the Canaanite woman: "Yes, Lord, for even the dogs eat of the crumbs that fall from their master's table" (Mt. 15:27). At other times take up some spiritual book and read it with attention until your spirit is awakened and restored in you. Sometimes you may arouse your heart by some position or action of exterior devotion, such as prostrating yourself on the ground, crossing your hands before your breast, or embracing a crucifix, provided you are alone or in some private place (*Introduction,* II, ix).

None of the means which favor mental prayer, although they demand much humility and simplicity, are negligible. But the most painful and most dangerous trial is that of dryness, prolonged despite all efforts to banish it. It makes all souls suffer. The page written on this subject by St. Francis de Sales is truly fine: "But if after all this you should receive no comfort, do not be disturbed, no matter how excessive the dryness may be, but continue to remain in a devout posture in the presence of God." Imitating the courtiers who, he said, "enter a hundred times a year into the prince's presence chamber without hope of speaking to him," we must

come to prayer, purely and merely to do our duty and affirm our fidelity. Should it please the divine Majesty to speak to us and aid us by his holy inspirations and interior consolations, it would certainly be a great honor and the sweetest delight. But should it not please him to grant us this favor, and should he leave us without speaking to us any more than if he did not see us or we were not in his presence, we must not depart for that reason. On the contrary, we should respectfully and devoutly remain in the presence of his adorable Majesty. Without fail, he will be pleased by our patience. He will notice our diligence and perseverance so that when we come before him another time he will favor us with his consolations and grant us the sweetness of his holy prayer. Yet if he should not do so, let us assure ourselves, Philothea, that it is an exceedingly great honor for us to stand before him and in his sight (*Ibid.*).

Perhaps we imagine that these elementary directives are destined solely for novices, for beginners in the spiritual way, and that they are not useful for souls advanced in prayer, to whom it would be more useful to expose the method to be followed in uncommon, extraordinary ways. The correspondence of St. Francis de Sales shows clearly that some souls most privileged by the Holy Spirit spent hours and sometimes years of darkness, dryness, impotence, and that they needed to be directed like beginners.

It was not to a novice but to a soul very advanced in prayer and happy to enter Carmel to give herself over to contemplation that he wrote on March 11, 1610:

As to the precepts of prayer which you have received from the good mother prioress (of Carmel at Dijon) . . . I only pray you to learn all you can of its principles. To speak plainly to you, although two or three times during the past summer I put myself in the presence of God without preparation or design, I found that I was extremely near to his majesty, with one very simple and continual affection of a love that was almost imperceptible, but very sweet. . . . Yet I would not have dared to make it a custom to take myself away from the usual road in order to follow this extraordinary one. I do not know how it is, but I love the simple way of those who have gone before us and to make a custom of no preparation, no thanksgiving, no offering, no expressed prayer at the end, is somehow repugnant to me.

The following year he insisted on the necessity of the presence of God. "Guard against strong applications of the intellect." When we become conscious of distractions, we should turn simply "to actions of the will." It is important to keep oneself in the presence of God.

To remain in the presence of God and to put oneself in the presence of God are two very different things in my opinion; for, in order to put ourselves there, we must recall our soul from every other object and make it attentive to this presence at this moment, as I said in the book (*Treatise*, VI, xi). But after we have put ourselves there, we keep ourselves there always, while, either by intellect or by will, we make acts toward God, either regarding him or regarding something else for love of him, or . . . simply remaining where he has placed us as a statue in its niche.

Then follows a graceful comparison with the statue which does not wish to move from the place where the Master has placed it. " 'I am where my Master placed me and his pleasure is the one satisfaction of my being.' Ah, my dear daughter, what a good prayer that is, and what an excellent manner of staying in the presence of God it is to remain in his will and his good pleasure."

It is my opinion that Magdalen was as a statue in her niche when without saying a word, without moving, and perhaps without looking at him, seated at his feet, she listened to what our Lord was saying. When he spoke, she listened; when he ceased speaking, she left off listening, and yet she was always there. . . . How happy we are when we wish to love our Lord! Let us love him then very well, my daughter; let us not spend any thought on the little that we do for his love, provided that we know that we wish never to do anything except for his love. As for me, I think that we keep ourselves in the presence of God even when sleeping, for we sleep in his sight, at his pleasure and at his will, and we place ourselves there on the bed like statues in their niche. When we wake up we find that he is near us; he has not moved, nor have we; we are, then, as it were, held in his presence, but with our eyes closed tight.

Shall we say that Francis de Sales forgets that he is writing to the Baroness de Chantal, or that he is ignorant of her gifts of prayer? At the end of her life, Mére de Chantal had to undergo terrible mystical trials. But like all great souls, she knew dryness well.

Alas, my dear daughter, how happy we are to be thus crushed and held close by our heavenly Teacher. . . . My Lord, I wish no enjoyment of my faith nor of my hope nor of my charity except to be able to say truly, although without taste and without feeling, that I would die rather than leave off my faith, hope and charity. Alas, Lord, if it is in your good pleasure that I have no other pleasure from the practice of the virtues than what your grace has conferred on me, I acquiesce with all my will, even though against all my feelings.

It is the greatest point of holy resignation to be content with bare, dry, insensible acts, exercised by the superior will alone. . . . You have expressed your suffering very well, and can do nothing as a remedy except what you are doing, protesting to our Lord, even vocally and sometimes even in singing, that you wish to live by death and to eat as if you were dead, without taste, without feeling and without consciousness. Finally, this Lord wishes that we be perfectly his and that nothing remain to us so that we may abandon ourselves entirely to the mercy of his providence, without reserve.

Here is a clear directive, leaving no doubt about the manner of sanctifying ourselves through aridity. The Baroness de

Chantal was not, let us repeat, a novice who did not know how to converse with God. Madame de Brulart was not a beginner, either. And yet Francis de Sales gave her the same counsels that St. Ignatius Loyola gave:

What do you want to do at prayer save what you are doing, laying your misery and your nothingness again and again before God? The most successful beggars are those who show their ulcers and necessities. But sometimes even that, you say, is beyond your power, and all you can do is to remain there like a phantom or a statue. Well, that is no small thing. . . . Trees do not bear fruit except by the presence of the sun—some sooner, some later, some every year, some only every three years, and some in no set pattern. We are happy to be able to remain in the presence of God, and let us be content that this presence will make us bear fruit sooner or later, or every day, or only sometimes, according to the good pleasure toward which we must fully resign ourselves.

Another time he returned to this essential point of prayer which consists in loving, willing and not thinking or imagining. That is also elementary, and yet all souls must sometimes be reminded of it. He wrote to his dear Philothea:

Not to make use in prayer of the imagination or of the intellect is impossible but to make use of them only for moving the will and, the will being moved, to use it more than the imagination or the intellect—that must undoubtedly be done. There is no need (said this good mother, the Carmelite Marie de la Trinité), of making use of the imagination to represent to oneself the humanity of the Savior. Nor perhaps for those who are already far advanced on the mountain of perfection, but for us who are still in the valley, although desirous of climbing, I think it expedient to make use of all our faculties, including our imagination. Nevertheless I have not marked on any paper that this imagination must remain very simple and be used like a needle to thread its affections and resolutions into our spirit. . . . Let us remain, my dear daughter, a little while here in these low valleys, let us kiss again the feet of the Savior; he will call us to his holy mouth when he pleases. Do not depart from our method until we see each other again.

And in June, 1607, he repeats to Mme Brulart, eager to advance in prayer:

I approve of your keeping to a little method in regard to your prayer, preparing your mind by reading and arranging the points, yet using your imagination only in so far as it is necessary to recollect the mind. Now I know very well that when one is so fortunate as to find God, it is a good thing to occupy oneself with him and repose in him. To imagine that we are always going to meet him without preparation, would not, I think, be desirable for us who are still novices and need to consider the virtues of the crucifix one by one in detail rather than admire them all collectively. If, after you have applied your mind to this humble preparation, God still does not give you consolations, you must then wait patiently, eating your bread quite dry and doing your duty without any immediate reward.

Accustomed to speaking to our Lord in vocal prayers, Madame Brulart was worried when she happened to remain silent in his presence. St. Francis reassures her (November 2, 1607):

Do not worry about your prayer, which you tell me passes without words; if it leaves good effects in your heart, it is a good prayer. Make no violent efforts to speak; in this divine love he who looks and is looked at speaks enough. Follow the impulse of the Holy Spirit. But do not leave off your preparation for prayer, for this is your duty. You ought not of yourself undertake any other method. But if, when you are beginning to pray in your usual way, God draws you by another path, follow him. According to our reach, we must make our preparation, and when God extends our reach, to him alone be the glory.

Addressing himself to a young lady whose name we do not know but whom her letters reveal as very eager to advance in prayer, St. Francis de Sales suggests that we place ourselves in the presence of God for two reasons: the first, to render him the homage we owe him; the second, to hear his word, his inspirations, his interior movements. Then he proceeds to the method, which is always the same: "If we can speak to

God, let us speak. If we are unable to speak, let us remain silent in his presence and pay him reverence. Our patience will please him and he will look with favor on our silence. Presently, in awe, we shall see him take us by the hand, talk with us, and lead us hither and thither through the bypaths of his garden of prayer. And should he never do this, the great honor and grace of his allowing us to be in his presence should satisfy us."

These quotations may appear excessive to those who have not understood our purpose, but they show the identity of views of St. Ignatius and St. Francis on the practice of prayer.

25 *Meekness, a Salesian Virtue*

ALL THE VIRTUES which St. Francis de Sales recommended because of his own genius, St. Ignatius had already described in his own fashion as essential to spirituality. St. Thomas Aquinas had also made them the main object of the *Secunda Secundae* of his *Summa*. But there are a few of which St. Ignatius spoke little. We could believe, because he passed over them almost in silence, that he did not consider them essential for his disciples of the Society nor for souls in general. That would be a mistake. He recommends them in a different manner.

Among these virtues we point out only four which seem to be Salesian in a special manner and to which false applications have not been lacking: meekness, simplicity, liberty of spirit, abandonment. Although Francis de Sales wrote on these virtues, the pages which best manifest, perhaps, his soul and his spiritual genius shall be omitted in our comparative study with St. Ignatius in order to avoid useless length (See Roffat, p. 312 ff.).

"As for meekness properly so called," wrote Henri Bremond, "who will be naturally meek if he is not? Is not this meekness made up of benevolence, compassion, worldly kindness, and Christian charity? Is it not exactly the tenderness which we could believe, or, if we prefer, that tenderness which is more spiritual than profound?"

Why did St. Francis de Sales esteem meekness, and why did he wish to practice it and counsel its practice until the end of his life? For two reasons: (1) to imitate Jesus in his love for God and man; and (2) to gain souls for Jesus Christ. In order to present the true character of Jesus, St. Matthew (12:20) recalls to us the prophecy of the prophet Isaia who announced especially the sweetness of the servant of Yahweh: "Whom I have called my servant, whom I have chosen and will not cast off" (41:10). St. John calls him the Lamb, the symbol of meekness, as soon as he appears in his Gospel. And the Apocalypse even describes the triumph of the Lamb in great pomp.

His kingdom is that of a "pure and saving victim." The kingdom that he restores to his Father is the kingdom of truth and life, of holiness and of grace, a kingdom of justice, love and peace. He is the peacemaker par excellence—divine, eternal. And so he is in every circumstance of the Gospel.

In his *Introduction to the Devout Life*, Francis speaks with love of those dear and well-beloved virtues which gleam in the person of our Lord, those he has especially recommended to us as if by them our heart might be especially consecrated to his service and applied to his imitation: "Learn of me for I am meek and humble of heart" (Mt. 11:29). Humility perfects us toward God and meekness toward our neighbor.

Francis does not cease to repeat this example and this word of our Lord to all his correspondents, when the occasion presents itself. On June 8, 1605, he wrote to a lady who wished to put herself under his direction: "Remember the principal lesson, the one which he (our Lord) has left us in three words, so that we would never forget it and which a hundred times a day we might repeat: 'Learn of me for I am meek and humble of heart.' That is all. Just keep your heart meek in regard to your neighbor and humble in regard to God" (*Œuvres*, XIII, 358).

St. Jane de Chantal reported in her deposition that "no one ever saw him troubled or distressed when affairs surprised him one after the other. He received them with meekness from the hand of God and not according to human reason. Thus he was always at prayer, since he continually held his heart exposed to the good pleasure of God, to whom he acquiesced simply, without distinction or exception whatever" (3–174). "I have a great desire," she added, "that we should imitate him in this, for it is the shortest and easiest road to acquire the true and solid perfection of the spirit of the Visitation." According to St. Francis, whoever can "preserve meekness among troubles and torments and peace in the midst of uproar and the multiplicity of affairs, he is almost *perfect.*"

To study the other Salesian virtues, too numerous to be analyzed in this study, we enthusiastically advise the reading of the *Introduction to the Devout Life* and the *Spiritual Conferences* which are from several points of view more perfect and fruitful than the *Christian Perfection* of Rodríguez.

BIBLIOGRAPHY

Henry Bordeaux, *François de Sales et notre coeur de chair* (Paris, Plon).

Henri Bremond, *Histoire littéraire du sentiment religieux en France* (1916–1936). 11 vols.

P. Brodrick, *Saint Ignace de Loyola* (Paris, Spes).

Charles-Auguste de Sales, *Histoire du bienheureux François de Sales*.

Louis Cognet, *La Mère Angélique et saint François de Sales* (Paris, Flammarion).

Paul Dudon, S.J., *Saint Ignace de Loyola* (Paris, Beauchesne: 1934).

Antoine Dufournet, *La Jeunesse de saint François de Sales* (1567–1622).

H. Fouqueray, *La Compagnie de Jésus en France* (Paris).
2 vols. *Œuvres de saint François de Sales,* évêque et prince de Genève, Docteur de l'Eglise. Edition complète (Annecy, Imprimerie Nierat, 1892–1932).

Hamon, *Vie de saint François de Sales,* évêque et prince de Genève, Docteur de l'Eglise. New edition, revised by M. Gonthier and M. Letourneau (Paris, 1909). 2 vols.

Maurice Henry-Coüannier, *Saint François de Sales et ses amitiés* (Paris, 1922).

E. Le Couturier, *Lettres de direction de spiritualité de saint François de Sales.*

P. Leturia, S.J., *El Gentil hombre Iñigo Lopez de Loyola* (Barcelona).

Antanias Liuima, S.J., *Aux sources du traité de l'amour de Dieu de saint François de Sales* (Rome, 1959: Librairie éditrice de l'Université grégorienne). 2 vols.

Claude Roffat, *A l'école de saint François de Sales* (Paris, Spes, 1948).

Sainte Jeanne-Françoise Frémyot de Chantal, Sa vie et ses oeuvres (Plon, 1874). 6 vols.

Francis Trochu, *Saint François de Sales,* évêque et prince de Genève, fondateur de la Visitation Sainte-Marie, Docteur de l'Eglise (1567–1622), d'après ses écrits, ses premiers historiens et les procès inédits de sa canonisation (Lyon, 1946). 2 vols.

Francis Vincent, *Saint François de Sales,* directeur d'âmes (Paris, 1933).